The Fundamentalist Movement
1930-1956

The Fundamentalist Movement
1930-1956

Louis Gasper

BAKER BOOK HOUSE
Grand Rapids, Michigan 49506

PHOTOLITHOPRINTED BY CUSHING - MALLOY, INC.
ANN ARBOR, MICHIGAN, UNITED STATES OF AMERICA

Preface

An attempt was made in this book to present an objective and definitive account of the developments within the organized fundamentalist movement in American Protestant Christianity since 1930, with particular reference to the contributions of two distinct groups of fundamentalists to Christianity in America, each of which are characteristically different in temperament and in the methods employed in the propagation of fundamentalist doctrines. The heirs of the older or original fundamentalists are represented by the American Council of Christian Churches. This group is extremely aggressive and often vituperative in their militancy, especially against those whom they regard as apostate or theologically modernist or liberal. The second group is represented by the National Association of Evangelicals. The latter group emerged during the forties primarily because certain leaders arose at that time who believed that the older fundamentalists behaved disgracefully and had brought embarrassment to Biblical Christianity. They are eager to propagate fundamentalist doctrines and to achieve their social goals through suasion. Hence, the National Association of Evangelicals is characteristically conciliatory toward other theological groups within Protestantism. Their leaders are reputably intellectual and they have gained the notice of other theologians through their scholarship.

Religious fundamentalism is rooted in apostolic doctrine, Medieval-Reformation theology, and American revivalism. Since 1910 it represents an interaction against twentieth century liberalism and modernism, particularly against the teachings of science and the higher criticism in Biblical research which tends to undermine certain fundamentalist tenets. In their first skirmish with modernism the fundamentalists were without any effective national organization to direct their efforts and as a consequence they were left demoralized by 1930.

635 39

During the thirties the fundamentalists formed local organizations, but it was not until the forties that effective national organizations emerged. In 1941 the American Council of Christian Churches, known as the exclusivist or separatist fundamentalists, was organized, admitting into its membership only those who were separated from the Federal Council of the Churches of Christ in America and its successor, the National Council of the Churches of Christ in the U.S.A. In 1942 the National Association of Evangelicals, known as the inclusivist fundamentalists, was formed, including in its membership all those regardless of their relationship with any other Protestant organization who willingly subscribed to the fundamentalist creed. Thus, instead of one national association the fundamentalists were divided into two organizations primarily because of their differences over the method of combatting modernism and liberalism.

A transition from liberalism in theology to neo-orthodoxy occurred during the thirties, and this development became the prevalent theological mood in the United States. Because the neo-orthodox accepted the methods of higher criticism and directed their efforts toward ecumenicity, the fundamentalists fought them as a new form of modernism and attacked them as promoters of socialism, communism, anti-capitalism, pacifism, internationalism, and a world church for the United Nations.

During the forties the fundamentalists spent millions of dollars annually to broadcast the gospel over the radio. The Federal Council and later its successor, the National Council, sought to encourage the radio industry to restrict the time allocated for religious broadcasts, and also demanded the imposition of higher standards for religious broadcasting and the elimination of religious racketeering over the air. To protect their rights and freedom of speech, the fundamentalists organized theNational Religious Broadcasters in 1944 to establish a religious broadcaster's code and to convince the radio industry of their desire for high standards and fiscal accountability.

During the thirties and thereafter a spontaneous outburst of mass evangelism was noted, beginning with such new fundamentalist organizations as the Youth for Christ, High School Christian Clubs, and the Inter-Varsity Christian Fellowship. These youth organizations helped condition American youth to accept fundamentalism. Americans became more conscious of a need for religion in part because of the international tensions caused by the cold war with Russia and the threat of global annihilation from nuclear warfare. Religion became popular as attested by the appearance of religious subjects in books, magazines, and newspapers. Church membership reached a new high in American history and the construction of new churches was phenomenal.

Suddenly Billy Graham was catapulted into national and international prominence as a mass evangelist starting with his Greater Los Angeles (Evangelistic) Crusade in 1949. Afterwards Graham conducted massive rallies in the larger cities of the United States, England, Scotland, and Australia. On May 15, 1957 Graham launched a New York Crusade, which was originally scheduled for six weeks, but the interest was so great the campaign was extended two times until September 1. During the New York Crusade Graham was attacked by the American Council, on the one hand, for permitting modernists of the New York Protestant Council to be represented on his crusade committee. On the other hand, he was attacked by liberal theologians for preaching primitive doctrines, and the Protestant Council was attacked for aiding the crusade.

During the thirties and forties Bible Institutes met the needs of fundamentalist higher education. In 1947 the Accrediting Association of Bible Institutes and Bible Colleges was formed to raise the educational standards of fundamentalist schools. With this fundamentalist education entered a new phase of development with a recognition of the value of general education and sound scholarship, although the Bible remained the central textbook and unifying principle of fundamentalist education. The National Association of Christian Schools was organized in 1947 to meet the growing demand for fundamentalist primary and secondary education and to combat the secularism in public school instruction.

The fundamentalist revival was also reflected in part in the resurgence of extreme nationalism. Congress was persuaded to alter the pledge of allegiance to the American flag by the inclusion of the phrase 'under God.' Congress also enacted legislation making the slogan 'In God We Trust' the official motto of the American people and provided that the motto be inscribed on American coins and currency. Finally, the Christian Amendment Movement, which received some support from fundamentalists, revived the nineteenth century plan of the National Reform Organization to amend the Constitution of the United States in order to recognize Jesus Christ as Saviour and to declare the United States to be a Christian nation.

Acknowledgments are in order. I owe a great debt to my teachers in college and university whose accumulated wisdom helped shape my thought and whose encouragement fortified my interest in things scholarly. In particular, I acknowledge the guidance I received during the writing of this book from my graduate professors at Western Reserve University, Cleveland, Ohio. Dr. Clarence H. Cramer, Dean of Adelbert College and Professor of History, supervised the writing of this manuscript and offered many valuable suggestions for its improvement. Dr. Rolland Emerson Wolfe, Harkness Professor of Biblical Literature and chairman of the Department of Religion, permitted me to use several personal letters which proved valuable in this study. Dr. Lyon N. Richardson, Professor of English and chairman of the Department of American Studies, and Dr. Carl F. Wittke, Elbert Jay Professor of History and Dean of the Graduate School, read the original manuscript and offered suggestions for its improvement. Dr. Harvey Wish, Professor of History, encouraged me to write on this subject in order to bring the story of fundamentalism up-to-date. Dr. Elgin S. Moyer, Librarian at Moody Bible Institute of Chicago, generously permitted me to peruse the books, brochures, pamphlets, and periodicals under his care. During my years of study, I was encouraged and assisted by my wife Nellie, who deserves all the recognition that should come to a devoted helpmeet. Much of my success must be attributed to her sacrificial assistance and inexhaustible patience.

LOUIS GASPER

Los Angeles, California
July 2, 1962

Contents

List of tables

CHAPTER ONE

The Fundamentalist Heritage

Various attempts have been made to explain the reasons for the present resurgence of conservative theological belief in America. The consensus is that the current international tensions, coupled with the inability of world political leaders to find a satisfactory solution for world problems short of war, is largely responsible for the revival of religion of the more pessimistic sort; that is, religion which distrusts human nature and scorns the dependence upon reason as a guide to salvation. It seems that not only the masses, but many intellectuals, have little faith in the optimistic concept of the perfectibility of man, which had dominated liberal thought at the start of the twentieth century. Many people have returned to the ancient Christian doctrine of the depravity of man and his inability to reason his way to an acceptable solution of the problems which beset him. The prevalent view today regarding man is that he is a sinner who must be redeemed by divine power. The neo-orthodox theologians, who are prominent in American Protestant circles at present, have also come to regard the unregenerate state of modern man as the primary problem in religion, although they reject many other fundamentalistic doctrines. But the significant point to remember, is that many theologians are afraid to rely upon reason alone. They have come to rely more on divine power and intervention.[1]

Since the end of World War II the enthusiasm for religion has been noticeable in church attendance, revival crusades, and in the greatest program of church construction ever experienced before in the United States. Church membership has risen to the phenomenal figure of approximately 100,000,000, the highest in American history.[2] This upsurge in religious interest is seen in the popularity of religious themes in music, in books, in motion pictures, and in the expansion of religious sections in many local newspapers. Religion is discussed in every-day conversation and church attendance has become both popular and fashionable.[3]

The names most frequently heard and associated in connection with mass evangelistic efforts during the current resurgence of religious interest and revivals are those of fundamentalist preachers, with Billy Graham leading the group. The neo-orthodox, perhaps the closest rivals of the fundamentalists, by their own admission do not command the attention of the masses as do the fundamentalists. This is significant when one considers the fact that neo-orthodoxy is prevalent among the leaders in the major Protestant denominations and seminaries in the United States. Even so, they have not been successful in reaching the masses through any of their preachers as has Billy Graham. The reason for this probably can be explained by suggesting that a latent fundamentalism exists among most Protestants in the United States, and that their inherent religious interest has suddenly come to the surface to be expressed more actively than in recent years. However, it should be stated that the same existent conditions which stirred the Protestant masses have had a similar effect upon other religious groups, for example the Roman Catholics and the Jews.[4]

The European Legacy
Although religious fundamentalism as an organized movement in American Protestant Christianity is comparatively youthful, the tradition from which it sprang is very old: some scholars trace the spirit of fundamentalism back to the Reformation. There are fundamentalist leaders, however, who declare that it goes back to the New Testament period and the apostles, and that the Reformation only restated the neglected fundamentals of the gospel. William Ward Ayer, a popular radio evangelist in New York City, emphasized this point in a speech he delivered during the Cleveland convention of the National Association of Evangelicals in April, 1956. He said:

Fundamentalism represents a resurgence of ancient practices, which began not with Martin Luther but at Pentecost. Fundamentalism is apostolic, and the doctrine of justification goes back to Paul. That branch from which the fundamentalist movement sprang lived obscurely through the ages and had never been completely silenced even in the Dark Ages.[5]

Ayer was probably trying to establish what is commonly believed by the fundamentalists: (1) that they do not owe any former allegiance to the Roman Catholic hierarchy or to any other denomination for their existence, and (2) that the source of fundamentalist theology is the Bible. Thus, in no sense can the fundamentalists be accused of being a disaffected religious body suddenly severed from the main stream of Christianity or from Catholicism and Protestantism.[6] They still claim their loyalty to the primitive teachings of the New Testament church. Ayer said:

What fundamentalism did was to awaken the slumbering apostolicism from lethargy. The theme of the Reformation, like the cry of the fundamentalists today, was 'back to the Bible and the Apostles,' with no mediator between men and God except Christ. Fundamentalists are in the direct line of succession to those preaching this same message.[7]

On the other hand, it is safe to conclude that much of what the fundamentalists teach today are doctrines which were delineated during the Reformation period and were further clarified through subsequent developments in Protestant Christianity. The Reformers did not appeal for a revolution in theology, as though what they were teaching was something new, but they complained that the Roman Catholic Church had permitted certain fundamental principles to become obscured by their ecclesiastical authority and by some of their ritual. It was during the Reformation that the cry for less ecclesiastical authority was heard and an appeal for more reliance on the Bible was demanded. The fundamentalists are still echoing the Reformers in this respect.[8]

Martin Luther, the most familiar figure during the Reformation, rebelled against what he and his followers considered to be a mechanical operation of the Roman Catholic ritual. The Reformers declared there was little or no concomitant moral change in those who observed the Roman Catholic rites. Luther turned to the Pauline doctrine of justification by faith, a doctrine he accepted after reading Augustine's views that salvation from sin cannot come by human merit, but by the gracious act of God. In defense of this principle Luther appealed to the authority of the Bible, which he regarded as infallible, and to which he said before his Roman Catholic inquisitors, 'my conscience is captive.'[9]

History shows that the Lutheran movement successfully detached itself from papal authority, and since the Reformation Protestantism generally has been characteristically anti-Catholic. Since the twentieth century, with the rise of liberal influences in thought, this anti-Catholic spirit has subsided to a great extent. However, the fundamentalists have continued the anti-Catholic attitude, largely because of their stern and rigid dependence upon

the authority of the Bible and their enmity against any organization or people
not showing a similar regard for it. William Ward Ayer declared in his
Cleveland speech: 'Anti-Catholicism is found in the Bible and the evangelicals, therefore, are on scriptural grounds when they resist the papal claims of
apostolicity.'[10]

The doctrines which first became important in American churches were
enunciated by John Calvin (1509-1564), who found Luther's doctrines acceptable in most of their essentials. But Calvin, who has been rated by scholars
as a cold logician, took Luther's doctrines several steps further and developed
a theological system that was more rigid in many of its demands. Besides
teaching the doctrine of God's sovereignty, which in itself was stern enough,
Calvin viewed the church as a factor in the rest of life, and he extended the
scope of its responsibility and its authority to include civic and social matters
as well as religious concernments. Calvin's ideals for all Christians were
'thrift, industry, and sobriety,' which permitted men to prosper economically
without the fear of being regarded as tainted by the sin of avarice. However,
Calvin's ideals were eventually misconstrued to mean the regulation of all
petty activities among church people, such as card playing, dancing, and
unnecessary frolicking. Thus, both the logical aspects of Calvin's theology
and the illogical interpretation of it were synthesized into one system of
religious thought. This modified version of Calvinism, surviving to the present, has been inherited for the most part by the fundamentalists with only
minor variations.[11]

The American Legacy
Calvinism first came to America during the early part of the seventeenth
century by way of the Pilgrim and Puritan migrations from England, and
both were irreconcilable enemies of the Roman Catholic Church. These two
groups were originally members of the Anglican Church, but because the
parent body procrastinated and refused to eliminate the vestiges of popery
from its worship, they separated and formed independent religious bodies,
although the Puritans preferred to remain as a reforming body within the
Anglican Church. Thus, besides introducing the Calvinistic version of Protestant Christianity into America, these two groups immediately established
two fundamentalistic traditions for dissenting groups to follow. They were:
(1) the emphatic anti-Catholic spirit of Protestantism, and (2) the principle
of separation as a method by which religious minorities might safeguard
their beliefs and protect themselves from the domination of the majority.[12]

The source and vitality of Puritan theology was reliance upon the authorized King James Version (1611) of the Bible, which came to be regarded as the official Protestant version of Scripture. The King James Version soon became part of the common tongue. Even to this day in certain mountain areas of the South people still speak the English in ordinary conversation which was common during the seventeenth century, and much of this must be attributed to the influence of the English Bible.[13] Recently, following the publication of the Revised Standard Version of the Bible in 1952 by the National Council of the Churches of Christ in the United States of America, a preference for the King James Version of the Bible was vociferously demonstrated by most fundamentalists, who called the new version a corruption imposed upon Christians by the modernists.[14]

Until 1690 the churches which favored church-state unity and an intellectual approach to religion were supreme in colonial America. But after that date left-wing evangelical sects, largely comprised of non-English stock from German pietist and independent Lutheran and Reformed groups, began to increase very rapidly in the colonies. The pietists for the most part came from the common people who, by the nature of their case, stressed personal piety and rejected institutional religion and state-church unity.[15] These groups, along with the Pilgrim separatists and the Baptists, created a condition in the religious life of the colonies that had some direct bearing upon the uniquely American development of revivalism. It was first tried by Jonathan Edwards (1703–1758) to induce those in New England whose religious ardor had cooled to take a more positive part in the life of the church.[16] Revivalism 'was a way of bringing Christianity to individuals, and it stressed the fact that salvation depended upon individual decisions, that religion was a personal concern and not primarily an institutional matter.'[17]

The development of revivalism came about fortuitously, after Edwards, preaching in his Northampton church, rose to defend the principles of Calvinism, which at that time were believed threatened by the inroads of Arminianism. Edwards was noted for his intellectualism, but to accomplish his task of revivifying New England Calvinism he began to appeal to the average as well as to the more educated people of his community which he served from 1727-1750. Thus Edwards resorted to emotionalism in preaching, and because of his reputation as an intellectual, his doing so made emotionalism in religion respectable. No doubt, this helped left-wing sects everywhere which were basically emotional in their approach to religion. A revival began in Edwards' church in 1737 and spread quickly to other communities after reports of remarkable conversions in his meetings were circulated. Critics of revivalism, showing a concern for the survival of polite religion of a scholarly nature, spoke of these occurrences as evidence of revivalistic distemper.[18]

The revival that started in Edwards' church was actually a prelude to the Great Awakening of 1740; it not only had its immediate effects upon all of the colonies, but set the pattern in American religion for over a century and a half.[19] At the same time of the Great Awakening the English were also having a revival which had started among the Methodists. Soon the Methodists were sending preachers to the new world to add their distinctive character to American revivalism. Like the evangelicals already here, the Methodists were humble folk who were often crude, outspoken, and ill-mannered in their approach. Most of them were untutored and erudition in the pulpit began to decline rapidly, particularly at the cutting edge of the frontier where illiterate Baptist farmer preachers and Methodist circuit riders usually were found. These ministers justified their lack of education on the simple, though psychologically satisfying, ground that no theological training had been required of the apostles before any of them were permitted to preach the simple gospel.[20]

George Whitefield, referred to as the 'hot gospeler' of his time, was influenced by the Methodists while he was in England. He preferred to preach extemporaneously, which he could do with facility.[21] However, his omission of evidences of erudition from the pulpit, such as manuscripts, probably encouraged the anti-intellectuals, who were trying to do the same thing. This was easily done, because revivalist preaching did not involve complicated argumentation. The primary objective of all revivalists was not an appeal to the intellect but to the heart of the hearer, for the purpose of bringing about their conversion. Thus, revival sermons became homiletically simple, their structure being determined for the most part by three basic requirements: conviction of one's sinfulness, repentance, and commitment to Christ.[22] In his famous sermon on 'The Danger of an Unconverted Ministry,' William Tennent, one of the many reputable evangelists during the Great Awakening, indicated his disapproval of those coming into the ministry without any other qualification than one's learning. He stated, as has often been repeated since, that the primary qualification for all those who enter the ministry is their own conversion. Only then could one hope to minister effectively, since God works only through the regenerate and enables them to overcome their personal handicaps to accomplish His purposes among men.[23] Charles Finney, America's most successful evangelist during the period preceding the Civil War, also said:

Oftentimes I went into the pulpit without knowing what text I should speak, or a word that I should say, I depended on the occasion and the Holy Spirit to suggest the text, and to open up the whole subject to my mind; and certainly in no part of my ministry have I preached with greater success and power.[24]

Furthermore, the gauge of an evangelist's success was not demonstrated by his erudition, as though preaching was solely a scholarly exercise, but by the numbers who responded to the invitation given by the speaker at the conclusion of the sermon. This was the end of all evangelical preaching. 'That is the reason why,' Finney said, 'formerly, the ignorant Methodist preachers and the earnest Baptist preachers produced so much more effect than our most learned theologians and divines.'[25]

The period from the eighteen-thirties to the Civil War showed the people to be restless, confused, and dissatisfied. This restlessness was manifested in all aspects of life, including religion. During this period a number of utopian schemes with a religious foundation were tried; various religious organizations, some of them bizarre, were proliferated in the 'burned-over-district' of central and western New York, an area in which revivalists had worked intensively. The fear of popery reached a new high as a consequence of the immigration of a large number of Irish Catholics. The disappearance of William Morgan in 1826, which was charged to the Masons, resulted in the rise of anti-Masonry among most Protestant groups. Some of the developments in religion during this period lasted but a short time. However, many of the organizations which were spawned at that time, such as Mormonism, Adventism, and Spiritualism, have been subjects of concern to the fundamentalists.[26] The fundamentalists regard the Mormons and Spiritualists as unscriptural cults, and have proliferated a body of literature to convince others why this is true. Spiritualism, which came into existence after reports of the Fox sisters were circulated telling of their experiences with unseen spiritual powers, has been described by the fundamentalists as a religion controlled by the devil and his demons. The fundamentalists support their contention with Scripture.[27]

The most important development during this period for the future of fundamentalism was the rise of millenialism to a new prominence in American religious life. William Miller, a farmer with varied religious experiences, became the leader of millenialism or Millerism, as the movement was called. Those people who probably were impatient with conditions as they found them at that time, longed for the establishment of a divine utopia on earth which would be realized when Christ returned to the earth with His saints to rule in person for a thousand years. Miller discovered a formula after studying the books of Daniel and Revelation, which enabled him to prognosticate the date for the second advent of Christ to take place on March 21, 1843. Of course the event never occurred and the Millerites were disappointed, but their hopes did not fade completely.[28] Millerism is still perpetuated in contemporary adventist groups, and it is one of the fundamental principles of the fundamentalist movement.

However, since Miller's time the fundamentalists have had sufficient time to eliminate the unfortunate errors of prognostication made by Miller. Instead of trying to establish a definite date, the fundamentalists use the term 'imminency' with respect to the second coming of Christ. Therefore, the fundamentalists live in a constant state of expectancy with regard to the second coming of Christ, but because no dates are set for this event there is no danger of any disappointment should it not be forthcoming.[29]

The period after the Civil War to 1900 was one during which two distinct cultures began to clash, the spiritual and the secular. Various discoveries in experimental science not only revealed the potential capacity of men's minds, but they also began to change men's views regarding biblical cosmology, because the new scientific outlook had challenged the place of revelation as a source of knowledge. Churchmen were shocked when colleges eliminated many religious courses, while adding secular subjects in their curricula. They became alarmed when evolution became a working hypothesis in almost every discipline, including religion. Darwin's hypothesis of no fixity in the species, together with the postulations of the geologists, struck at the base of the theological cosmology that the earth and men had been created in six days by divine fiat. The geologists postulated the materialistic origin of the universe eons before 4004 B. C., the date which had usually been given by the older theologians.[30]

Biblical scholars known as higher critics also alarmed the conservative theologians. The higher critics, most of whom had studied in Germany, began to employ the empirical method to the study of the Bible, thereby striking at the roots of evangelical Christianity, which depended for its epistemology upon an infallible Revelation. The basic principle of the higher critics 'was that the Bible was a collection of human documents subject to the same literary criticism as other human writings.'[31] Therefore, they sought to discover the original purpose and distinctive message of each book of the Bible, actual authorship, the correct or approximate date of writing, and other pertinent facts to show the relevance of each book to its time. They proceeded on the assumption, using comparative religion as one of their supports, that the Hebrew religion developed from the primitive to the more advanced ethical concepts.[32] Accordingly, the predictive element of the Bible was discarded, and the prophets came to be regarded not as foretellers but as devoted men with profound spiritual motivations and insights. Jesus Christ was also included in the line of succession from the prophets.[33] His teachings were re-examined and the conclusions drawn from them was that He had been motivated by a desire to save men by reforming their institutions; this new view inspired the development of the social gospel.[34]

These challenges to traditional theology concerned the conservative theologians, and the first stirrings of the fundamentalist controversy were observed, a controversy which also was a result of a rapid and turbulent transition from an agrarian society to a highly technical urban social order with different sets of beliefs. America's homogeneous population began to change into a heterogeneous type after the Civil War. The rapid rise of science and industry, with its need for a new and increased supply of labor, brought with it a massive immigration mostly from countries having Roman Catholic traditions. Their languages proved to be a formidable defense against their being proselyted by the Protestants; at the same time it also formed a barrier that prevented hospitable relations between them to develop. Consequently, the ancient enmity between the Protestants and the Roman Catholics was accentuated.[35]

Out of the needs of the immigrants a new system of religious ethics began to compete with older American religious ethics. The latter was founded upon the evangelical tradition which held that the primary responsibility of the church was religious. On the other hand, economic life was regarded as a separate area where character was stimulated and developed through competition between individuals. The new ethics was largely European, being transmitted to America by a preponderently Roman Catholic immigration, by people conditioned to expect ecclesiastical intercessions for them. In this system, the sphere of activity of the church was not restricted primarily to doctrine; the church was expected to act in the economic and political realms as well, where the individual could not do very well by himself. The latter interpretation of the role of the church coincided in certain respects with the philosophy of the Protestant modernists who were beginning to propagate their ideas of the social gospel about the same time.[36]

The chief impetus for the social gospel came from two clergymen, Washington Gladden and Walter Rauschenbusch. Both were meliorists and believed that the environment was largely responsible for evil, a view that was in opposition to the traditional theological concept of human depravity. Both of these clergymen influenced the development of a philosophy of religion which was based not in terms of some ethereal future life, but in terms of service in a collective Christian world or kingdom.[37]

Gladden directed his attacks against laissez-faire economics and proposed that the government should intervene to help labor achieve economic justice. In his *Theology of the Social Gospel*, Rauschenbusch stated that the church must accept a part of the responsibility for a more equitable social order. The climax of their efforts came in 1908 after several denominations, already having established their own social service agencies, united to form the inter-church Federal Council of the Churches of Christ in America to implement the principles of the social gospel. The Federal Council immediately adopted a social creed which was based on the one established by the Methodist Episcopal Church in 1908.[38] The fundamentalists were aroused, and from that time to the present have objected to any teaching which viewed the kingdom of God as something separate from a redemptive society.[39]

The nineteenth century ended with a decomposition of medieval theology. The chief issues in religion at that time were between a prescientific and scientific expression of it. The conservatives, who comprised those who held the Bible was the absolute revelation of God, were regarded as adherents of a pre-scientific epistemology hardly compatible with modern developments.[40] Those who applied the methods of science to the study of the Bible and religion were referred to as modernists.[41] The conservative leaders became alarmed as they saw their theological foundations crumble and a paralyzing indifference engulf their own constituency. Of course, modernity was blamed for all this. And it probably never occured to the conservative leaders that the growing heterogenous character of American life, with its multifarious social and economic problems, was largely responsible for the shifting of the attention of the rank-and-file of conservativism to more immediate problems.[42] The conservative leaders were convinced that the age of apostasy had begun, and that the stage was being prepared for the coming of the anti-Christ.[43]

The conservatives tried desperately to stem the tide of liberalism by consolidating their own position and by resorting to vilification in order to accomplish their purpose. Their leaders began to meet in Bible conferences where the chief emphasis was the prophetic portions of the Scriptures, teachings which not only emphasized the second coming of Christ but also those which provided a warning against the apostasy which was destroying faith in the Bible through devastating scholarship. Scholars were not frightened by these ominous declarations. The only success the conservatives probably enjoyed was among themselves, for their own warnings seemed to fortify them in their efforts to defend the Bible and their historic principles. Between 1876 and 1900 several such conferences were held in strategic points in the United States. These must be regarded as embryonic stirrings of the fundamentalist movement. The most important conference was conducted in 1895 at Niagara, where a declaration anticipating the fundamentalist five-points of 1910 was formulated. The conservatives at that conference declared that traditional Protestant Christianity must be regarded as having five important and indispensable poles: (1) the inerrancy of the Scriptures, (2) the virgin birth, (3) the deity of Jesus Christ, (4) the substitutionary atonement,[44] and (5) the physical resurrection of Jesus Christ and His bodily return.[45]

The conservatives were also disturbed by the rising tide of secularism in the nation's schools and the modernizing influences in seminaries. They tried to meet this situation in two important ways. First, they sought to maintain their grip on those schools which seemed to be loyal to their tradition, and they succeeded in some instances. Next, they began to direct their energies toward the establishment of conservative schools with the Bible as the central textbook. This effort gave rise to the Bible Institute movement.[46]

The conservatives were relatively fortunate in the latter case in that several Bible schools had already been organized during the 1880's. The first Bible school was founded in 1882 as the Missionary Training Institute of Nyack-on-the-Hudson, called Nyack for the purpose of brevity.[47] Dwight L. Moody founded the Chicago Evangelistic Society in 1886. This school later became the Moody Bible Institute.[48] The Providence (Rhode Island) Bible Institute, now known as Barrington College, was founded in 1900 as the Bethel Bible Training School in Sutton, Massachusetts.[49] Two other schools, which eventually evolved into colleges, were also founded during this period. They were the Union Missionary Training Institute of Brooklyn, founded in 1885, and the Boston Bible and Missionary Training School, which was organized in 1889. The former school later merged with the National Bible Institute of

New York where it remained until it changed its name to Shelton College and moved to Ringwood, New Jersey, where it occupies an extensive mountain campus. Gordon College of Boston evolved from the Boston Bible and Missionary Training School.[50]

Thus at the beginning of the twentieth century, when the temper of thought was against their tradition, the conservatives had begun to launch a new form of educational system which was destined to affect American culture tremendously. Since the 1880's more than one hundred-sixty Bible schools enrolling over 25,000 students annually were founded in every section of the country 'deliberately non-conforming to the conventional secondary-college-seminary pattern' of American education.[51] When these early schools were organized they did not try to emphasize scholarship, since the purpose of their founding was to provide a short cut method of preparing leaders for Christian service as evangelists, pastors, Sunday School teachers, and missionaries which other schools were not doing. Many of the existing educational centers in the United States were gradually turning to secular and non-biblical subjects so the conservatives felt the only reliable place where leaders could be trained was in these Bible schools.[52] The battle lines were being drawn and tightened between the theological conservatives and liberals; and the conflict has never ended, although the intensity of the controversy has risen and fallen several times.[53]

The Fundamentalist Controversy

The fundamentalist movement in Protestant Christianity was intensified in 1910 with the publication of a series of essays which were compiled into twelve booklets entitled The Fundamentals: A Testimony to the Truth. The entire series, paid for by funds provided by two wealthy Los Angeles businessmen, Lyman and Milton Stewart, were published and distributed without charge to clergymen, evangelists, missionaries, Sunday School teachers, theological students, and others interested in the propagation of the Christian faith.[54] The Fundamentals set forth the historic doctrines regarded as essential. They were: (1) the verbal and inerrant inspiration of the Bible, (2) the virgin birth of Jesus Christ, (3) the substitutionary atonement of Jesus Christ, (4) the physical or bodily resurrection of Jesus Christ, and (5) the imminent second coming of Jesus Christ. Other doctrines which supplemented these were: (1) the deity of Jesus Christ, (2) the depravity or sinful nature of man, (3) salvation and justification by faith through the grace of God, and (4) the promise of the physical or bodily resurrection of believing or regenerate Christians.[55] The books also contained the fundamentalists' refutation of evolution and higher criticism, and an attempt was made to show the unscriptural character of Roman Catholicism, Mormonism, Millenial Dawnism (now Jehovah Witnesses), Christian Science, and Spiritualism, all of which were anathematized as perversions of the Christian faith.[56]

Various attempts have been made to define correctly the fundamentalist movement. Some of the definitions were inaccurate simply because they tended to expose the fundamentalists to ridicule rather than to describe the principles for which they stood.[57] Folk definitions also cropped up, most of them more humorous than true. One fundamentalist recently revealed his personal resentment toward those who defined fundamentalism in a satirical manner when he wrote:

I have found that there is an idea abroad among certain religious liberals that if a person believes in what is usually called the 'old-time religion,' he must, so to speak, have a greasy nose, dirty fingernails, baggy pants, and he mustn't shine his shoes or comb his hair.[58]

Historically, fundamentalism may be defined as that 'movement which arose in opposition to liberalism, reemphasizing the inerrancy of the Scriptures, separation and Biblical miracles, especially the Virgin Birth, the physical Resurrection of Christ and the Substitutionary Atonement.'[59] In this respect, therefore, it represents a conservative reaction against the teachings of the modernists who declared that historic Protestant theology was incompatible with modern scientific discoveries and religious knowledge. The position of the modernists, in opposition to the fundamentalists, can be briefly stated as the rejection of 'the authority of the Bible as the inerrant Word of God, tending to interpret it in the light of modern-day science and philosophy.' In its extreme form its final step is humanism.[60]

Nothing extraordinary resulted from the publication of *The Fundamentals* to cause anyone outside the fundamentalist movement to become concerned for the preservation of intellectual freedom. It was not until World War I had ended that the fundamentalists could muster their own forces and emerge with a national organization; at that time a threat to intellectual freedom in the public schools became distinct.[61]

Before 1919, the fundamentalists were loosely organized in a plethora of undisciplined societies, most of them held together by the will and ambition of energetic clergymen like argumentative John Roach Straton of New York

City, who was called the 'fundamentalist pope'; William Bell Riley from Minneapolis, who was an indefatigable organizer; and Evangelist Paul Rader from Chicago. These three were probably the most familiar figures during the pre-war years. After the war new leaders from different sections of the country appeared and the movement became national in scope. The outstanding clergymen who joined the movement after the war years were the controversial Rev. Frank J. Norris of Fort Worth, Texas; Rev. Gerald Winrod of Kansas; and Rev. Harry Rimmer of Los Angeles, who founded the Research Science Bureau with the intention of establishing harmony between science and the Bible. In many respects Rimmer was the most constructive representative of the group.[62]

Although local fundamentalist societies were formed in various localities, none of them came near meeting a plan for correlative action, which the ministers meeting at Montrose, Pennsylvania in 1916 said was necessary, if the fundamentalists were successfully to withstand the modernists. Meetings were conducted each year after the Montrose convention, but it was not until the 1919 convention at the Moody Bible Institute of Chicago that a permanent organization on a national scale was formed. The World's Christian Fundamentals Association was formed at that time with a definite plan of action to purge schools, seminaries and pulpits of heretics. In 1924 William Jennings Bryan, thrice defeated candidate for the presidency on the Democratic ticket, made an appearance at the World's Christian Fundamentals Association convention at Minneapolis. This event raised the enthusiasm of the fundamentalists to a new high. They now had a nationally known and popular figure to lead them in their crusade.[63]

The next year was a climactic one for the fundamentalists, and perhaps for other Protestants as well. In 1925 their case against evolution finally reached a sympathetic judge and jury after John T. Scopes, a school teacher, had been arrested for violating the Tennessee statute which prohibited the teaching of evolution in tax supported schools of the State. This farcical episode, as it turned out to be, attracted the attention of the nation and other parts of the world, but it did not seem to have helped the fundamentalists to any great extent, even though Scopes was found guilty. In the following year the attendance at their Toronto meeting was disappointing. Interest had fallen. By 1930 the fundamentalists had lost their ardor for a fight, and at their convention during that same year 'none of the scheduled speeches contained any reference to modernism or evolution.'[64] The fundamentalist controversy appeared to be dying.

During the height of the controversy the fundamentalists were generally discordant and divisive, because 'when one quits fighting it is an indication of either compromise or death.'[65] When they were not fighting modernists, Catholics, and evolutionists, they fought among themselves. There was a struggle for power going within fundamentalism.[66] This internecine struggle goes far to explain why it was that the fundamentalists lost every major ecclesiastical battle in which they had been engaged. Their own leaders stated that the fundamentalists had shown that they were utterly incapable of co-operative action.[67] One minister, long associated with Frank J. Norris and his World Baptist Fellowship (which the latter dominated until his death in 1952),[68] made this revealing confession after he joined the Southern Baptist Convention recently, a confession which also explains how Norris advanced his own personal ambitions:

The dissident preacher will manipulate himself into a position where the denomination will have to take some steps to protect its work from his inroads and from the discordant note he injects into the work. When this is done the brother sets up a loud wail of 'persecution, overlordship, dictatorial control, totalitarianism, and denominational oppression.' He invariably publishes a paper in which these matters are widely publicized.[69]

Once a splinter organization was formed, the important decisions for the new group were usually made by one man, and those who disagreed with his decisions were eliminated. In the judgment of one critic, 'It would be impossible to find a more dictatorial machine than Fundamentalism itself had throughout its course.'[70]

Denominational strife was rampant during the 1920's, particularly in the North among the Baptists, Presbyterians, and Disciples of Christ. By 1929 the Disciples of Christ, however, discovered a formula to settle its differences without division, something which the other two churches were unfortunately unable to do. The first explosive issue which rocked the Presbyterian church was centered around Harry Emerson Fosdick, a Baptist minister serving in the First Presbyterian Church of New York City. Fosdick preached a sermon expressing his liberal religious views. Ivy Lee, a layman, was so impressed he had it published and distributed widely without Fosdick's knowledge; in doing so Lee inadvertently exposed Fosdick's liberalism outside his church. The fundamentalists in the denomination immediately exerted pressure to oust him for denying the virgin birth, the inerrancy of the Bible, and the second coming of Christ. However, the liberals in the church, recognizing what this might mean to themselves later, finally 'caused' Fosdick to resign in 1924 on the grounds that he was not a Presbyterian, a solution which displeased the fundamentalists.[71]

A feud which had been smoldering for some time over the question of the infiltration of liberal professors on the faculty of Princeton Theological Seminary finally erupted and caused J. Gresham Machen (a teacher at Princeton noted for his erudition) and his colleague Robert Dick Wilson to withdraw and form the fundamentalist Westminister Theological Seminary in 1929. Later Machen also became displeased with the treatment accorded by the regular Presbyterian mission board to conservative missionary candidates. As a consequence he led a contingent of fundamentalists in 1933 to organize an independent mission board. J. Oliver Buswell, then president of Wheaton (Illinois) College, and Carl McIntire, pastor of the Collingswood (New Jersey) Presbyterian Church, were included in the contingent. This action brought their expulsion from the denomination in 1936 on the charge of insubordination. Following their expulsion the trio organized the Presbyterian Church in America.[72]

Machen died on January 1, 1937 and within six months the church he had helped form was divided. One group formed the Orthodox Presbyterian Church while a second group, lead by Carl McIntire, organized the Bible Presbyterian Church and its official seminary, Faith Theological Seminary in Wilmington, Delaware. As a result, Carl McIntire came to the forefront as a leader of the separatist branch of the fundamentalist movement.[73]

The Northern Baptist Convention, more than any other denomination in America of any appreciable size, suffered most as a consequence of the fundamentalist controversy. Some people feel that the battle has only begun and that the American Baptist Convention (the new name of the Northern Baptist Convention) can expect to lose much of its present constituency in the near future, especially in the western part of the United States. The fundamentalists, operating through their conservative associations within the denomination, have already succeeded in establishing control of the Baptist state convention in Minnesota and of the Western Baptist Theological Seminary in Portland, Oregon. They have also organized the new Conservative Baptist Theological Seminary at Denver, Colorado.[74] F. M. Kepner, executive secretary of the Southern California Baptist Convention (a branch of the American Baptist Convention), said in 1954 that he expects the fate of the American Baptist Convention to be decided in the Los Angeles area within the next ten years.[75]

The battle within the American Baptist Convention first became vigorous in 1920 when a dissident group organized the Fundamentalist Fellowship within the denomination. Its purpose was to fight modernism and to maintain the autonomy of the local congregations, which the fundamentalists feared would disappear as soon as the denomination tightened its ecclesiastical control over each church. In 1923 William Bell Riley, J. Frank Norris, and others were responsible for the formation of the Baptist Bible Union, which began to encourage individual Baptist churches to secede from the parent denomination and unite as a separatist body to harass the Northern Baptist Convention. The Baptist Bible Union acquired a school of its own in 1927 when it relieved the Convention of the heavily indebted Des Moines University. However, an internal dispute in 1929 over the dictatorial administration of the University president, T. T. Shields, forced the school to close after the students refused to attend classes. This event also brought the demise of the Baptist Bible Union.[76]

The separatist Baptists were without an organization after the disintegration of the Baptist Bible Union until the General Association of Regular Baptists, North (usually known as GARB) was organized in 1932 to continue the crusade against the Convention and to encourage other Baptist churches to separate from the denomination and to join their organization.[77]

Meanwhile, the Fundamentalist Fellowship continued its work within the Convention, seeking the adoption of a clear-cut creedal statement designed to break down the inclusivist policy which permitted a divergency of belief in the denomination. At the same time, the fundamentalist faction sought to force the denomination to withdraw from the Federal Council of the Churches of Christ in America, and demanded that the trend toward centralization of the Convention machinery, which endangered the autonomy of each local church, be halted. Their efforts were repulsed on every occasion. In 1946 they did come close to achieving victory, lacking 350 votes of the required two-thirds majority to accomplish their purpose. It is evident that the defections from the Convention to the General Association of Regular Baptists, North, which at that time numbered about 500 churches, had cost the fundamentalists an important victory.[78] Dejected and stunned, the Fundamentalist Fellowship outlined new plans in the pursuit of their goal; this resulted in the formation of the Conservative Baptist Association in 1947. The struggle among the Baptists in the North has continued without relaxation ever since.[79]

There was less tension during the fundamentalist controversy in the South than in the North, simply because the Southern churches for the most part were essentially conservative. The only discordance of any consequence that did follow occurred in 1924 when J. Frank Norris began to accuse the Texas Baptists and the Southern Baptist Convention of inaction against modernism and evolution. The chief issue, however, was not modernism or evolution, although Norris continued to make charges along this line. The matter which disturbed Norris most was that the Southern Baptists showed some tendency toward tightening their grip on their constituent churches, which meant less autonomy for the local congregations and more ecclesiastical power for the denomination.[80]

Despite Norris' accusations and harassments, by 1929 the Southern Baptists became relatively free from internal dissension and tranquility began to prevail. Norris, however, was dissatisfied and succeeded in leading a contingent of dissenters out of the Southern Baptist Convention (a phenomenon which seems to be normal in all Baptist Conventions in all sections of the United States). This dissident group organized the World Baptist Fellowship, the Bible Baptist Seminary, and *The Fundamentalist*, a weekly newspaper. Norris edited this newspaper until his death in 1952, and through its pages maintained an incessant campaign against the Southern Baptist Convention. Since his death his followers, who probably more than any others represent the separatist fundamentalist movement in the South and the Southwest, have continued the campaign.[81]

Perhaps it can be stated without danger of contradiction that the Scopes trial in 1925 was the highest peak of and the turning point in the fundamentalist controversy. Within five years public interest in the controversial issues had declined appreciably and even the fundamentalists had lost their ardor for a fight to keep the issues alive.[82]

In his *The Fundamentalist Controversy*, Furniss has outlined and summarized what seem to be the most significant reasons for the decline in the controversy. First, the inopportune death of William Jennings Bryan immediately after the Scopes trial left the fundamentalists with no outstanding national leader who could hold them together. Second, the fundamentalists had dissipated their energies uselessly and as a result failed to consolidate their forces to produce an effective, permanent national organization. Third, the reappearance of the prohibition question divided the attention of the fundamentalists, many of whom turned to the immediate question of repeal. Fourth, the economic 'crash' of 1929 turned the attention of the churches to the need of alleviating human misery caused by the depression, and as a consequence dispelled much of the theological strife. Fifth, there was the spread of knowledge. Furniss contended that many people were stimulated by the controversy to read scientific books and thereby learned the facts of evolution without the distorted interpretations of the fundamentalists. The radio, then in its infancy, also helped spread knowledge. Harry Emerson Fosdick, for example, preached on the air and many people liked what he said and saw him in a different light than he had been pictured by the fundamentalists. Finally, the fundamentalists modified the nature of their propaganda and method of attack. They became petulant, passive, and in some instances less vitriolic. They began to appear harmless and chose to become martyrs serving God as an abused remnant.[83]

There was another factor which Furniss did not mention. A reaction against liberalism had begun to be manifest by 1930. This undoubtedly softened the nature of the fundamentalists' attack for a while. A re-alignment of theological forces was taking shape during the thirties with the rise of Karl Barth's school of neo-orthodoxy which showed that theologians were becoming disillusioned with liberalism, particularly after the rise of dictators like Hitler and Mussolini. Repentant liberals and moderate conservatives were united by the Barthian view that man is a sinner who needs to be encountered by God before he can alter his ways and improve his surroundings. This was one of the doctrines which the fundamentalists had insisted upon as being essentially biblical. However, the Barthians accepted the principles and the methods of the higher critics and like them denied the verbal and inerrant inspiration of the Bible. The fundamentalists were sorely displeased with this. Nevertheless, the Barthian movement for the moment dulled the cutting edge of the fundamentalists' argument.[84]

Even though the fundamentalist controversy had quieted down immeasurably during the thirties, this does not mean that the fundamentalists had been completely silenced and that they would eventually become extinct. During the thirties the fundamentalists were active in positive and constructive ways. The things they did during this period were foundational and no doubt prepared them for the developments which followed World War II. They explored the various possibilities for an effective national organization which came to fruition during the war.

Newspapers, magazines, books, tracts, and other types of literature flowed from fundamentalist presses in an endless stream. Evangelists continued to conduct revival meetings wherever possible. Meanwhile, many fundamentalists began to utilize the new medium of radio, which probably more than anything else, kept the doctrines of the fundamentalists before the American people. Charles E. Fuller, preacher on the Old Fashioned Revival Hour, first started broadcasting the gospel over an independent station in California in 1925. By 1933 he had expanded his program to a network of stations. Others began to follow Fuller with broadcasts of their own. It was not very long before most people of the United States could hear the gospel if they so desired. Certainly, the fundamentalists had kept their own hopes alive during the thirties, and their efforts helped condition the American people to be receptive to their theological viewpoints.[85]

CHAPTER TWO

The Dual Alignment of Fundamentalism

The demise of the World's Christian Fundamentals Association indicated that the fundamentalists had not made any long range plans to maintain their testimony; everything in the way of an organized movement had been haphazardly tried. This in part explains why the fundamentalists acted in an intolerant manner towards the modernists, without any consideration of honest differences in belief. After the waning of the World's Christian Fundamentals Association few expected the fundamentalists would again become a significant force in American religious life. Furniss concluded in the last paragraph of his book, published in 1954, that the fundamentalists remain 'today not by any means extinguished but unable to capture the headlines.'[1] The fundamentalists were aware of their plight and they were distressed about their possible fate during the thirties; hardly anyone among them was optimistic. For the most part they acted like martyrs and regarded themselves as the 'faithful remnant' of modern times suffering for Jesus Christ. This was a psychological stimulant, because they believed their faithfulness would be rewarded posthumously.[2]

The Independent Church Movement
In the early efforts to maintain rigid orthodoxy and safeguards against modernist 'corruption,' fundamentalists on the congregational level had to choose between secession from those denominations which had gone over to modernism, thereby risking the loss of all their church properties, or to remain as they were as unwilling, but 'contaminated' members of apostate denominations. In the churches controlled by the congregation, such as the Baptists, Congregationalists, and Disciples of Christ, the fear of any loss of property by the local congregation to the denomination was not a serious problem. In these churches the deed to the property usually remained in the hands of the Board of Trustees of the local congregation. Therefore, in these

churches convincing agitators for secession frequently incited a significant majority in their congregations to make this bold step. This was the beginning of the independent church movement of modern fundamentalism.[3]

The road ahead was more rugged for fundamentalists in the churches controlled by a centralized body such as the Methodists and the Presbyterians, since the denomination rather than the local congregation held the title to the property. Secessionists in these denominations lost the right to any use of the property which had been supported by their contributions. One fundamentalist minister, commenting on the difficulty he and his congregation faced when they decided to secede from the Presbyterian denomination, said:

We had to make a more difficult decision as Presbyterians than the Baptists. Our sacrifices were much greater from the physical standpoint. When we seceded we had to give up our property and start anew. We were not as fortunate as our fundamentalist Baptist brethren who could steal a church from their denomination whenever they decided to sever their connections with their denomination.[4]

Nevertheless, numerous churches decided to secede from regular denominations to start independent fundamental churches. During the thirties, independent denominations came into being such as the General Association of Regular Baptists, North, known briefly as GARB; the Bible Presbyterian Church, which Carl McIntire helped organize; the Bible Protestant Church (formerly the Methodist Protestant Church), a group of dissenters refusing to enter into the Methodist union in 1939; and the Independent Fundamental Churches of America, whose membership was drawn from several denominations. There were many smaller independent churches which remained unaffiliated, although their sympathies for the most part were with other fundamentalists.[5]

Independence was only a transitional stage which prepared the way for an organized fundamentalist movement that soon followed. But even after the fundamentalists finally became organized nationally they continued to think and act as independents, primarily because of the fear of ecclesiastical control of local congregations. This state of mind has persisted among many fundamentalists to this day, and those who would understand their temperament must always keep this in mind. This explains, for example, why the fundamentalists are militantly opposed to the ecumenical movement in Protestantism, which they believe is only a step away from a 'super-church' or a Protestant ecclesiasticism.[6]

The American Council of Christian Churches

The independents soon were persuaded that their survival depended upon the united defense of their historic faith. Several abortive attempts were made to organize a national council of fundamentalist churches. However, nothing significant developed along this line until the leaders of the Bible Protestant Church, meeting in Westville, New Jersey, sanctioned the formation of an official committee of three on September 27, 1940 to explore with the leaders of the Bible Presbyterian Church the possibility of a union of fundamentalist forces at the national level. The Bible Presbyterian Synod subsequently approved the formation of a similar committee in a meeting at Chester, Pennsylvania in October of the same year. The two committees immediately began to study the problems connected with formation of such a council and to seek the means to implement their common desires by the formation of a national organization.[7] Approximately a year later the two groups met in New York City where a draft of a constitution providing for the formation of the American Council of Christian Churches (hereafter referred to as the American Council) was formally adopted on September 17, 1941.[8] It was 'militantly pro-Gospel and anti-modernist.'[9]

The principles upon which the American Council was founded were incorporated into the preamble of its constitution:

Whereas, it is the duty of Christian believers to make common testimony to their glorious faith, especially in darkening days of apostasy, the bodies forming this council do now establish it as an agency unreservedly dedicated without compromise or evasion as a witness to the glory of God and the historic faith of the church universal, including adherence to these truths among others, equally precious: the full truthfulness, inerrancy, and authority of the Bible, which is the Word of God; the holiness and love of the one sovereign God, Father, Son, and Holy Spirit; the true deity and sinless humanity of our Lord Jesus Christ, His virgin birth, His atoning death, 'The just for the unjust,' His bodily resurrection, His glorious coming again; salvation by grace through faith alone; the oneness in Christ of those He has redeemed with His own precious blood; and the maintenance in the visible church of purity of life and doctrine.[10]

The stated purpose of the American Council was dual, 'of a testimony and of separation.' It was established to maintain and advance the 'historic faith' embodied in the five articles of fundamentalism and in the preamble of the American Council.[11] Its constitution also provided for an exclusivist or separatist organization, barring individual churches and denominations from its membership as long as any of them were associated with modernism[12] or remained affiliated with the Federal Council of the Churches of Christ in America. Only those who renounced modernism or separated from the Federal Council were eligible for membership in the American Council.[13]

Carl McIntire became the first president of the new fundamentalist council. He was well known by his opponents as one ready and eager to engage anyone in debate in defense of the historic position of fundamentalism. McIntire was not visibly disturbed by those who criticized his controversial mannerisms. Criticism apparently stimulated him into further aggressiveness, which his sometimes befuddled foes never seemed to have observed. McIntire expected to be criticized and he was always ready for it. He declared his intention to challenge the right of the Federal Council to speak as the sole representative of Protestantism in America. Thus an article published in the *Presbyterian*, an organ of the Presbyterian Church in the U.S.A., properly described the new fundamentalist organization as a protesting council of churches.[14] *Newsweek* described the American Council as a group of dissidents explicitly organized to fight the Federal Council.[15] Obviously, there were many who recognized that the future held no bright prospects of religious peace in the United States.

After the American Council was organized its leaders began to question the allotment of free radio time which the Federal Communications Commission allocated to the three main branches in religion in America: Roman Catholics, Jews, and Protestants. The American Council demanded that the Protestant share of free radio time be apportioned between them and the Federal Council. This was done. Before the American Council was formed, the Federal Council also decided the Protestant quota of chaplains for the armed forces of the United States. The American Council protested to the Government and they were allowed a quota of chaplains. These two incidents made it abundantly clear that the American Council was in a fighting mood, and that henceforth the Federal Council would not enjoy these privileges undivided.[16]

The American Council immediately began a concerted drive to encourage other dissident fundamentalists to separate from the Federal Council. Its spokesman contended that this was necessary because co-existence between liberals and fundamentalists in one church was not only impossible but also scripturally wrong. Therefore, the American Council began to publish a newspaper – along with pamphlets and brochures – to promulgate their program and to point out the errors of the Federal Council. Carl McIntire became the editor of the *Christian Beacon*. In its pages he warned fundamentalists about the danger to their faith and he encouraged them to separate from liberal churches. To show the slightest departures from fundamentalism, he published photographic exposures and analyses of sermons, statements, articles, and books by leaders of the Federal Council.[17]

The National Association of Evangelicals
In 1944 Carl McIntire proudly wrote that the fundamentalists had finally emerged with a permanent national organization. He said:

The groups that have been called fundamentalists have been chided because they cannot get along together, but they are now proving to the world that the charge is false and that they can work together; for in the American Council they are uniting and helping to mold and lift the whole level of the evangelical testimony in America.[18]

Those unacquainted with the situation within the fundamentalist movement probably gained the impression from McIntire's statement that only one fundamentalist organization existed and that all was well within it. However, the fundamentalists were badly split. On October 27-28, 1941, slightly more than a month after the American Council was organized, another distinct group met at the Moody Bible Institute in Chicago to consider the formation of an organization which 'was determined to break with apostasy but . . . wanted no dog-in-the-manger, reactionary, negative, or destructive type of organization.' This group was 'determined to shun all forms of bigotry, intolerance, misrepresentation, hate, jealousy, false judgment, and hypocrisy.'[19] Actually, this second group, which became the National Association of Evangelicals, was determined not to embark upon a program similar to that of the American Council.[20]

The representatives of the American Council were given an opportunity to present their proposals at the Chicago convention of the National Association of Evangelicals. The purpose was to discover a formula which might result in the formation of one national fundamentalist organization. After hearing the views of the American Council, however, the National Association of Evangelicals rejected their plan for one national organization, because it did not 'properly express and implement the constructive ideals which they had in mind.'[21] The National Association of Evangelicals proposed to follow an inclusivist policy wherein its constituent members were not required to separate from denominations or churches affiliated with the Federal Council – a policy the American Council adamantly opposed. Furthermore, the National Association of Evangelicals was opposed to the American Council's vitriolic attack upon the Federal Council, because they thought it might be more harmful than beneficial. The two fundamentalist groups agreed doctrinally, but they were divided in method.[22]

A group of ministers in the New England Fellowship, led by J. Elwin Wright as chairman, was responsible for initiating the resolution calling for the Chicago Convention that prepared the way for the establishment of the National Association of Evangelicals in 1941. After invitations were mailed by the New England Fellowship, ministers from various sections of the United States attended the Chicago meeting, and before the conference adjourned a Constitutional convention was scheduled for April 7-9, 1942 in St. Louis. Wright was chosen as chairman of a temporary committee to prepare a draft of the constitution.[23]

Approximately two hundred leaders and delegates from thirty-four denominations, missionary organizations, and educational agencies convened in St. Louis on the night of April 7, 1942. The first session was described as a time of agonizing prayer for divine guidance to discover a formula for an effective national organization. The next day the Convention got down to the practical aspects of its business and listened to the speeches of various fundamentalist leaders. Representatives of the American Council were also present and were given an opportunity, as in Chicago a year earlier, to present their proposals to the Convention. They again warned that a radical separation from the Federal Council must take place before fundamentalism could advance. Some of their arguments were convincing because a division of opinion over the issue of exclusivism or inclusivism had occurred, and some of the delegates demanded that the issue be debated. However, the majority of delegates favored an inclusivist organization with a constructive approach toward liberal Protestantism.[24]

These issues finally caused a dual alignment of fundamentalism, and this disagreement has been bitterly debated to the present day. In some respects the division has been advantageous. The inclusivist policy of the National

Association of Evangelicals has enabled it to bore from within the major trunk of American Protestantism, while the exclusivist American Council attacks the liberals from without. This two-prong attack has been effective. It would appear, however, that of the two groups, the National Association of Evangelicals has profited the most because of its inclusivist policy.[25]

Steps were taken by the delegates at St. Louis to establish a tentative constitution which provided for voluntary membership of denominations and churches, which could conscientiously subscribe to the doctrinal statement of the National Association of Evangelicals. The constitution imposed a restriction against denominations affiliated with the Federal Council, making them ineligible for membership in the National Association of Evangelicals. In this respect the National Association of Evangelicals established an exclusivist policy in line with that of the American Council. But this restriction did not apply to individuals or groups of churches, which were involuntarily affiliates of the Federal Council through the action of their ecclesiastical superiors. A large part of the membership of the National Association of Evangelicals came from churches with no voice in the matter of affiliation with the Federal Council.[26]

Before the St. Louis conference adjourned Harold John Ockenga, who was rated as an intellectual of promise in the fundamentalist movement, was elected president of the new provisional organization. J. Elwin Wright was appointed in charge of a temporary office, later established in Boston, where the affairs of the new organization were conducted. It was not long before applications for membership from thousands of interested fundamentalist churches, which declared they could no longer support the Federal Council, began to flood this office. Additional staff members were employed to process the applications, and additional office space was acquired. The formula discovered by the National Association of Evangelicals appeared to be effective.[27]

Approximately 1,000 delegates representing fifty denominations, with a potential constituency of 15,000,000, converged upon Chicago on May 3, 1943 for the second annual Convention of the National Association of Evangelicals. The delegates were extremely jubilant, and by song and prayer created an atmosphere like a second Pentecost. This can be readily explained. There were only two hundred delegates from thirty-four denominational organizations at the Convention in St. Louis in 1942. In one year this number had expanded tremendously. The delegates at the Chicago Convention were sure their movement was being divinely directed. No one seemed to be able to explain it in any other way, and this historic moment called for rejoicing.[28]

President Ockenga delivered the keynote address to the Convention, in which he blamed modern liberal thought for the destructive forces endangering the security of the world. By speaking as he did, Ockenga seemed to have veered from the announced constructive approach which leaders in the National Association of Evangelicals had proclaimed they would follow. However, in speaking as he did Ockenga sought only to emphasize the real theological differences which separated all fundamentalists from liberal or modernist ecclesiastical leaders. Ockenga was determined to make it clear that the National Association of Evangelicals did not intend to surrender to those whom they regarded as apostate. The earlier pronouncement of tolerance was meant to be applied not to liberals or modernists, but only to fundamentalists or to those still within denominations controlled by liberals or modernists who were faithful to the *fundamentals*.[29] His attack on the liberals differed little from those of McIntire and the disputants connected with the fundamentalists during the twenties.

The leaders of the Federal Council were disturbed by the criticisms which came from both fundamentalist groups. In its report of the formation of the National Association of Evangelicals in 1943 the *Christian Century* (regarded by the fundamentalists as the voice of liberalism) referred to their action as an effort to promote atomistic sectarianism by members dissatisfied with the Federal Council and largely recruited from dissident groups, such as the Baptists, Disciples of Christ, Presbyterians, and Congregationalists.[30]

The first matter considered by the delegates at the Chicago Convention was a statement of faith on which the delegates representing forty denominations could agree. After careful deliberation a minimal statement – the common denominator of united evangelical action – was formulated, essentially on the principles of 'the deity of Christ and the Bible as the Word of God.' A detailed statement covering seven points and reiterating the five articles of fundamentalism was approved by the delegates without a dissenting vote. They were:

1. *We believe the Bible to be the inspired, the only infallible, authoritarian word of God.*

2. *We believe that there is one God, eternally existent in three persons, Father, Son and Holy Ghost.*

3. *We believe in the deity of our Lord Jesus Christ, in His virgin birth, in His sinless life, in His miracles, in His vicarious and atoning death through*

His shed blood, in His bodily resurrection, in His ascension to the right hand of the Father, and in His personal return in power and glory.

4. *We believe that for the salvation of lost and sinful men regeneration by the Holy Spirit is absolutely essential.*

5. *We believe in the present ministry of the Holy Spirit by whose indwelling the Christian is enabled to live a godly life.*

6. *We believe in the resurrection of both the saved and the lost; but they that are saved unto the resurrection of life and they that are lost unto the resurrection of damnation.*

7. *We believe in the spiritual unity of believers in our Lord Jesus Christ.*[31]

Those who accepted this statement by signature were admitted into fellowship of the National Association of Evangelicals. The founders sought to be as inclusivist in their policy as possible, but exclusive only of 'those who do not accept the Bible as God's Word.'[32]

The national Association of Evangelicals recognized at once the necessity of forming certain functioning units in the various fields of interchurch cooperation. A Committee on Policy and Fields of Endeavor was formed and it established promotional headquarters and various regional offices under the direction of a central board of administrators. The Committee also suggested the formation of other committees on evangelism, missions, education, moral and social welfare, quotas for chaplains in the armed services of the United States, separation of church and state, and radio broadcasting. The program of the National Association was to be as comprehensive as possible.[33]

At the founding of the National Association of Evangelicals there was concern over the matter of separation of church and state. In 1939 President Franklin Delano Roosevelt had appointed Myron C. Taylor as his personal representative to the Vatican. The National Association of Evangelicals and the American Council became alarmed; they feared a sinister plot to violate the American principle of separation of church and state. The Committee of Policy and Fields of Endeavor waged a campaign against any sanction, support, or legislation (including the allocation of any public funds for the benefit of any sectarian institution), which might foster one form of religion and thereby restrict or abridge the rights of others. In this respect the fundamentalists were in accord with most Protestants and humanists in America.[34]

The growth of the National Association of Evangelicals
Various reports were issued by the National Association to indicate its success in attracting members. Three years after its formation, it claimed over 1,000,000 members drawn from twenty-two denominations, one hundred individual churches, and other organizations and institutions. In 1947 the membership had increased another half million. In 1956 the National Association of Evangelicals claimed that it was the 'fastest-growing interdenominational, conservative body in American Protestantism.'[35]

Editor James DeForest Murch of the *United Evangelical Action*, official journal of the National Association of Evangelicals, estimated in January, 1957 that there were 58,000,000 Protestants in a total church membership of 100,000,000 in the United States. Among the Protestants he stated that 21,000,000 were fundamentalists outside of the National Council of Churches (successors of the Federal Council). He estimated there were 3,000,000 additional fundamentalists in the National Council. According to Murch's calculations, therefore, one-half of the Protestants in America were fundamentalists.[36]

In Tables I and II, which appear at the end of this chapter, the official membership of the National Association of Evangelicals as given in 1956 is shown. One of the significant aspects of this tabulation is that many Pentecostal or 'tongue' groups are represented in the membership of the National Association of Evangelicals. The Pentecostals, also known as holiness people and sometimes opprobriously called holy rollers, originated during the 1890's for the most part in the southwest and in the mountain areas of the south among the poorer folk. They were extremely conservative in doctrine, Bible-centered, millenarian, and stressed the necessity of personal religious experience.[37] They were also 'inimical to modern scholarship, which they called 'modernism.'[38]

Because of the inclusivist policy which proffered unimpaired fundamentalist fellowship to all who subscribed to a belief in the inerrant Bible, the Pentecostal groups began to gravitate toward the National Association of Evangelicals. Carl McIntire and others in the American Council regarded the Pentecostal movement as a disruptive force not 'in the historic succession of the evangelical church.' The American Council felt that their presence in any association of evangelicals was obnoxious, perhaps subversive, and likely to result in a hybrid fundamentalist movement.[39] Because of its separatist position, the National Bible Institute (now Shelton College and a member of the American Council) stated in its bulletin its reluctance 'to graduate, or to certify as

competent leaders, those who make propaganda of such views.'[40] McIntire
also said that before a union of the American Council and the National
Association of Evangelicals could be effected, the latter must be willing to
eliminate the Pentecostals from its membership.[41]

The Revolt within the American Council
For an undetermined time an undercurrent of discontent in the Bible Presbyterian Church, primarily among its youthful leaders (but also supported by
some of its old ones), threatened to flare up into an open revolt. The reasons
were disapproval of the leadership of Carl McIntire, of the rigid separatist
position of the American Council, and over discrepancies in the statistical
reports which it was charged exaggerated the actual membership of the
American Council. An open rupture finally occurred in 1954 in Greenville,
South Carolina during the meeting of the General Synod of the Bible Presbyterian Church. Robert Rayburn, president of Highland College in California,
led the revolting faction. It charged the leaders of the American Council with
deliberate deception, falsification, and exaggeration.[42] This 'underground'
movement, as it was called, directed its attack upon Carl McIntire and other
leaders of the American Council charging they assumed too much authority
and presumed to speak without prior approval about the policies of the Bible
Presbyterian Church. These 'self willed' leaders, as they were described by
the revolting group, refused to accept criticism no matter how constructive,
but instead embarked upon a subtle program to silence their detractors.[43]
Rayburn repudiated Carl McIntire's leadership when he was asked if he
accepted the latter's position on separation. Rayburn answered: ' . . . I do not
accept the doctrine of separation as defined by Carl McIntire; I accept the
doctrine of separation as defined by the Word of God.'[44]

   In 1955 the issues which precipitated the revolt were made much clearer
when the General Synod of the Bible Presbyterian Church decided to form
a new committee on Christian Education, debated whether the Synod should
control the agencies and institutions of the church, proposed that an official
magazine be founded, and approved the establishment of a college controlled
by the Synod.[45] Up to that time the various agencies, schools, and institutions
of the Bible Presbyterian Church (such as Highland College, Faith Theological
Seminary, The Bible Presbyterian Home for the Aged, the *Christian Beacon*,
and missionary boards) had operated independently, free from the control
of the Synod.[46]

   This independent arrangement of the various agencies, schools, and institutions of the Bible Presbyterian Church was the work of Carl McIntire and others, and was an aftermath of the struggle in the 1930's with the Presbyterian Church in the U.S.A. It will be recalled that Carl McIntire, J. Gresham Machen, and others were expelled in 1936 by the Presbyterian Church for their independent action in the formation of the Independent Board for Presbyterian Foreign Missions, which operated free from control by the Synod. When McIntire and others founded the Bible Presbyterian Church in 1936 as an aftermath of their expulsion, they were determined this would not happen again. They incorporated a clause in the constitution of the Bible Presbyterian Church permitting the establishment of both independent and controlled agencies, schools, and institutions. However, under the influence of McIntire independent agencies, schools, and institutions predominated and by the fifties tended to weaken the growth of the Bible Presbyterian Church. Therefore, the newer leaders rising to power in the church demanded that the various agencies, schools, and institutions be placed under the direct control and operation of the Synod.[47]

Another important factor in the revolt centered around the question of inaccuracies in the statistical reports released by the American Council. It was charged that figures were inflated to make it appear that the membership of the American Council was larger than it actually was. The protesters complained that the inaccuracies had caused them embarrassment, because the liberals and even the National Association of Evangelicals began to impugn their honesty.[48]

An explanation is necessary at this point with respect to the method of determining membership and the status of members in the American Council. There are two types of members in the American Council, constituent and auxiliary members. Both must be in full accord with the purposes of the American Council before admission into membership. The real difference between the two types of members, however, is that constituent members are fully separated from the Federal Council and therefore are permitted to vote, while auxiliary members are quasi-affiliates and hence partly separated from the Federal Council. Auxiliary members are therefore not permitted to vote.[49] Constituent membership is determined by the following provision of the American Council's constitution:

No national church or association which is a member of the Federal council of Churches of Christ in America[50] is eligible for membership in this Council so long as it retains connection with that body, nor shall local churches or individuals connected with national bodies holding membership in the said Federal Council be eligible for constituent membership.[51]

Auxiliary members, although still technically connected with the Federal Council, are admitted into membership in the American Council provided they repudiate the Federal Council as required by the constitution of the American Council as follows:

Every applicant for either local or individual membership connected with a body belonging to the Federal Council of Churches shall with their application to the American Council certify that a written statement has been forwarded to their or his denomination and local church Council or Federation, if one exists, certifying to such bodies that they should no longer consider themselves as representing the applicant.[52]

The Constituent membership of the American Council for 1950 and 1957 is compared in Table III, which appears at the end of this chapter. The Table shows that the American Council's membership has changed rapidly without any appreciable permanent gains. Several new churches or associations joined the American Council between 1950 and 1957, while some had seceded or had been dropped for disciplinary reasons. The Independent Fundamental Churches of America (one of the largest Constituent members) and two other churches, the Evangelical Methodist Church and the Iowa Eldership of Churches of God in North America, voluntarily withdrew from the American Council.[53] However, the American Council continued to list the Evangelical Methodist Church as a constituent member in 1957, although it had united with the National Association of Evangelicals in 1956.[54] Another reason for the rapid change in membership of the American Council was that some associations either ceased to exist or had merged with other organizations and had taken a new name. Finally, some were expelled for disciplinary reasons as in the case of the American Episcopal Church (Evangelical), which was dropped in 1945 after its self-styled Bishop D. Scott Swain had been exposed as a religious racketeer and an ex-convict – an unusual and unenviable preparation for the ministry.[55]

In 1948 the American Council claimed a combined constituent and auxiliary membership of 1,213,000. Less than 200,000 were constituent members who were accountable. This left approximately 1,000,000 auxiliary members. A major portion of auxiliary members, probably five-sixths, were also members of churches or denominations affiliated with the Federal Council. In this connection, Stephen W. Paine, president of Houghton (New York) College and one of the prominent leaders in the National Association of Evangelicals, criticized the American Council for inaccuracies in its statistics. Writing on the subject in 1951, Paine stated that the tabulations were exaggerated both to offset the numerical advantage of the Federal Council and to challenge the latter's right to speak for all Protestants in America.[56]

The question of free radio time, mentioned earlier in this study, was also a factor in the controversy over the American Council's statistics. In 1943 and 1944 the American Council conducted a campaign to obtain signatures on petitions it circulated throughout the United States. These petitions were produced as evidence before the Federal Communications Commission supporting the claim of the American Council that it represented a large segment of Protestants in America. Therefore, it was entitled to a proportionate share of Protestant free radio time, which until that time had been allotted wholly to the Federal Council. Those who signed the petitions approximated 800,000. Of this figure 250,000 were presumed to be non-members of the Federal Council so they were counted as constituent members of the American Council. The remainder, approximately 550,000 were presumed to be in the Federal Council so they were counted as auxiliary members of the American Council without voting privileges. Perhaps many who signed the petitions were unaware that the American Council construed their act as a repudiation of the Federal Council and that for that reason they met the constitutional requirement of, and were counted as, members of the American Council.[57]

In 1950 fifteen denominations with a reported membership of 263,311 were classified as constituent members in the American Council.[58] Robert Rayburn said that of this number 19,423 were not actually members of any denominations then listed by the American Council. Another 40,000 persons, who were members of the National Fellowship of Brethren Churches should not have been counted since they cooperated with the American Council in radio matters only, but never united with it. Thus, if in these two cases the disputed members were dropped it would show only 203,888 constituent members in the American Council in 1950, 59,423 less than the American Council had claimed.[59]

Furthermore, there were errors in the statistical report of the Bible Presbyterian Church. Rayburn stated that the actual membership of the Bible Presbyterian Church in 1954 was only 8,428, not 15,662 as had been listed by the American Council.[60]

Robert Ketcham (national chairman of the General Association of Regular Baptists, North) was irked by the allegations of dishonesty against those who had prepared the American Council's statistical report. He charged that the Stated Clerk of the Bible Presbyterian Church was responsible for the disputed statistics. He explained that the Stated Clerk had combined the Sunday School membership with the church membership (the latter amounting to 7,234). This explained the difference in the total figures questioned by Rayburn. In 1955 the Stated Clerk avoided this confusion by separating the Sunday School from the church membership, and that settled one minor item in the dispute.[61] Thus, the statistics of the American Council for 1954 should only show 196,654 constituent members. This figure approximates the estimated 200,000 membership given in 1951 by Stephen W. Paine when he criticized the American Council for inaccuracies in its statistics.[62] Obviously, both sides in the controversy were not clear on what was being reported, and if the statistics were inaccurate as charged, both factions must be held responsible for the errors. However, it is apparent that the membership of the American Council had remained relatively stable during the period between 1951 and 1954.

Another factor leading to the schism in the American Council was the failure of the Bible Presbyterian Church to grow during the period between 1951 and 1954. This stagnation was attributed to the domination of the independents within the Bible Presbyterian Church whose policy it was to promote independent agencies, schools, and institutions free from the control of the Synod. The dismissal of Robert Rayburn from his post as president of Highland College and J. Oliver Buswell, Jr., from a similar position at Shelton College, for example, resulted partly from the fear on the part of the independents that the two had planned for Synod control of the two schools.[63] The pro-Synod faction also attributed the stagnation of their church to the tendency of the independents to neglect evangelism while engaging in separatist polemics which repelled people from the church. Furthermore, the growth of the Bible Presbyterian Church and the fundamentalist movement, it was charged, was hindered by the vitriolic campaign the independents waged against the National Association of Evangelicals over the separatist-inclusivist issue. Kenneth A. Horner, member of the pro-Synod faction, wrote that while the Bible Presbyterians were definitely committed to separatism, there was a feeling among those in his faction that there was need of some liberty in its observance because 'strict adherence to such 'rules' has so completely cut us off from fellowship or contact with many of our fellow-believers that we have removed ourselves from any possibility of assisting them to understand and adopt our separationist position.'[64]

The two factions could not come to any appropriate agreement to settle the differences between them. However, the pro-Synod faction was in the majority when the Nineteenth General Synod of the Bible Presbyterian Church convened in St. Louis in April, 1956. During that conference a vote was taken to disassociate the Bible Presbyterian Church from the American Council and the International Council of Christian Churches. The latter organization had been formed in 1948 on the same principles of the American Council; actually it was an international extension of the American Council.[65] Action was also taken in St. Louis to reaffirm a decision made in 1955 to establish certain missionary and educational agencies under the control of the Synod. Covenant College and Theological Seminary, which had been established in 1955 and temporarily located in Pasadena, California, was relocated in St. Louis where it opened in September, 1956 with twenty-two students. Robert Rayburn was installed as president of the new college and J. Oliver Buswell, Jr. was appointed dean of the graduate school and seminary.[66]

The decision of the Nineteenth General Synod to disassociate the Bible Presbyterian Church from the American Council placed McIntire and other extreme separatists in a peculiar situation. They were removed from influence in the Bible Presbyterian Church, and technically detached from constituent membership in the American Council as a result of the action of the General Synod. However, McIntire, always a strategist in church controversies, quickly united his dispossessed faction to form the Bible Presbyterian Church Association for the purpose of maintaining representation in the American Council and the International Council.[67]

McIntire and those who formed the Bible Presbyterian Church Association complicated matters still further because they remained within the Bible Presbyterian Church and their action in forming the new organization was regared as an act of insubordination. However, no formal action was taken to censure McIntire and his associates until 1957, when McIntire was dropped from membership in the Bible Presbyterian Church after the Collingswood Synod of which McIntire is a member separated from the national body.[68] Meanwhile, the pro-Synod faction discussed the implications of McIntire's independent actions. Horner wrote:

The question of the nature of Presbyterianism is again raised at this point because it is held by those who support the actions of the Church that a

Presbyterian Church acts as a church in such matters. It is their feeling that for individuals, local churches, and Presbyteries to form an actual association within the framework of a Presbyterian Church to act contrary to the decisions of the Church itself is tantamount to a revolution against the decisions of the Church and borders closely on the formation of an actual denomination within a denomination.[69]

Thus, McIntire maneuvered himself into a position similar to the one over two decades ago when he and others in the Presbyterian Church in the U.S.A. established the Independent Board for Presbyterian Missions which resulted in their expulsion from their denomination. Then McIntire and his associates had established the Bible Presbyterian Church, which repudiated McIntire in 1956. These situations illustrate the reasons for, and the sources of, new churches in America.[70]

TABLE I

CHURCHES, ASSOCIATIONS, AND DENOMINATIONS AFFILIATED WITH
THE NATIONAL ASSOCIATION OF EVANGELICALS IN 1956
INCLUDING THEIR TOTAL MEMBERSHIP *

Assemblies of God	400,000
Association of Fundamental Ministers and Churches	1,000
Brethren in Christ Church	6,000
Christian Church of North America, Inc.	18,000
Christian Union	15,000
Church of God (Cleveland, Tennessee)	200,000
Church of the United Brethren in Christ	20,000
Churches of Christ in Christian Union	10,500
Congregational Methodist Church	12,500
Church by the Side of the Road	2,000
Conservative Congregational Conference	10,000
Elim Missionary Assemblies	5,000
Evangelical Free Church of America	30,000
Evangelical Mennonite Brethren Church	2,000
Evangelical Mennonite Church of North America	2,000
Evangelical Methodist Church	20,000
Evangelistic Tabernacles	2,000
Free Methodist Church of North America	51,000
General Six-Principle Baptists	280
Grace Gospel Evangelistic Association	1,000
Holiness Methodist Church	1,000
International Church of the Foursquare Gospel	88,000
International Pentecostal Assemblies	5,000
Krimmer Mennonite Brethren Conference	2,000
Mennonite Brethren Church of North America	15,000
Missionary Bands of the World, Inc.	250
Missionary Church Association	7,000
Missionary Methodist Conference	2,000
New England Fellowship of Evangelical Baptists	2,000
National Association of Free Will Baptists	400,000
Ohio Yearly Meeting of Friends	7,000
Open Bible Standard Churches	27,000
Oregon Yearly Meeting of Friends	6,500
Pentecostal Church of God of America	45,000
Pentecostal Holiness Church	45,000
Primitive Methodist Church of the USA	12,500
Reformed Presbyterian Church of North America	5,000
United Fundamentalist Church	1,000
United Holy Church of America	27,000
United Missionary Church	10,000
Wesleyan Methodist Church of America	35,500
TOTAL	1,551,530

* Source: Murch, *Co-operation Without Compromise*, pp. 202–203.

TABLE II

CONFERENCES OF DENOMINATIONS AFFILIATED WITH THE NATIONAL ASSOCIATION OF EVANGELICALS IN 1956 INCLUDING THEIR TOTAL MEMBERSHIP *

Advent Christian Church, Massachusetts Conference	5,000
Advent Christian Church, New Hampshire Conference	1,200
Baptist General Conference of New England	3,000
California Conference of United Brethren In Christ	600
North Central District of the Pilgrim Holiness Church	5,000
Pacific Northwest Conference of Evangelical United Brethren Church	11,000
Western Conference of Evangelical Congregational Church	3,000
TOTAL	28,800

Total from Table I	1,551,530
Total from Table II	28,800
Total Membership	1,580,330

* Source: Murch, *Co-operation Without Compromise*, pp. 202–203.

TABLE III

THE AMERICAN COUNCIL OF CHRISTIAN CHURCHES IN 1950 AND 1957 SHOWING CHANGES IN ITS CONSTITUENT MEMBERSHIP *

Membership in 1950	Membership in 1957
Associated Gospel Churches	Associated Gospel Church
Bible Presbyterian Church	Bible Presbyterian Church Association
Bible Protestant Church	Bible Protestant Church
Conference of Fundamental Church	Congregational Methodist Church
Evangelical Methodist Church	Conservative Baptist Association of
General Association of Regular Baptists, North	Canada
Independent Fundamental Churches of America	Evangelical Methodist Church
Iowa Eldership of the Churches of God in North America	General Association of Regular Baptists, North
Methodist Protestant Church	Independent Churches, Affiliated
National Fellowship of Brethren Churches	Methodist Protestant Church
Old (Evangelical) Catholic Church	Militant Fundamental Bible Churches
Southern Methodist Church	Southern Methodist Church
Tioga River Christian Conference	Tioga River Christian Conference
Union of Regular Baptist Churches of Ontario and Quebec	United Christian Church
United Christian Church	World Baptist Fellowship

* Source: 'American Council of Christian Churches' (pamphlet published by the American Council, No. 108, n.d.), 'American Council of Christian Churches' (pamphlet published by the American Council, n.d.); also see Roy, *Apostles of Discord*, pp. 397–398.

CHAPTER THREE

The Resurgence of Militant Fundamentalism

The fundamentalist controversy, as had been shown in Chapter I, abated after the Scopes trial with the result that not much was heard from the fundamentalists during the thirties when they were without a significant leader (such as William Jennings Bryan) who could command national attention. Their own leaders have stated that during this period despair rather than hope engulfed them. They had no effective national organization to provide identity of interest, and they failed to produce an educated clergy and a scholarly literature with which to combat modernism.[1] The atmosphere in which they moved was negative and reactionary. This meagre intellectual climate, as one commentator has noted, was 'not . . . conducive to the production of brilliant, flexible, highly trained, sensitive and scholarly trained minds.'[2]

The Transition from Liberalism to Neo-orthodoxy
From the twenties and well into the thirties the prevailing mood in Protestantism in America had been liberalism, with its 'theology' of the social gospel. Generally, American liberalism was world-affirming, i.e., it taught that harmony and peace could be attained by bringing Christian ethics to bear upon all human problems, and that negotiation among nations as a common brotherhood could be effectively substituted for war in settling international disputes. However, by the thirties many who might have preferred to follow liberalism were already unnerved by the disastrous effects of World War I, the economic depression, and the rise of the dictatorships of Hitler, Mussolini, and Stalin. Clergymen in American churches were turning from liberalism and looking for something to supplant it.[3]

In Europe following World War I, while political insecurity was still fresh in men's minds, the doctrines of Karl Barth and Emil Brunner, both outstanding European theologians, received widespread acceptance as more realistic for the human situation and the most practical answer to liberalism. The doctrine they elaborated was called the 'theology of crisis' because of its emphasis upon divine judgment. When individuals were encountered by God, at a critical moment in their lives, they surrendered their wills to and admitted their finitude before God.[4] Thus man stood 'at the bar of divine justice hearing God's verdict or judgment . . . and though hearing the condemning judgment of the sovereign, unknown God, he nonetheless ventured to confide in this condemning, unknown, unknowable.'[5] The books of Barth and Brunner began to circulate widely in America during the thirties. Their doctrines were readily accepted by both repentant liberals and moderate conservatives. These two groups provided the realignment for a strong central bloc in the churches affiliated with the Federal Council, and they declared their opposition 'to humanism on the left and fundamentalism on the right.'[6] By 1940 neo-orthodoxy, as the 'theology of crisis' was more familiarly known was firmly established in American Protestantism.[7]

Neo-orthodoxy drew its cardinal principles from orthodoxy. This does not mean, however, that it completely returned to medieval theology, though many of the teachings of Augustine, Luther, and Calvin were revived. For one thing, neo-orthodoxy rejected the fundamentalists' teaching regarding the infallibility and verbal inspiration of the Bible and adopted the higher critical method of biblical research instead. It regarded certain biblical statements as nothing more than pre-scientific legend, and for that reason studied them critically.[8] Therefore, unlike the fundamentalists, the neo-orthodox taught the Bible not as *the* objective Word of God but as a source of Christian truth that *becomes* the Word of God and acquires meaning 'in the moment of revelation.'[9] Revelation took place after God, having taken the initiative, encountered an individual while reading it. Because of the finitude of man, no one could be certain that any meaning or interpretation thus received was authoritative or final, although each individual was to render obedience to these tentative instructions, and make a decision to either follow or reject Jesus Christ as Savior.[10]

The neo-orthodox also accepted the social gospel, inherited for the most part from the liberals, with some slight differences. They believed that liberalism had been naive in placing too much faith in human nature and in the inevitability of progress. Consequently, they looked to an external authority, the transcendent God, to help them as Christians to reduce inequality and disharmony among men. However, even with God's help nothing lasting could be accomplished in history. Reinhold Niebuhr, one of the leading exponents of neo-orthodoxy in the United States, wrote that 'the final completion of history must include God's destruction of man's abortive and premature efforts to bring history to its culmination.'[11] Nevertheless, the requirement for responsible Christian social action was made no less urgent. Thus, the idea of the social gospel was the leavening influence through which the individual and society might expect to be slightly improved.[12]

The neo-orthodox agreed with the fundamentalists that man is essentially a fallen creature and that his salvation is not dependent upon personal merit but upon the grace of God through justification by faith. However, since the neo-orthodox tended to be more abstract than literal in interpreting the Scriptures, they regarded the Genesis account of the Fall as a myth having only a symbolic explanation. For the neo-orthodox the historical origin of sin is unknown; it is a secret of pre-destination and belongs to superhistory. But they were certain that man could not be otherwise than a sinner.[13]

It is difficult to determine the exact position of the neo-orthodox on other cardinal doctrines of fundamentalism such as the virgin birth, the deity of Christ, the atonement and resurrection, and the second coming. There are as many opinions and theories about these doctrines as there are original thinkers aligned with the neo-orthodox school of theology. The virgin birth has been referred to as an illegitimate rationalization, on the one hand, and an indispensable part of the Christian faith on the other. The mystery of the incarnation was sometimes explained as a miracle independent of the virgin birth; 'what was born was primarily of God and not of man,' as it was stated.[14] The biological doctrine was not as important as the idea which influenced its acceptance, that Jesus was born with a divine nature.[15]

The atonement of Jesus Christ was a necessary adjunct to neo-orthodoxy's doctrine of the sinfulness of man. However, it was their judgment that Christ's death on the cross was only a symbol of self-abnegation in which He conformed to divine love and by it became 'the moral mediator of the Father's will toward men.'[16] Neo-orthodoxy stated that through the cross the sinner was reminded of God's judgment, but as he appropriated the work of Christ by faith to himself he was also reminded of the triumphant mercy of God. Nels F. S. Ferré, another leading neo-orthodox theologian in the United States, wrote: 'The Atonement is the supreme revelation that *God* suffers to save a sinful world.'[17]

In the matter of the credibility of the resurrection there are many neo-orthodox theologians who doubt it, regarding it as perhaps an afterthought of the disciples of Christ as they later talked or wrote about Him.[18] Despite certain logical difficulties surrounding the resurrection, most neo-orthodox leaders have accepted it as a historical fact without which there would be very little hope left in Christianity,[19] since eternal life is not a matter '*of man's nature, but God's faithfulness as seen and experienced* in Christ Jesus.'[20] For these leaders, the doctrine of the resurrection points to a miraculous consummation of the immortal soul beyond history.[21]

Finally, it appears that neo-orthodox leaders in the United States have rejected any cataclysmic interpretations of the second coming of Christ as ordinarily taught by the fundamentalists. Instead they speak of the second coming of Christ as 'the eventual manifestation of divine love, and its completed victory over all evil . . .'[22] The second coming of Christ refers to an interim period during which the true meaning of history would be disclosed 'and the fulfillment of that meaning.'[23] Thus, 'just as creation is a necessary concept of the beginning of our history, so the Second Coming is a necessary concept of its end.'[24]

By mid-century neo-orthodoxy had become the dominant theological school of thought in Europe and the United States. On the surface, neo-orthodoxy appeared fundamentalistic, having revived the main emphases of St. Paul, Augustine, Luther, and Calvin. It stressed 'the insufficiency of human reason, the depravity of human nature, the inexorability of divine judgment, and the absolute need of divine grace if man is to be saved . . .'[25] The neo-orthodox retained the terminology of Protestant orthodoxy, although they changed the meaning of the terms in a large measure to fit their own presuppositions.[26]

At first the fundamentalists were pleased with the rise of neo-orthodoxy because they believed the latter had exposed 'the utter barrenness and inadequacies of modernism,' and had proved that the impact of liberalism on American religious thought to be less than had been supposed.[27] The fundamentalists were to discover, however, that neo-orthodoxy was not slavishly attached to the literal details of traditional orthodoxy, and had apparently retreated to a liberal position, reinterpreting the Bible according to scientific knowledge. This interpretation appeared to question the divine origin of the Bible. The orthodox could not agree and began to denounce the neo-orthodox as a new expression of modernism. Consequently, the warfare against liberalism (as at the beginning of the twentieth century) was resuscitated against the neo-orthodox or the new modernism, as the fundamentalists sometimes called neo-orthodoxy. Stephen W. Paine based the objections of the fundamentalists against the neo-orthodox in the following succinct statement:

The neo-supernaturalists generally accept the results of the higher criticism and reject the full authority and accuracy of the Scriptures. They tend to accept emergent evolution as accounting for the beginning of man and to reject the Genesis account of creation as a myth. Concerning the miracles of the Bible, and particularly those recorded concerning Christ, they tend to believe these 'in a spiritual sense,' but are not greatly interested in whether they ever actually took place.[28]

Futhermore, the fundamentalists objected to the use of orthodox terms which they believed obscured the liberalism of neo-orthodoxy. Paine said they called men back to the Word of God but made 'it clear that the Word of God was not to be confused with the Bible.'[29] For these reasons the fundamentalists charged the neo-orthodox belonged in the same catagory with modernism.[30]

The Ecumenical Movement and the Fundamentalists
Plans for the official formation of an ecumenical organization or the World Council of Churches, which had been unofficially functioning since 1938, were rapidly completed in 1948 after a delay caused by the outbreak of World War II. Before the constituent assembly of the World Council convened in Amsterdam from August 22 through September 5, 1948, Carl McIntire assembled a delegation of separatist fundamentalists in the same city from August 11 through August 19, 1948. He formed a counter-organization, the International Council of Christian Churches, designed to encourage 'a loyal and aggressive revival of Bible Christianity all over the world' and to 'awaken Christians everywhere to the insidious dangers of modernism and Roman Catholicism.'[31]

The formation of the International Council several days before the assembly of the World Council not only annoyed the World Council's leaders but also confused the press and the public. The meeting of the International Council, its critics charged, was no coincidence, rather it was an intentional arrangement by Carl McIntire for propaganda value. The confusion it created caused newspaper correspondents to seek clarification. This is what McIntire desired and provided him with an opportunity not only to explain the purpose of the counter-organization but to list his charges against the modernism of the World Council. Because of the sensational nature of his statement, the newspapers readily published them. From that time, whenever the World Council or its national counterparts assembled, McIntire tried to convene a delegation several days in advance of these meetings.[32]

Critics charged that it had been difficult to obtain accurate statistical data from Carl McIntire regarding the number of delegates that were assembled to form the International Council. The *New York Times* quoted McIntire to the effect that forty-five Protestant churches from eighteen countries had been represented.[33] A later issue of the *New York Times* quoted McIntire as saying that sixty-five Protestant denominations from twenty-nine countries had been represented.[34] Later McIntire published a list which claimed that forty-seven churches had sent official delegates while other churches were represented by observers. The convention consisted of one hundred fifty persons, and these assembled in Amsterdam's English Reformed Church, which had been dedicated in 1419 as a Roman Catholic chapel. It had been refitted for Protestant services in 1607. McIntire thought it was significant that Christians from all over the world were gathered there for 'genuine Twentieth Century Reformation.'[35]

J. Howard Pew (chairman and former president of Sun Oil Company, director of Sun Shipbuilding and Drydock Company, and director of Philadelphia National Bank) contributed $50,000 to the McIntire fund to pay the expenses connected with the establishment of the International Council.[36] McIntire admitted to a newspaper correspondent that 'he had no trouble raising $50,000 from one industrialist in order to finance plane trips for delegates to meetings of the International Council of Christian Churches.'[37]

Some observers noted as significant Pew's apparent dual alliance in the field of religion. In the above instance he supported the fundamentalists. Later when the National Council of Churches was formed in Cleveland in November, 1950 he became the chairman of its National Lay Committee. Upon assuming this position he stated that the primary task of the church must be evangelism. Pew's primary interests were (1) the maintenance of Christian libertarianism (free enterprise) and (2) evangelical Christianity. Whenever the clerical leaders of the National Council went beyond evangelism and issued proclamations on political and economic matters, Pew sought to have them censored because they were trying to 'impose a philosophy of statism on the council.'[38] However, Pew's activities were resisted not only by the clergy in the National Council but also by less conservative members on the National Lay Committee of the National Council of Churches. As a consequence the committee was finally dissolved on June 30, 1955.[39]

The delegates at the constituent assembly of the International Council unanimously adopted the usual fundamentalist doctrinal statement, and agreed to pattern their organization on a separatist basis similar to that of the American Council. The preamble of its constitution stated the purpose of the International Council as a cooperative fellowship of true believers united internationally for the proclamation and defense of historic Christianity, especially 'the great doctrines of the Protestant Reformation.'[40] A condemnatory resolution was also adopted characterizing the World Council as a conglomeration of religious negativists consisting of 'conspicuous modernists,' 'near-blasphemous unbelievers,' and 'ecclesiastical opposites.'[41] The World Council was also referred to as 'anti-Biblical, anti-evangelical, and anti-Protestant' because it included the Greek Orthodox Church in its membership. The International Council said this would 'nullify the entire work of the Reformation.'[42] The resolution also mentioned that members of the World Council had demonstrated by their principles 'that they are fellow travelers with systems of totalitarianism and authoritarianism.'[43] It was clear that the International Council intended to engage in a controversy with the World Council not only on biblical issues but also on political and economic grounds.

Some fundamentalists did not agree with McIntire and his strategy. Donald Grey Barnhouse, editor of *Eternity* (a fundamentalist magazine), was annoyed by the conduct of the International Council in Amsterdam. He stated their meeting was a side-show before the main event that suffered because it lacked enthusiasm, and the entire proceedings were a fiasco consisting of a little group of less than fifty seeking to extend the divisive work of the American Council in the churches of Europe. Barnhouse also said:

So that there might be as large a number as possible, the American Council took several men from various parts of Europe who should not have been at any Christian meetings, men who had been fired from work, one at least on moral grounds.[44]

The Communist Issue

During its constituent assembly in Amsterdam the World Council released a report on communism and capitalism to the newspapers which immediately precipitated heated debate. The original draft of the controversial report contained a clause declaring both communism and capitalism to be incompatible with the Christian view of life. The report stated:

The Christian Church should reject the ideologies of both communism and capitalism, and should seek to draw men away from the false assumption

*that these are the only alternatives. Each has made promises which it could
not redeem.*[45]

The writers of this section of the report elaborated on what they meant in
declaring communism and capitalism were at variance with Christianity.
They said that communism was at variance with Christianity because of its
materialistic and deterministic teachings and its emphasis upon economic
justice at the immediate expense of freedom (communism promised that
freedom would come ultimately, but only after the revolution of the new
communistic order was complete). They stated that capitalism was at variance
with Christianity because of its emphasis upon freedom at the immediate
expense of economic justice (capitalism promised economic justice would
'follow as a by-product of free enterprise').[46] Meanwhile, they stated that
capitalism tended 'to subordinate human needs to economic advantage, to
stress the importance of making money and to subject people to mass unemployment,' whereas justice demanded that the economic be subordinated
to social ends.[41] The authors of the report declared that it was the responsibility of Christians 'to seek new creative solutions which never allow either
justice or freedom to destroy each other.'[48] The section concluded with the
following statement:

*The church cannot resolve the debate between those who feel that the
primary solution is to socialize the means of production and those who fear
that such a course will merely lead to new and inordinate combinations of
political and economic power, culminating finally in an omnipotent state.
In the light of the Christian understanding of man we must, however, say
to the advocates of socialism that the institution of property is not the root
of the corruption of human nature; we must equally say to the defenders of
existing property relations that ownership is not an unconditional right; it
must, therefore, be preserved, curtailed or distributed in accordance with
the requirements of justice.*[49]

The response of the fundamentalists to this report on communism and
capitalism was immediate. They vehemently protested the propriety of
condemning capitalism in the same breath with communism as though the
two were twin evils deserving to be equally excoriated. In the United States
other voices, including those of American capitalists, were heard in con-
demnation of the report. As a consequence a revision of the report followed

these protests. Charles P. Taft, lay delegate to the World Council and brother of United States Senator Robert A. Taft of Ohio, explained that the revision was not an attempt to soften the report but to clarify what its authors meant by capitalism. The original report was amended by the inclusion of the qualifying phrase 'laissez-faire' before the word 'capitalism;' with the result that the revised report stated:

The Christian Church should reject the ideologies of both communism and laissez-faire capitalism, and should seek to draw men away from the false assumption that these are the only alternatives. Each has made promises it could not redeem.[50]

The amendment did not end the criticisms. Instead criticism increased and became more relentless because it was thought that the revision was only an ameliorative deception. The authors of the report did their best to explain that they had not been influenced by Russian propaganda and that the World Council did not prefer communism over capitalism. This explanation did not satisfy Carl McIntire. He not only attacked the World Council but he also criticized John Foster Dulles, prominent member of the Republican Party in the United States and an expert on foreign affairs, who had attended the assembly as a lay delegate. McIntire called Dulles a tool of the radical and pacifist church leaders of both the Federal Council and the World Council, and a supporter of the social gospel and a planned economy for America.[51]

   The charge that the World Council had been influenced by Russian propaganda was difficult to sustain. The pronouncements of various leaders in the World Council revealed primarily a preference for some modified form of socialism and capitalism, and the prevalent feeling was that communism and capitalism 'both regiment and dehumanize men.'[52] Emil Brunner stated that communism was more dangerous because it prohibited discussion and correction. He declared that the churches must oppose both statism and totalitarianism, particularly the latter, which was the contemporary devil.[53] John C. Bennett, a member of the faculty of Union Theological Seminary, thought that something like the program of the English Labor Party might be the eventual form that would evolve out of the current dissatisfaction with communism and capitalism.[54] Reinhold Niebuhr regarded the communist hope to be delusory, but he also thought that the means of production should be controlled by society, and that any societal struggle should be for the benefit of the laboring class.[55] E. Stanley Jones, Methodist missionary to India, frequently emphasized in his books and public lectures that capitalism was breaking down and the cooperative motive should take its place.[56]

To summarize what apparently was, and still is, the thinking of the leaders of the World Council, it seems that most of them were dissatisfied with both communism and laissez-faire capitalism. Although the leaders of the World Council were not clear as to what system should finally take the place of communism and capitalism, apparently all of them clung to the Lockean concept of government that man and not the state, and that man and not production, should be the proper directive for society.[57]

The Super-church and the United Nations

The postwar drive for Protestant unity resulting in the establishment of the World Council in 1948 almost coincided with a similar drive for political unity resulting in the establishment of the United Nations in 1945. These two important historical events for unity, one political and one religious, were not regarded as coincidental by the fundamentalists. They were convinced the World Council or the ecumenical movement, as the effort of the World Council was called, was the embryonic beginnings of a universal ecclesiastical system, perhaps the forerunner of the universal church 'to serve as the harlot queen of the United Nations.'[58] The fundamentalists associated the ecumenical movement with the United Nations as though the two organizations were specifically designed to work together in some type of ecclesiastical-political alliance. It is difficult for a student of international affairs to discover any clear evidence to substantiate the fundamentalists. On the other hand, the fundamentalists, relying upon their biblical prognostications and assumptions in the absence of external facts, declared the World Council and the United Nations were not operating independently. Furthermore, the fact that the World Council supported the United Nations was accepted as proof that an unholy alliance for an ecclesiastical-political state existed.[59]

It will be remembered that the Eastern Orthodox Church accepted the invitation of the World Council to become a member. Although the Roman Catholic Church refused to accept a similar invitation to be represented in the World Council the fundamentalists were convinced, on the basis of the invitation to the Catholics and from certain biblical statements, that union between the Roman Catholic Church and the World Council would ultimately be achieved. The Fundamentalists literally believed that 'the woman arrayed in purple and scarlet' in Revelation 17:4 prefigures the establishment of a corrupted, though colorful world church which would include the

Catholics and Protestants.[60] Walter M. Horton, a delegate to the World Council assembly, was among those who denied the allegations of the fundamentalists. He wrote that the World Council was interested, not in organic unity, but only in an ideal Christian arrangement based on Catholic unity and Protestant liberty.[61]

The World Council disavowed 'any pretensions to be a 'super-church' or even to foster organic union among separate bodies.'[62] W. A. Visser 't Hooft, one of the prominent delegates in the World Council assembly, stated in a letter to James DeForest Murch (who wrote a series of critiques on the World Council calling it the coming super-church) that the World Council explicitly declared itself to be nothing more than a council of churches to serve the churches and encourage them to stay together in a spiritual fellowship. The World Council, he added, did not seek to control churches nor did it desire to act for them without a specific mandate.[63]

Carl McIntire quoted from an address delivered in 1951 by Leonard Hodgson, professor of Divinity in the University of Oxford, in which Hodgson stated the World Council was the beginning of a program to seek the means for full union. The major stumbling block to this achievement, Hodgson reportedly stated, was the fundamentalist movement, because of their incoherent and unintelligible beliefs and use of the Bible. McIntire followed with this reply:

In other words, the acceptance of the Bible as God's inerrant and infallible Word creates a puzzle for these leaders of the ecumenical movement, and it is a part of the ecumenical movement's program to tear down this so-called fundamentalist position in order that they may build 'the coming great church'.[64]

The National Association of Evangelicals and the American Council jointly condemned the World Council. James DeForest Murch stated that the World Council blindly followed the 'ecumaniacs' and were unable to see the dangerous implications of their movement.[65] Carl McIntire associated the ecumenical movement with the biblical last days or period of apostasy preceding the cataclysmic second advent of Christ. He concluded:

The so-called fundamentalist or Bible believer looks to the Book of Revelation and sees Babylon the Great. He knows what the Reformers called it and how they identified it with the Roman Catholic Apostasy. It is a harlot church. *He then looks at the structure and program for the World Council of Churches. Nothing like this has appeared on the scene since the power of Rome was broken. The elements, the principles, the situation is there described in the Book of Revelation . . . Rejection of an infallible Bible leads to the building of an infallible church. The acceptance of an infallible Bible enables man properly to evaluate the apostasy and the rising structure of a supertotalitarian church. For these reasons the Bible must be discredited before the Ecumenical Church can capture the minds of men.*[66]

The fundamentalists generally adopted an isolationist and non-pacifist position in foreign affairs. This position was in effect long before the World Council or the United Nations were established. After these two international bodies were formed, the fundamentalists commented on the World Council's attitude toward war and American nationalism. Before the World Council was formed the fundamentalists had criticized the Federal Council for adopting a radical pacifism, which they said was the fruit of modernism and the result of the evolutionary doctrine that there was nothing drastically wrong with human nature.[67] Carl McIntire stated that 'this radical pacifism stems logically and naturally from the denials of the faith and the departure of the Federal Council from the teachings of the Bible.'[68]

It is true the World Council believed that war was characteristically un-christian and contrary to the will of God. But it is only fair to state that none of the utterances of the leaders of the World Council gave any indication of radical or even moderate pacifism. The World Council took the position that no war is inevitable. They did scorn the idea of preventive war which some fundamentalists, particularly McIntire, advocated against Russia. Considering the terrible prospects of total destruction in a nuclear war, the World Council promised to support the United Nations because it believed the United Nations to be the only hope of preserving international law and order.[69]

However, the World Council did not rule out the possibility of war and in no instance was any statement released denying the right of defensive war. The World Council said:

In the last resort, we are in conscience bound to turn to force in defence of justice even though we know that the destruction of human life is evil. There are times when this can be the lesser of two evils, forced upon us by our common failure to achieve better relations.[70]

The general attitude of the fundamentalists was that a Christian should be prepared to fight when necessary. Obviously this did not differ materially from the general attitude of the World Council. However, in the case of Russia, some fundamentalists thought it might be best if America struck first, because of their assumption that peaceful co-existence with Russia is impossible. 'America's only salvation,' one fundamentalist wrote while Russia ostensibly was friendly to the United States, 'may lie in obeying the slogan of her early western days, 'beat Russia to the draw'.'[71]

Although the fundamentalists were generally opposed to the United Nations and criticized it vehemently, they did not make any organized attempt to place pressure upon Congress to cause the withdrawal of the United States from it. Their opposition was usually expressed in the form of statements and resolutions which were adopted at frequent intervals to indicate their general disapproval of the United Nations. They protested any attempt to grant the United Nations more power than its original charter had allowed, and on occasion the fundamentalists rallied to support isolationist leaders in Congress seeking to safeguard American sovereignty. The fundamentalists supported United States Senator John W. Bricker's proposed amendment to the Constitution designed to protect United States sovereignty in treaty arrangements with foreign powers.[72] The American Council urged Congress to enact enabling legislation which would make the proposed Bricker Amendment the law of the land, because 'restraints must be written into the Constitution to protect us from the schemes and the subtleties of those who are working for a One World Church.'[73]

The fundamentalists agreed that world government was necessary because they believed sinful men must be curbed from carrying out their cruelties against one another. The fundamentalists did not believe, however, the United Nations or any other similar organization could ever solve the primary problem of national interest. Leaders in the National Association of Evangelicals called any proposal for world cooperation an invitation to national disaster and an opening wedge 'for world socialism and world dictatorship.'[74] V. Raymond Edman, president of fundamentalist Wheaton (Illinois) College, wrote:

To be realistic in the matter one must recognize that there must be one sovereign power in the world, a World Government, if you please, to make secure the peace thereof, for autonomous sovereign powers will always have interests vital to the selves which they will defend even to waging warfare.[75]

Edman repudiated the United Nations because he charged it was erected on the same principle of concert of powers as was the old League of Nations. Edman warned against any American attempt to yield any part of its sovereignty in a world rapidly becoming communist. Instead, he encouraged American isolationism and objected to the United Nations on strictly nationalistic principles. He said there would be world government some day, but it would not come from tinkering with the United Nations or trying to improve its machinery. 'It will come to pass,' he said, 'when the World Sovereign Himself, The Lord Jesus Christ, returns to the world, as He promised.'[76]

While political leaders within and outside of the United Nations tried to find a satisfactory formula which might lessen international tension caused by the cold war between Russia and the Western powers, the fundamentalists were trying to draw attention of people everywhere to an alternative hope for mankind. The alternative offered by the fundamentalists was premillenialism,[77] by which current history could be explained, including the postwar activity of Russia and of the Jews in the Near East. In their premillenial doctrine most fundamentalists taught that a regrouping of nations involving Russia, Germany, the Jews in Palestine, and the peoples of the Orient would occur, marking the end of the age immediately preceding the second coming of Christ.[78]

It was the supposition of the fundamentalists that the Jews were the key to the future, and they would await the coming of their Messiah.[79] The fundamentalists believed, however, that the Jews, before the Messiah came, would be deceived through the cleverness of a false Messiah (anti-Christ) who would betray them into the domination of Russia. Armageddon or a period of tribulation would follow, culminating in the total destruction of anti-God and anti-capitalist Russia by Jesus Christ. Later Christ would establish a chiliastic or millenial age of peace and prosperity with Palestine fully restored to the Jews according to the ancient promise of God to His chosen people. Jesus Christ, their rightful Messiah and heir to the throne of David, would then govern them as a glorious and righteous monarch.[80]

This analysis explains the rejection by the fundamentalists of the United Nations, because it sought to solve the problems causing international disharmony through better understanding between fallible nations and peoples. The fundamentalists' apocalypse does not offer any hope for any progressive moral development in human character which might cause men to be less warlike. Without the aid of divine grace, man would be incapable of bringing a peaceful order into existence.[91] By the mid-twentieth century the fundamentalists had become extremely nationalist and isolationist, and spoke in favor of military preparation (and in some instances urged preventive war) as a deterrent of aggression. Meanwhile, it appeared that nothing constructive could be done to secure international harmony, except to evangelize the world until Jesus Christ returns.[82]

The Attack upon UNESCO

Because the fundamentalists opposed the United Nations, it was only natural for them to object to one of its functioning units, the United Nations Educational, Scientific, and Cultural Organization (or UNESCO, as it is more familiarly known). One of the important proposals of UNESCO was an exchange of teachers among foreign nations, in which Russia became interested. James DeForest Murch saw sinister motives behind this, and concluded that Russia and UNESCO were conspiring to betray America. He wrote:

The growing interest of Moscow in the use of the World Council of Churches, the National Council of Churches (USA) and UNESCO to further Communist aims needs to be watched carefully. Evangelicals both within and without will probably become another major battlefield in the cold war.[83]

Other fundamentalists fulminated against UNESCO, among them Wilbur M. Smith, bibliographer and member of the faculty of Fuller Theological Seminary of Pasadena, California. Smith criticized UNESCO because of the announcement that its primary philosophy 'must be evolutionary as opposed to static or ideal humanism,'[84] and because nowhere in its constitution did UNESCO mention God. He also attacked the appointment of Julian Huxley, British biologist, as director of UNESCO in 1946, because as a scientist Huxley denied that God existed as a person. Smith wrote: 'In our Declaration of Independence, we begin by recognizing God; in the Preamble for the Constitution of UNESCO, God is never mentioned, but it begins with a recognition of the goodness and sufficiency of man.'[85] Finally, Smith was disturbed because UNESCO was working to establish a single world culture, which implied among other things a possibility of an eclectic religion or perhaps 'a universal atheism.'[86] Thus, the fundamentalists not only objected to UNESCO on nationalistic grounds but also because of theology.

CHAPTER FOUR

The Aggravation of Militant Fundamentalism

The period after World War II was a time of adjustment and transition for religion and governments. During this period the United Nations and its agencies were in their infancy and were seeking to encourage international understanding, now made necessary by the prospect of global annihilation through nuclear warfare. Almost coincidental with the formation of the United Nations was the establishment of the World Council of Churches and the National Council of the Churches of Christ in the U.S.A. Both Councils were prevalently neo-orthodox in theology and ecumenical or world-wide in scope. Those who promoted the United Nations, and the leaders of the World Council and the National Council, were motivated by similar ideals of internationalism, though none were less patriotic and loyal to their own nations. Thus, the same universalism in thought was affecting both religion and politics simultaneously.

Perhaps no controversy of any significance between the fundamentalists on the one hand, and the World Council and the National Council, on the other, would have emerged had the latter two religious organizations avoided involvement in economic matters which stirred various conservative groups in the United States against them. It will be remembered that the World Council attacked laissez-faire capitalism and urged some other economic order offering a more equitable distribution of economic wealth should take its place. As a result the World Council incurred the wrath of economic conservatives and threw some of them into the waiting arms of the fundamentalists, who immediately exploited the situation to gain support in the defense of their historic doctrines.

Another factor in the controversy was the unsettled international situation during the post-war period, resulting for the most part, from Russia's actions in Europe and the upsurge of nationalism in Asia and Asia Minor. It was natural therefore, that many Americans, particularly those with no reasoned understanding of the situation, should become frightened with any rapid alteration in American modes of economic, political, and religious conduct. Some of them reverted to nationalism and isolationism. Although not all Americans turned to religious fundamentalism, a favorable climate had developed in which the fundamentalists could work.

The National Council of Churches

On November 26 to December 1, 1950 delegates from the Federal Council, eight interdenominational agencies, twenty-five Protestant denominations, and four Eastern Orthodox churches met in Cleveland, Ohio to form the National Council of the Churches of Christ in the U.S.A. The primary purpose of the National Council was stated as an effort on the part of the churches in the United States to cooperate in those areas of Christian service where none could expect to do much separately. The National Council believed that 'those who live under the Fatherhood of God must as never before work for an understanding brotherhood of men.'[1]

The American Council was disturbed by this rising trend toward Protestant unity in the United States. The Gallup Poll had shown in 1950 that fifty percent of the people favored a single Protestant church, thirty-nine percent were opposed, and eleven percent were indifferent. This was much different from the situation which existed in 1937 when another Gallup Poll revealed that fifty-one percent opposed and forty percent favored a single Protestant church. Carl McIntire attributed this rising sentiment in favor of a single Protestant church to the constant flow of propaganda from the Federal Council. McIntire was determined to counteract this propaganda, and promised that the American Council would wage a great battle against religious inclusivism. He said that every means, 'propaganda, facts, campaigns, tours, radio broadcasts, would be employed to keep the issues alive before the people.'[2]

It will be remembered that the International Council arranged to meet in Amsterdam several days before the convention of the World Council in 1948. The American Council discovered the propaganda value of this arrangement and followed a similar plan by convening from November 22 to 26, 1950 in Cleveland, two days before the meeting of constituent assembly of the National Council. Carl McIntire, later reflecting on this arrangement, said that the American Council benefited from such scheduling of their meetings because they received excellent newspaper publicity and obtained free radio time through the generosity of local broadcasting stations.[3]

It is no surprise that the American Council issued statements to the newspapers in Cleveland criticizing the National Council before it was formed. W. O. H. Garman, one of the principal speakers for the American Council, reiterated that the American Council intended to contend for the faith; by this he meant, a belief in an infallible Bible, the virgin birth of Jesus Christ and His deity, the substitutionary or vicarious atonement of Jesus Christ, His death and resurrection, justification by faith, and the literal second coming of Jesus Christ. Furthermore, Garman said, it was the intention of the American Council to identify those who failed to accept these doctrines.[4] Carl McIntire, who seemed to have been quoted more often by the newspapers, issued various statements in which he declared that the proposed National Council was 'another mile-post on the road to a super-church,' a 'whistle-stop on the train back to Rome,' and ' a twentieth century hybrid' which 'reflected a conglomeration of opinion regarding even the divinity of Christ.'[5] Thus, in a few statements Carl McIntire outlined the issues which would be emphasized in the future in the American Council's struggle with the National Council.[6]

Apparently some of the leaders of the National Council were annoyed by the presence of Carl McIntire in Cleveland as the latter watched the proceedings of the constituent assembly of the National Council on a press pass. During one session, when attendance was largely curtailed because of a sudden crippling snowstorm requiring the declaration of martial law and use of National Guardsmen, Charles P. Taft, a member of the National Lay Committee of the National Council, spoke before a group of approximately forty persons. He related an anecdote about the American Council and mentioned Carl McIntire by name. This episode indicated that the National council intended to reciprocate the fundamentalists' attack. McIntire reported the incident in the *Christian Beacon:*

He told a story about the American Council. They, he said, are like the story he heard about Texas. A visitor who had been to Texas was asked, 'What's wrong with Texas?' He replied, 'They need more water and a better class of people.' The questioner replied, 'That's all hell needs.'[7]

After the prolonged laughter which followed the recitation of the anecdote had subsided Taft mentioned McIntire by name, saying, 'When we really try we can do better than Carl McIntire any day.'[9]

Carl McIntire did not expect the recognition he had received in Cleveland.

But, he said, 'I considered it a tribute. Yet there is real bitterness and hatred on the part of these F(ederal) C(ouncil) men who speak of the 'brotherhood of men'.[9] McIntire was elated over the incident because he believed the leaders of the National Council had begun to chafe under his constant attack. He stated:

Something has happened to their tranquility. The 'new' council definitely has been placed on the defensive; there has been a public unmasking; and telling blows have been struck, the extent of which we were not aware.[10]

The Road back to Rome

The fundamentalists were as suspicious of the ultimate purpose of the National Council as they had been of the World Council after the latter had been formed in 1948. The National Council was immediately referred to as a contrivance which would eventually evolve into and become 'the One Church for the One World,'[11] the same charge, it should be remembered, which had been made against the World Council after its formation. The fundamentalists looked upon the National Council as a companion of the World Council in the drive for an ecumenical church which would eventually include the Protestants and the Roman Catholics. Thus, when the fundamentalists spoke of the ecumenical movement they meant both the World Council and the National Council.[12]

The most disturbing event which occurred during the formation of the National Council was the inclusion of the Eastern Orthodox Churches in the Council's membership. The fundamentalists looked upon their inclusion as an ominous departure from strict Protestantism. In this connection, Carl McIntire thought it was significant that the National Council was formed amid pageantry, with vested boys, banners, cross-bearers, candles, Eastern Orthodox clergy in their ecclesiastical vestments, and Protestant clergy in their robes. McIntire said their pomposity was not unlike the 'papal pageantry in the Vatican at St. Peter's.'[13] McIntire also reproduced an article in the *Christian Beacon* that had originally appeared in a Roman Catholic publication, which lent support to the fundamentalists' charge that the National Council was slowly reverting to Catholicism. The article stated: 'It is not hard to see that all this yearning for a single visible Church is a return to Catholic tradition. In this respect the movement should be welcomed.'[14]

However, the leaders of the National Council denied that the ultimate goal of the National Council or the World Council was one Catholic Church.

The fundamentalists were disbelieving and continued to charge that ecumen-icists were moving in the direction of establishing a World Church that would include the Roman Catholics. James DeForest Murch examined the literature of the ecumenicists and published his conclusions in articles and inexpensive books in which he expressed the fears of the fundamentalists that the ecumenicists were gradually moving away from a distinctly Protestant church to one more Roman Catholic in nature.[15] In one of his discourses Murch used harsh language to describe the National Council and the World Council as adulterous organizations having 'all the Babylonian admixture of truth and error found in the Church of Rome, universal in scope, and even-tually leading up in the Romish abomination itself.'[16]

THE ANTI-COMMUNIST CRUSADE

Preparation for the Anti-communist Crusade
Conservative factions in the United States became directly or indirectly allied with the fundamentalists in the anti-communist crusade which gained mo-mentum about 1949 with the publication of several controversial articles, books, and pamphlets. Several outstanding conservatives, among them John T. Flynn (author of *The Roosevelt Myth* and other controversial works), Verne F. Kaub (a retired utilities agent in Madison, Wisconsin who described himself as a Christian American), Stanley High (one of the editors of the *Reader's Digest*), Captain Edgar C. Bundy (former United States Air Force Intelligence Officer), and a confessed former communist named J. B. Matthews declared in speeches or in print that the leaders in the Federal Council or the National Council advocated the over-throw of American capitalism. The entrance of these conservatives into the anti-communist crusade provided fuel and ammunition for the fundamentalists and helped change the character of the fundamentalist crusade from a strictly religious controversy, which always remained primary, to a struggle for social, economic and political conservativism as well.[17]

Coincident with the growing attacks of the fundamentalists against the Federal Council and its various leaders was the publication in 1949 of *The Road Ahead*, Flynn's book on 'creeping socialism.' In the tenth chapter of this book, from which the fundamentalists often quoted, Flynn named the Federal Council in general and more specifically E. Stanley Jones, Methodist Bishop G. Bromley Oxnam, J. Henry Carpenter (executive secretary of the

Brooklyn Federation of Churches) and John C. Bennett (chairman of the Congregational Christian Council for Social Action) as advocates of socialism and communist policies under the guise of the Kingdom of God. Most of these men and the Federal Council supported various social welfare projects and the New Deal's economic measures such as: consumer cooperatives, T.V.A., subsidies to farmers, and other federal aid projects. However, they denied Flynn's charges that the Federal Council or any of its leaders advocated socialism or communism and stated they were only interested in a more equitable distribution of American productive wealth spread over a wider base for the greater well being of American citizens. At no time, the Federal Council stated, had it advocated ownership of the means of production by the State.[18]

Verne F. Kaub became an active participant in the anti-communist crusade in 1950. He organized the American Council of Christian Laymen which assisted in an organized campaign to blanket the United States in 1950 with copies of Flynn's controversial book. Kaub's personal contribution to the anti-communist campaign was in the form of a pamphlet entitled 'How Red is the Federal Council of Churches?' The pamphlet depicted the Federal Council as a pro-communist organization, whose activity in the United States aided and abetted the socialists and the communists. The front cover of the pamphlet displayed a cross with hammer and sickle superimposed upon it.[19]

Kaub named John C. Bennett, J. Henry Carpenter, Harry Emerson Fosdick, E. Stanley Jones, Reinhold Niebuhr, Bishop Oxnam, Abraham Muste (secretary of the Fellowship of Reconciliation), Ralph W. Sockman (minister of Christ Church in New York City), and Henry Van Dusen (president of Union Theological Seminary in New York City) as pro-communists and pro-socialists. He also attacked organizations such as the American Civil Liberties Union, the Fellowship of Reconciliation, and the National Religion and Labor Foundation.[20] However, Kaub cautiously avoided any statement that these men and organizations were directly connected with the communists. He sought to accomplish his purpose by creating the impression that the projects or programs they espoused aided the communists. He qualified his statements, saying:

While some affiliated with the Federal Council are undoubtedly members of the Communist Party, most of them who have been actively aiding and abetting Socialism and Communism are fellow travelers rather than actual members of the party.[21]

Regardless of this qualifying statement, Kaub succeeded in some quarters in establishing the guilt of these men and organizations by association. Kaub himself said that his pamphlet became powerful ammunition in 'the battle against apostasy and evil aims of the Federal Council of Churches.'[22] Erwin A. Gaede, a Unitarian minister who knew Kaub personally, interviewed him twice. After these interviews, Gaede said he was convinced that Kaub was less interested in religious doctrines than in his extremely conservative economic principles. Gaede said that Kaub associated Christian individualism with economic individualism and for that reason was opposed to any form of social planning.[23] Because of the sensational nature of the criticisms of the Federal Council and its leaders, the secular press readily published them, and 'these attacks,' Gaede said, 'serve to confuse popular opinion on the nature of the Federal Council and undoubtedly weaken the confidence of others in the Federal Council.'[24] Gaede concluded:

The attacks by Mr. Kaub like those by Mr. Flynn, attempt to associate liberalism in economics with socialism and communism. Actually, the leaders in the Federal Council are vigorously anti-communist and would not associate with any organization if they suspected the presence of communists.

But these attacks may have the effect of tempering any future statements, pronouncements, or activities of Federal Council leaders or the organization itself.[25]

In February, 1950 Stanley High published an article he had written for the *Reader's Digest* on 'Methodism's Pink Fringe.' In the article he accused the Methodist Federation for Social Action (an un-official organization of Methodists) of discrediting America at home and abroad by their characterization of capitalism as un-Christian, thus giving aid and comfort to the communists. High's statement that the Federation (which comprised in its membership many laymen and seventeen bishops, including Bishop Oxnam) was under surveillance by the House Committee on Un-American Activities, proved to be embarrassing to the organization and immediately caused widespread comment and stormy discussion about the Federation's activities. Members of the official board of St. Luke's Methodist Church in Oklahoma City, for example, were aroused and they declared their opposition to any economic changes in America which might lead to British socialism as an alternative to laissez-faire capitalism. They also demanded that use of the name Methodist in connection with the Federation be discontinued.[26]

The fundamentalists immediately recognized the explosive nature and the propaganda value of the literature that was proliferated against the Federal Council and its leaders. They immediately began to quote from Flynn's book, Kaub's pamphlet, and High's article. Carl McIntire, it should be noted, had been making similar charges against the Federal Council and its leaders for several years. By 1950, Flynn, Kaub, High and others outside of the fundamentalist movement were beginning to add credence to his charges. McIntire expected to exploit the communist issue alongside of the religious one; by this device he hoped that certain advantages would accrue to the American Council of Christian Churches in their controversy with the Federal Council.

Ernest Gordon, fundamentalist editor of the *Sunday School Times*, published an article on February 11, 1950 covering Kaub's allegations. He indicated that Kaub's pamphlet was available to the churches and to the clergy, and urged them to write for bundles of them for distribution to the public. A month after Gordon's article was published Kaub released a printed letter under his signature in which he stated that churches affiliated with the American Council of Christian Churches were distributing his pamphlet on 'How Red is the Federal Council of Churches.' He noted that these churches had 'nothing short of duty to give this information to the public.'[27] Kaub also included a copy of the pamphlet to all ministers on the mailing list of the American Council of Christian Churches.[28]

The Attack upon E. Stanley Jones

For some time before the formation of the National Council, E. Stanley Jones, one of the leading exponents for church union, appeared before church audiences and clerical associations in the United States to determine their sentiment toward his federal plan of church union, which was patterned after the United States federal structure. In this plan denominations would cease as separate sovereign entities, but would become subordinate branches of a single sovereign union of churches. He discovered through his tours about the country that the people and clergy overwhelmingly favored his federal plan of church union as the most realistic and practical approach to the union of Protestant churches in the United States.[29]

Jones was also one of those who criticized laissez-faire capitalism because it was based on selfish competition.[30] He became an indefatigable proponent of profit sharing to meet his ideal of widening the base of economic wealth according to the principle of 'the greatest good for the greatest

number.' The foundation of his economic theory was Christianity and enlightened self-interest. Profit sharing would be sustained, Jones maintained,
through social feeling of men toward each other and a practical desire for
unity of all men with their fellow-creatures. Jones said:

I believe in the profit motive and would like to change it from more indivi-
dual profit to the profit of the many. Profit-sharing in industry would be a
symbol of that conversion of the profit motive . . . This conversion of the
profit motive would save the profit motive. A growing number of capitalists
would agree with me.

I believe in competition. It is the driving principle in life. But I would
convert competition from selfish competition for oneself alone to com-
petition that would harness competition to the good of the many . . . They
do it through enlightened self-interest.[31]

In espousing these two proposals, church union and his economic plan, Jones
incurred the wrath of the fundamentalists and became a target of their attack.
At the time of the formation of the National Council, Jones appeared as the
principal speaker during the religious emphasis week sponsored by the Pasadena (California) Council of Churches. When Jones arrived in Pasadena he
discovered that the fundamentalists had been waiting to harass him by
accusations of socialist tendencies. M. H. Reynolds, Jr., chairman of the
southern California branch of the American Council of Christian Churches,
had prepared a list of charges,[32] and asked two Pasadena newspapers, the
Independent and the *Star-News*, to publish them. The latter newspaper
refused to become involved in the controversy, but the *Independent* took the
prepared copy and published the following charges against Jones: (1) Promoting socialism under the guise of the Kingdom of God, (2) seeking to bring an
end to free enterprise as something incompatible with Christianity, and (3)
advocacy of pacifism.[33]

Two pages of quotations taken from several books Jones had written over a
period of several years, and published long before the cold war between Russia
and the Western Powers, were mimeographed by Reynolds and distributed to
clergymen and newspapers in the southern California area. Some of the books
from which quotations were taken were: *The Choice Before Us*; *Christ's*
Alternative to Communism; *The Christ of the American Road*; and
Abundant Living. Reynolds also cited Flynn's *The Road Ahead*, which
stated that Jones was one of those the Federal Council periodically sponsored

'to preach the glory of Red Christianity.'[34] Flynn said that Jones had found a new name for socialism – the Kingdom of God – and was using the church to promote a social and economic revolution in the United States.[35]

The Star-News, which refused to publish the manuscript Reynolds had given it, said that publication of these charges would amount to nothing less than an engagement in religious controversy. The editor of that newspaper realized that the matter of freedom of religion and freedom of speech was involved in the controversy. However, Reynolds protested that no attempt was being made to hamper or deny free speech, but added that 'we don't want ministers preaching Socialism in the name of religion and undermining all those things we Americans hold essential.'[36] In a letter which showed no signs of vindictiveness Jones answered his critics:

I am neither a Communist nor a Socialist, but a Christian, at least a Christian-in-the-making. I believe the supreme order is God's order, the Kingdom of God. Everything must conform to that order or perish. I want to change our competitive, capitalistic order to make it conform to the Kingdom of God. Just as the individual needs to be changed from a self-centered interest, so I believe the social and economic order has to be changed from self-centeredness to a Kingdom-centeredness.[37]

Finally, Jones answered the fundamentalists on the third point of their charges – that he advocated pacifism. He replied that he had favored America's entrance into World War I, but afterwards lost faith in war as an instrument for settling international disputes. He noted:

From that time I have tried to do away with the causes of war. I advocate world government under which peace for all might be had. I believe there can be no peace without justice, no justice without law, no law without government and no government without power to enforce its laws. So my chosen strategy for peace is world government.[38]

The Attack upon Bishop G. Bromley Oxnam

While United States Senator Joseph McCarthy of Wisconsin investigated the extent of communist infiltration in government employment, Carl McIntire and other fundamentalists were equally active in their search for communists and their sympathizers in the churches. The methods employed by McIntire were similar to those used by Senator McCarthy. Senator McCarthy, it is interesting to note, approved of the work of Carl McIntire, the fundamentalist clergy, and the International Council 'as a militant anti-Communist Protestant group,' and its clergy, he said, were 'usefully serving the interests of America and God.'[39]

Perhaps more than any other person, Carl McIntire was responsible for the relentless attack upon Bishop G. Bromley Oxnam and was the person who forced the 'Red' issue upon him. McIntire quoted from Flynn's *The Road Ahead*, which accused Oxnam of promoting a social and economic revolution in the United States under the guise of the Kingdom of God, a charge not unlike the one made against E. Stanley Jones. Oxnam was a vulnerable object of attack because he had written many articles and made frequent statements on his social and economic views. McIntire quoted from Oxnam's study book *The Christian Vocation*, which was used by the Methodist Church in its missions study. In it Oxnam wrote about a new social order that he hoped to see realized:

It would be a co-operative social order in which the sacredness of every life was recognized and everyone found opportunity for the fullest self-expression of which he was capable . . ., in which the impulses to service and to creative action would be stronger than the acquisitive impulses . . ., in which differences of talent and capacity meant proportional responsibilities and ministry to the common good.

McIntire commented that 'the book uses the typical socialist or communist arguments against the capitalistic system, sanctified by the name mission study,' and that it urges cooperative planning through democratic action which could be just as effective in strangling free enterprise as totalitarian planning.[41]

The American Council of Christian Churches, spurred by McIntire, relentlessly conducted special meetings in various sections of the United States to get the message across to the people 'concerning the modernistic, pro-Red leaning and communist-front connections' of the National Council and Bishop Oxnam.[42] In practically every meeting audiences were referred to *The Road Ahead*, which was fast becoming the chief source book and ready reference for the fundamentalists in their campaign against 'creeping socialism' in America. McIntire kept his pen busy writing pamphlets, brochures, books, and articles to add fuel to the controversy. Some of the subjects he chose were: 'Bishop Oxnam, Prophet of Marx,' 'Communist Ministers,' 'How

Radical are the Clergy?,' 'Russia's Most Effective Fifth Column in America,' and the 'Truth About the Federal Council of Churches and the Kingdom of God.' Everyone of these titles indicate the character of the campaign the fundamentalists were waging against Oxnam.[43]

By 1953 the American Council had convinced a large proportion of the American people, and some members of Congress and the United States Senate, that there was some truth to their charges against Oxnam and the National Council. On March 9, 1953 Congressman Harold H. Velde, chairman of the House Committee on Un-American Activities, startled some people and raised the hopes of the fundamentalists with his announcement over the radio that an investigation of the churches and individual clergy was being planned to determine how much they had been infiltrated by communists. Velde's mail was immediately flooded with protests from those who declared that such an investigation would be a threat to America's traditional principle of religious liberty. As a result, Velde tried to avoid any embarrassment that might result to himself and his committee from such an inquiry. Instead he asked Senator William Jenner's Internal Security Subcommittee to launch the investigation.[44]

Nevertheless, the pressures on Bishop Oxnam and the National Council were becoming greater with each passing day. On March 17 Congressman Donald Jackson of California, a member of Velde's committee, suddenly created another sensation when he declared on the floor of the House of Representatives that Bishop Oxnam 'served God on Sunday and the Communist-front the other days of the week.' The leaders of the American Council of Christian Churches were jubilant. At their convention in Joplin, Missouri in late April and early May of 1953, they issued a challenge to Bishop Oxnam to appear voluntarily before the House Committee on Un-American Activities to answer under oath the charges against him.[45] The American Council was certain that the final show-down of Oxnam and the National Council was rapidly approaching.[46]

The American Council followed their Joplin convention with a pilgrimage to Washington, D.C. on May 8. Approximately 200 persons congregated on the platform of the railroad station. From that point they marched to Constitution Hall for a mass meeting, carrying banners reading 'Marx or Christ?,' 'Bible versus Communism?,' 'Put Oxnam Under Oath,' and 'Investigate Communist Clergy.'[47] Congressman Jackson had been invited to the meeting. There he was presented with two rolled bundles containing approximately 25,000 signatures, demanding that the House Committee on Un-American

Activities investigate the churches and clergy to determine how much they had been infiltrated by communists. W.W. Breckbill, president of the American Council, remarked as he handed the two bundles to Jackson: 'Our fathers came here for religious and political liberty. The only red that should be in the church of Jesus Christ is the blood of Jesus Christ.'[48] The audience cheered. Carl McIntire also spoke. He corrected Jackson on the statement he had made regarding Oxnam from the floor of the House of Representatives. McIntire said he doubted if Oxnam served God at any time.[49]

At this point the fundamentalists received support in their anti-communist crusade from another source. An article on 'Reds and Our Churches' appeared in *The American Mercury* in July, 1953. The author was J. B. Matthews, recently appointed by Senator Joseph R. McCarthy to the staff of the Senate Permanent Subcommittee investigating subversion in the United States. In the article Matthews charged that 7,000 Protestant clergymen were 'party members, fellow-travellers, espionage agents, party-line adherents, and unwilling dupes' of the communists.[50] A storm of protest immediately followed and three other Senators on the Subcommittee (Henry M. Jackson, Stuart Symington, and John L. McClellan) complained to McCarthy that Matthews' charges were unfounded and they angrily demanded his resignation. After McCarthy refused to relieve Matthews, the three Senators resigned from the committee. As expected, McIntire voiced his opinion in the dispute. He said that Matthews should be retained and that any action against him would be unwarranted because he had spoken the truth. Nevertheless, Matthews resigned a few days later.[51]

Non-fundamentalist clergymen vehemently denied Matthews had spoken the truth and called his article an exaggeration based on halftruth which bordered on political demagoguery.[52] Ministers in New York City referred to Matthews' attack as an example of McCarthyism, and an 'insidious threat to the American tradition of freedom'; they added that it was 'alarming to find that procedures resulting from the fear of communism are causing us to lose those things that most distinguish our way of life from theirs.'[53]

The climax of the fundamentalists' campaign against Bishop Oxnam was at hand. The Matthews charges against the Protestant clergy, although never substantiated, helped the fundamentalists immensely. On July 21, 1953, more than two months after the fundamentalists had dared him to do it, Bishop Oxnam appeared voluntarily before the House Committee on Un-American Activities, citing as his reason the fact that the committee had frequently released information about him 'without the group's acceptance of responsibility for their accuracy,' thus creating the impression he was sympathetic to communism and perhaps guilty of subversion.[54]

The atmosphere was tense when Oxnam appeared before one of the largest crowds ever to attend a single hearing in Washington, D. C. Captain Edgar Bundy (an associate of Carl McIntire and speaker in American Council of Christian Churches rallies) and other leaders of the American Council occupied the front row during Oxnam's hearing which, because of Jackson's relationship with the American Council, was called 'Jackson's Pew.' Carl McIntire was conspicuously absent; he was outside the country at the time. [55]

Bishop Oxnam fought back point by point as the committee interrogated him and introduced alleged evidence connecting him with communism. Newspaper clippings and letters dating back thirty years were placed before Oxnam; it is believed that many of these clippings and letters were collected by Carl McIntire during his private investigation of Bishop Oxnam. Bishop Oxnam admitted under oath that during the twenties he had been a member of organizations that were later cited as communistic, but he added that whenever he detected any leanings toward communism he withdrew at once from the organizations. He also admitted that he had lent his name on occasions to Soviet friendship during World War II; he noted, however, that this was at a time when Russia was an ally and when it was patriotic to do so. [56]

At the end of the gruelling session which lasted ten hours, the House Committee unanimously agreed there was no evidence linking Oxnam with the communist party. However, the committee could not agree on the question whether Oxnam might have given the communist aid and comfort through his associations, thus leaving the impression of his 'guilt by association.'[57] It is interesting to note that Oxnam received support from at least one fundamentalist during this controversy. Donald Grey Barnhouse, editor of *Eternity* and supporter of the policies of the National Association of Evangelicals, commented after the hearings that he had read many of Oxnam's writings. He said the only thing he could say about Oxnam was that he was a theological liberal who disbelieved the inspiration of the Bible and the absolute deity of Jesus Christ. Barnhouse wrote:

His religion . . . is that of a brotherhood of man, founded by a Jesus who was little more than the prophets. He is a social liberal as well, and, naturally, a political liberal. But it is a far cry from political liberalism to Communism . . . The separatists only weaken our case when they call Oxnam . . . a Communist.[58]

The House Committee's action disappointed the leaders of the American Council; they had expected a thorough unmasking of Oxnam. After the hearing, the communist issue in the churches quickly subsided, much like the evolution issue following the Scopes trial in 1925. Suspense was now absent from any mention of communism in the churches. This does not mean, however, that the campaign against Oxnam and the National Council had ended. The American Council made other attempts to discredit Oxnam. In October, 1955 when Oxnam appeared in Oakland, California as the Reformation Day speaker, he was greeted by a large crowd of fundamentalists carrying banners with the following slogans: 'Christ or Marx, not Marx *and* Christ,' 'Oxnam Display Your "Red" D.D. Degree,' 'Don't Let Reds Use Christian Pulpits,' 'Don't Smear; Answer McIntire's Facts,' and 'Co-existence Is the Red Program Today.' [59] However, this technique aroused little public opinion against Oxnam and the National Council.

The Campaign to Wreck the World Council's Second Plenary Session
The American Council did not succeed as expected in its anti-communist campaign against the National Council and its leaders. However, there was a faint hope that the public could be aroused against the World Council during its second plenary session in Evanston, Illinois in August, 1954. The American Council planned its strategy accordingly. In this respect it is unfortunate the World Council had decided to conduct its second plenary session in the United States. McCarthyism was still prevalent, and many politicians continued to thrive on American fears of Communism. Various patriotic groups, because of their extreme nationalism, were constantly watching the actions of foreigners for subversion.

Carl McIntire inaugurated the campaign to wreck the World Council's second plenary session in 1953. His plan was to block the admission of delegates from communist countries into the United States. Early in 1954 McIntire organized a 'truth team' of eight persons, including himself, to arouse public opinion against Professor Joseph L. Hromadka and other delegates who were planning to come to the United States. Hromadka was a member of the World Council Central Committee from Prague. McIntire had been publishing critical articles about Hromadka since 1951, accusing him of being a communist sympathizer.[60]

The National Association of Evangelicals refused to participate in this phase of the fundamentalists' campaign against the World Council. McIntire later criticized them for refusing to do so. However, Ralph Lord Roy, who by this time had become a severe critic of the fundamentalists and especially Carl McIntire, commended the National Association of Evangelicals for refusing to be a party in the campaign, as he described it, of hate, discord, and deliberate disruption planned by the American Council. [61]

The American Council received support from another source in its campaign against the admission of delegates from communist countries. In March, 1951 the Cook County (Illinois) Council of the American Legion prepared a resolution demanding that the State Department deny the admission of Professor Hromadka, Bishop Albert Bereczky of the Reformed Church in Hungary, Methodist Bishop Theodor Arvidson of Sweden, and W. A. Visser t'Hooft, general secretary of the World Council from Holland. The Legion described these men as antagonistic toward capitalism and the United States, and its National Executive Committee adopted a condemnatory resolution on May 4, 1954. In this resolution the Committee demanded that the State Department comply strictly with the provision of the McCarran-Walter Immigration Act. This Act denied admission into the United States of all delegates or visitors from communist countries, except those who have 'demonstrated five years of active opposition to totalitarianism.' [62]

Leaders of the World Council in the United States said this campaign of harassment and villification had been anticipated, but that it came much sooner than had been expected. The *Christian Century* said the attack upon Hromadka and Bereczky was understandable, since both admittedly had 'given their blessing to the communist regimes under which their countries suffer.' [63] However, the *Christian Century* stated that the attack upon the other two delegates was inexplicable. [64]

It was revealed, however, that Bishop Oxnam and Visser t'Hooft had called upon Secretary of State John Foster Dulles in December, 1953 in behalf of the delegates and received assurances they would be admitted without difficulty. In desperation Carl McIntire formed a delegation of twelve clergymen for a pilgrimage to Washington, D.C. On April 13, 1954 they filed a petition with Dulles and Attorney General Herbert Brownell protesting the admission of the delegates who had been 'under the domination and control of the communist authorities.' [65] The petitions also stated: 'These men are no longer representatives of the Christian Church but are agents of communists.' [66]

Donald Grey Barnhouse did not approve of the tactics of the American Council. He said that 'certain political reactionaries' had unjustly maligned

Hromadka and other Christians in the World Council by describing them as communists, Soviet spokesmen, and Russian agents. He also declared: 'A man who I believe to be a Christian but who has a reputation for inaccuracy in reporting' and who 'was adamant in his opinions' was largely responsible for the slander upon the controversial delegates from Europe.[67] McIntire later replied critically that he was the one of whom Barnhouse spoke.[68] Barnhouse also stated that he had interviewed Hromadka and obtained a reply from him that he was coming to the United States as a Christian delegate and not as a communist. Regarding his country, Hromadka said:

We must live where our Lord has placed us. I have not chosen the time in which I live. My God put me here into this era of history, and into my place in Prague. He demands that I administer His gospel in love. I must administer it to the people of my country among whom I live.[69]

When the second plenary session of the World Council began, all of the disputed delegates were present. Obviously the campaign against them had failed. McIntire admitted that the grant of visas to them was a defeat for him and the American Council. Their coming was a victory for Bishop Oxnam and Visser t'Hooft.[70] In addition, Barnhouse's interview with and subsequent statements about Hromadka vindicated the latter and placed Carl McIntire in an embarrassing position among the fundamentalists. It is interesting to note in this connection that McIntire has frequently criticized Barnhouse, whom he says is 'opposed to modernism but . . . did not believe in separation or in carrying the struggle to the breaking point.'[71]

The Campaign against the 'Modernist' Bible

Approximately thirty-two scholars labored some twenty years over old and recently discovered manuscripts to produce a new version of the Bible, which would correct the errors of existing versions and bring the Bible in line with present English usage. The National Council of Churches and the publishers of the new Bible, Thomas Nelson and Sons, conducted an extensive campaign and expended approximately $ 1,000,000 to promote it. It was expected that the new Bible, known as the Revised Standard Version, would replace the King James Version, published in 1611, and the American Standard Version, published in 1901.[72] The Revised Standard Version was placed on sale in September, 1952. Within eight weeks 1,600,000 copies were sold, attesting to the effectiveness of the promotional campaign on the one hand, and the popular demand for a readable and more modern English version of the Bible on the other.[73]

The scholars who produced the new Bible followed the methods of modern biblical scholarship for the most part, and for that reason their conception of the Bible was different from that of the fundamentalists, who naturally opposed and criticized them. Almost immediately after the new Bible went on sale, the fundamentalists conducted rallies throughout the United States as part of their campaign to discredit it. They described the new Bible as something inspired by the devil and the product of fraudulent scholarship, higher criticism, socialism, communism, modernism, Unitarianism, ecumenicism, and internationalism. Some fundamentalists called it the product of a Jewish conspiracy.[74] Dan Gilbert, a fundamentalist evangelist, concluded that the new Bible was not a 'Bible at all but a book contrived by the servants of anti-Christ to undermine the truths that are contained in the Bible of our fathers.'[75]

Others crusaded against the new Bible in stranger ways. The Reverend M. Luther Hix, pastor of the Temple Baptist Church of Rocky Mount, North Carolina was one of them. He consulted the fire department to ascertain if burning the new Bible in his church would create a fire hazard. Immediately the news spread across the United States that Hix contemplated a modern version of book burning. After his congregation and interested spectators were assembled in his church, Hix with eyes flashing tore a page from the new Bible and quickly set fire to it. As soon as the flames consumed the page he had torn from the Bible he began stabbing at another disputed passage. One was Isaiah 7:14 in which the word 'virgin' in older versions was changed to 'a young woman.' Hix shouted that this is 'a scheme of the modernists to make the Lord Jesus Christ the son of a bad woman.'[76] Then he hurled the new Bible into a waste basket. After the service Hix willingly posed for a newspaper photographer. He told those who interviewed him that he hoped this Bible burning episode was the beginning of a 'holy war' that would deal the new version its 'death blow.'[77]

Carl McIntire also participated in the crusade against the new Bible. He sponsored a 'Back to the Bible' rally in Denver on December 9, 1952, to coincide with the biennial congress of the National Council in the same city. Reports from across the country indicated that the contagion of the crusade had spread rapidly. Rallies similar to the one McIntire sponsored were conducted in Dallas, Houston, Winston-Salem, Baltimore, St. Louis, Grand Rapids, Atlantic City, and Philadelphia.[78] Kenneth Kinney, pastor of the First Baptist Church of Johnson City, New York explained the origin of the new Bible as 'Satan's masterplan' to take over the churches which began in the seventeenth century with the rise of the enlightenment and religious rationalism, finally culminating in the establishment of the National Council and the publication of the new Bible.[79]

The fundamentalists also received some help in their crusade against the new Bible when State Senator A. P. Decker of Michigan announced that he planned to introduce legislation barring the sale of the Revised Standard Version of the Bible in his state. No final bill was enacted, however.[80]

Several months passed before articles explaining the reasons for the controversy were published in the nation's periodicals. The fundamentalists finally stated their objections in concise and readable form for those who were interested enough to study the matter. They complained that the translators shared the viewpoint of the higher critics who did not accept the verbal inspiration of the Bible. They also raised the objection that the translators altered many of the texts in the Old Testament, doing violence to the predictive element in the Bible and obscuring the virgin birth and the deity of Jesus Christ. Examples were given to illustrate the way this was done. In the King James Version, which some fundamentalists regarded as the only true version of the Bible, Isaiah 7:14 states: 'Therefore the Lord himself shall give you a sign; Behold, a virgin shall conceive, and bear a son, and shall call his name Immanuel.' In the Revised Standard Version in place of 'virgin' a 'young woman' was substituted. However, the text in Matthew 1:23, which apparently quoted Isaiah 7:14, was not changed in the new version. In both the King James Version and the Revised Standard Version the word 'virgin' appears as the bearer of a supernatural child. The fundamentalists complained, therefore, that the change in Isaish 7:14 not only did violence to the predictive element of the Bible but also cast doubt on its infallibility, which was basic in fundamentalist theology.[81]

Gerald B. Winrod, noted for his anti-Semitism, charged that the translators were in league with the Jews. To support his thesis he drew attention to the fact that a Jewish scholar had been assigned to work on the Old Testament. Winrod warned those who read his *Defender* magazine that 'Jewish leaders made charges against the character of our Lord's mother when He was on earth, similar to those heard today.'[82] Winrod also said that the National Council of Churches, which held the copyright of the new Bible, was 'strongly supported by American Jewry,'[83] Only a small segment of fundamentalists listened to or accepted Winrod's explanation.

Other fundamentalists had varying explanations. In a rally conducted in

Baltimore in February, 1953, J. Oliver Buswell tried to explain that the new Bible had been inspired either by the socialists or the communists. To substantiate his charges he stated that Luther A. Weigle of the Yale Divinity School and chairman of the Revised Standard Version Committee, had been affiliated with organizations now cited as communist or socialist fronts.[84] Finally, James DeForest Murch and Carl McIntire agreed that the new Bible was created as an official version of the National Council for the coming super-church which would include Protestants and Roman Catholics. McIntire regarded it as more than co-incidence that the Roman Catholic version of the Lord's prayer in Matthew 6 had been reproduced in the new version.[85]

There were several fundamentalists, however, who were extremely cautious in their judgment of the new Bible. Paul Griffis, instructor at the Practical Bible Institute in Binghamton, New York wrote an article in which he reminded the fundamentalists that objections were also raised against the American Standard Version when it was published in 1901. Yet today, he noted, most conservative schools and theologians use it. Griffis criticized Allen A. MacRae, president of Faith Theological Seminary (a fundamentalist school), for his inconsistencies in pointing out the faults of the new Bible. Griffis pointed out that MacRae criticized the new Bible because it was called an 'authorized' version, yet he spoke kindly of the Douay version which the Roman Catholics called their 'authorized' version. MacRae also recommended the Williams' translation of the New Testament which states in Matthew 1:23: 'Behold, a maiden shall be pregnant . . .,' while he raised serious objections to the much disputed Isaiah 7:14 passage in the new Bible. Griffis pleaded with the fundamentalists to avoid such careless judgment against the new Bible. He pleaded: 'Let's be fair in our criticism. We must be exceedingly careful not to permit our prejudices to distort our judgment and destroy our Christian grace.'[86]

In summary, it should be noted that the fundamentalists had once again manifested their militancy as their predecessors did during the first quarter of the twentieth century. However, the fundamentalists today are strongly organized and capable of conducting a prolonged campaign against the National Council and the World Council. Although the fundamentalists did not succeed in every instance in winning their point, one fact is outstanding; they were never disorganized or routed by their reversals as their predecessors had been. Whenever they failed in one campaign they immediately waged another.

TABLE IV

DENOMINATIONS IN THE NATIONAL COUNCIL OF THE CHURCHES
OF CHRIST IN THE U.S.A. *

Denominations	Membership in 1953
African Methodist Episcopal	1,166,301
African Methodist Episcopal Zion	728,150
American Baptist Convention	1,554,304
Augustana Evangelical Lutheran	465,062
Church of the Brethren	186,358
Colored Methodist Episcopal	392,167
Congregational Christian	1,241,477
Czech-Moravian Brethren	4,090
Danish Evangelical Lutheran	19,899
Evangelical and Reformed	735,941
Evangelical United Brethren	720,544
Friends-Five Years Meeting	68,612
Friends of Philadelphia and Vicinity	5,743
Greek Orthodox Church in America	1,000,000
International Convention of Disciples of Christ	1,792,985
Methodist	9,065,727
Moravian	43,856
National Baptist Convention of America	2,645,789
National Baptist Convention U.S.A., Inc.	4,467,779
Presbyterian U.S.	702,266
Presbyterian U.S.A.	2,364,112
Protestant Episcopal	2,417,464
Reformed in America	187,256
Romanian Orthodox of America	50,000
Russian Orthodox of America	400,000
Seventh Day Baptist	6,187
Syrian Antiochian Orthodox	75,000
Ukranian Orthodox of America	40,250
United Lutheran	1,925,506
United Presbyterian	219,027
Total membership	34,681,852

* Roy, *Apostles of Discord*, pp. 390–391.

CHAPTER FIVE

The Rising Tide of Fundamentalist Evangelism

A primary feature of the fundamentalist-modernist controversy during the Scopes trial in 1925 was that the energy of the combatants was expended in destructive rather than on constructive enterprises. Instead of concentrating on evangelism, for which they had always been noted, the fundamentalists became involved in many side issues such as the instruction of evolution in the public schools. Furthermore, the fundamentalists were ill prepared intellectually during their controversy with the modernists and they saw themselves in a losing battle against liberalism, naturalism, and humanism – philosophies which had made such extraordinary 'inroads within the churches that evangelism was pretty largely discounted and looked upon as a relic of a bygone age.'[1] This state of affairs continued until recently when the fundamentalists once again began to capture the headlines, particularly because of the Billy Graham crusades and the fact they were once again stressing evangelism.[2]

The activity of the fundamentalists was once again directed toward the single task of evangelism. Clergymen and evangelists together with volunteer laymen began to expound the gospel, distribute gospel tracts, conduct youth rallies, and engage in radio broadcasts. They did anything, no matter how novel, to convince men in the pattern of past American revivalists 'that men without Christ are lost and that only as they heard the gospel, according to the Scriptures, and accepted it, according to the Scriptures, could they be saved.'[3] Since 1930 the fundamentalists have not only improved the old but have perfected new techniques for mass evangelism.

Radio Evangelism

Most radio audiences are aware of the innumerable religious broadcasts which can be heard, particularly on Sundays. One observer has commented that 'anyone who wants a religious program should be able to easily tune one in.'[4]

This is true anywhere in the United States. One might conclude that a significant proportion of available radio time had been preempted by religious groups. A partial listing in 1948 indicated that over 1,600 programs were broadcast by fundamentalists each week. It was estimated they spent $ 2,829,000 to broadcast approximately thirty-five gospel programs over a network of twenty or more stations.[5] In addition, there were more than a dozen stations which were operated either privately or by groups of fundamentalists. Most of these were supported through the sale of radio time to commercial accounts, but the profits were used primarily to disseminate the gospel.[6] Other stations were established by fundamentalists schools: WMBI by the Moody Bible Institute of Chicago; KUCA in Siloam Springs, Arkansas and KUGA in Los Angeles by John Brown University; WMUU by Bob Jones University in Greenville, South Carolina; and KBBI (FM) by the Bible Institute of Los Angeles.[7]

The following is a partial list of programs taken from a log published in 1954 (only those programs which were heard on a national network are shown here): Back to the Bible Hour, originating in Lincoln, Nebraska; Children's Gospel Hour, originating in Cleveland, Tennessee; Hour of Decision, originating in Minneapolis, Minnesota; Message to Israel, originating in New York City; Old Fashioned Revival Hour, originating in Long Beach, California; Radio Bible Class, originating in Grand Rapids, Michigan; and Unshackled, originating in Chicago.[8] In 1956 the Bible Study Hour, originating in Philadelphia, began broadcasting over the facilities of the National Broadcasting Company.[9]

The best known and the oldest fundamentalist radio program, the Old Fashioned Revival Hour, was established by Charles E. Fuller in Placentia, California in 1925. At that time Fuller was serving as a minister of a small church and was firmly convinced 'that radio would be a wonderful means of spreading the gospel.'[10] For several years he remained on an obscure radio station where he first began broadcasting. Gradually he expanded his program. By 1937 his program was heard as far east as Gary, Indiana.[11]

For some time there was danger that Fuller would be compelled to discontinue his expanded program unless he accepted the offer of the Mutual Broadcasting System for an entire network broadcast. Fuller did not have the necessary funds to pay for this expanded program, but he displayed courage and faith in the future of religion on the air, and accepted the contract rather than lose his place to a commercial account. At the time he made this important decision, Fuller's program was broadcast over sixty-five stations. In

1949, when other broadcasters began accepting religious programs, Fuller moved his Old Fashioned Revival Hour to the American Broadcasting Company's network. His program is now heard over three hundred stations.[12]

The Old Fashioned Revival Hour program is typical of most other fundamentalist programs which are heard every week over various stations. The music is spirited, with a fast tempo, and is easily sung by those with little or no musical training. Popular gospel choruses are employed to 'loosen' an audience which prefers less formality in religion. The climax in every program is an 'invitation' given at the end of the sermon. The American Broadcasting Company estimates that Fuller's audiences range from 15,000,000 to 20,000,000 persons every week. Mrs. Fuller participates by reading several selected letters from persons professed to have been converted or helped after listening to the program.[13] Similar results are repeated by other religious programs. One can therefore conclude that religious broadcasting conditioned a sizeable proportion of the people in the United States to accept fundamentalism as the normal expression of Protestant doctrine.

It is difficult to determine the source of financial assistance for any of these religious programs simply because responsible persons connected with them refuse to release this information. However, it is known that most of the money is contributed by the listeners and occasionally by a wealthy benefactor. Billy Graham obtained $ 25,000 during his Portland, Oregon crusade to launch his Hour of Decision program heard over three networks since 1955. The Billy Graham Evangelistic Association announced that most of the contributions were five dollars or less. One check for fifty dollars and another for $ 5,000 were the only unusually large contributions. This means that the program must reach large audiences to be able to remain on the air.[14]

Most stations disapprove of direct solicitation over the air, yet this is the one main source of income that maintains the religious programs. Where solicitation is forbidden, various devices are employed to circumvent the ban. Frequently radio evangelists remind their audiences that their program is not underwritten and that they depend upon the letters of those who listen and pray for the program for its continuance. This is an indirect method of solicitation. Oftentimes free gifts such as booklets of sermons, plastic crosses which glow in the dark, and other inducements are employed to induce people to write so that a mailing list of interested listeners can be compiled. These are subsequently solicited by mail. Frequently the letters contain money because people know this is the only way the programs remain on the air.[15]

One of the major problems for the radio stations, as well as for legitimate broadcasters, is the 'religious huckster,' as *Time* magazine described the 'fringe or marginal preacher.'[16] 'Religious hucksters' have been recognized as the real enemy of gospel broadcasting because their basic aim is to make money for themselves by appealing to credulous and unsuspecting listeners. One established evangelist reportedly received $ 35,000 weekly, without accounting how the money was spent.[17]

To combat this charlatanism the National Council of Churches recommended that radio and television broadcasting be limited to programs on a sustaining basis, that is, radio time should be allocated without charge to the Protestants, Jews, and Roman Catholics and should be apportioned among them. However, the American Council and the National Association of Evangelicals immediately protested and charged that the National Council's proposal was a deliberate plot to deny fundamentalists the constitutional guarantee of freedom of speech and religion.[18]

One fundamentalist program is unusually appealing to both children and adults, for this reason many radio and television stations are willing to provide free time to broadcast it. This program, known as the Children's Gospel Hour, was established by Henry C. Geiger of Cleveland, Tennessee, because of this firm conviction that seventy-five percent of all Christians were prepared for conversion during their formative years. The interest in this program is one that is natural whenever children perform. The substance of the program is simple: Bible stories, flannelgraph story presentations, Bible quizzes, and children singing. To finance his program Geiger makes appeals to individuals, churches, and other interested groups for funds for the production of recording and films which are sent to over one hundred stations carrying the program.[19]

Television programs require large financial resources, and only a very small proportion of fundamentalists have been daring enough to try to produce such programs. However, there have been few besides Geiger who have done so. Percy Crawford, indefatigable president of Kings College of Briarcliff Manor, New York earned the distinction of being the first to launch a fundamentalist gospel program on television. On October, 1949 he introduced his program, 'Youth on the March,' over the American Broadcasting Company's network. Crawford utilized as talent approximately forty students enrolled in Kings College. They presented a variety program of gospel songs, solos, quartets, and group songs. The Moody Bible Institute of Chicago also provided films from its 'Sermons from Science' on the nation's television networks. Finally, Donald Grey Barnhouse began his television debut on the

program 'Man to Man' in conjunction with the National Council of Churches.[20]

Barnhouse was immediately criticized by the American Council for working
in conjunction with the National Council of Churches to present the program. However, other fundamentalists defended Barnhouse and denied that
he had departed from the traditional fundamentalist position. Barnhouse
justified his actions as practical. He said the television program afforded him
an opportunity to minister in a way otherwise denied to the fundamentalists.
Several leaders in the National Council, on the other hand, wondered whether
it was wise to cooperate in presenting Barnhouse on a program with them.[21]
They finally decided, however, that regardless of theological differences it
should be continued. James DeForest Murch declared that the reason millions
of people from the Atlantic to the Pacific listen continually to their religious
broadcasts is because of 'the drawing power of the evangelical faith,' and because 'thousands who have been denied Bible preaching by liberal ministers
in their own churches rejoiced at the opportunity once again to hear the old
Gospel.'[22]

Fundamentalist religious broadcasters affiliated with the National Religious
Broadcasters (a fundamentalist agency), estimated that they paid the radio
industry approximately $ 10,000,000 annually for broadcasting time. Even
these statistics do not tell the complete story of the extent of fundamentalist
broadcasting and the virtual monopoly they apparently enjoyed over the air.
There are many fundamentalist broadcasters not affiliated with any organization to whom they are accountable. For that reason there is no way to force
them to release any statistical information to determine the extent of their
operation, or to accurately estimate their annual broadcasting expenditures.[23]

The Controversy over Radio Evangelism
Unfortunately religious racketeers have complicated matters, for those who
have sought to maintain high standards of ethics, by resorting to questionable
methods of extracting money for their own use at the expense of unwary
listeners. In some instances sick people were asked to touch the knobs of their
radio while the radio preacher prayed for their healing. Many of the sick,
either because they expected to be healed or because they found psychological
relief, sent money to the radio preacher in gratitude for his prayers. This
practice among others was repugnant to many. To combat this pernicious
practice, in 1943 the Mutual Broadcasting System, the only network then
selling radio time for religious broadcasts, submitted to the pressure of the

Federal Council of Churches. It announced a new policy of placing all religious broadcasts on a sustaining basis by allocating religious time to the three major religious groups in the United States. This practice was already in effect on other radio networks.[24]

The fundamentalists reacted promptly when they were informed that only programs with universal appeal 'giving only those truths that were common to all faiths' would be permitted on a sustaining basis. Carl McIntire objected on the grounds that each religious group (Catholic, Jew, and Protestant) should be accorded the privilege to buy time to present their message to win converts. McIntire blamed the Federal Council for this proposal, because it had frequently complained to the radio industry that the public received a distorted and one-sided picture, because the fundamentalists had monopolized most of the broadcasting time. The fundamentalists were convinced that the Federal Council was interested primarily in eliminating them from the air under the pretext of reforming religious broadcasting.[25]

On April 12, 1944 one hundred-fifty gospel broadcasters met in Columbus, Ohio to discover a judicious method to preserve their rights under the Constitution and the Bill of Rights to preach their theological views on purchased radio time, and to demand the right to share in time apportioned to Protestants on a sustaining basis.[26] These broadcasters, most of whom were affiliated with the National Association of Evangelicals, disputed the claim of the Federal Council that it represented American Protestantism. They declared that American Protestantism was divided between the liberals on the one hand and the fundamentalists on the other hand. They argued that to allocate all Protestant time to the Federal Council would be an unfair advantage granted to the liberals. The fundamentalists were alarmed over the prospect that free radio time would result in an end of freedom of speech and religion on the air for them. They believed their fight was right and that the only way freedom of speech and religion could be maintained was through equal opportunity for those who desired to purchase radio time, not to depend upon the grace of some powerful organization like the Federal Council.[27]

The Columbus meeting formulated plans to (1) meet with representatives of the radio industry to survey the problem, and (2) to meet in the Moody Memorial Church of Chicago on September 21, 1944 to adopt a constitution for the organization and a broadcaster's code which would be suitable to both the radio industry and the fundamentalists. Meanwhile, a committee remained in Columbus to draft a constitution. Legal consul was engaged, and other steps were taken to complete the plans for the new organization.[28]

The National Religious Broadcasters met as planned in the Moody Memorial Church in 1944. They adopted the constitution, which had been drafted in Columbus, and established a code of ethics to govern its constituency on the following basis: (1) all broadcasts should be solely on a non-profit basis and for the single purpose of propagating the gospel; (2) the message disseminated in such programs should be positive, concise and constructive; (3) the content, production, and presentation of the programs, including the music, should be consistent with the standards and requirements of the station, network, State and Federal laws, and the regulations of the Federal Communications Commission; and (4) all appeals for money should be of a bona fide character strictly for religious purposes. All donors should be given a receipt immediately, and members of the organization were required to give an accounting of their receipts whenever requested to do so by the Board of Directors of the National Religious Broadcasters.[29] James DeForest Murch was one of the principals in the establishment of the new organization. He declared: 'This code became a veritable 'Declaration of Independence' from radio racketeers on the one hand and ecclesiastical boycotters on the other.'[30]

Copies of this code were sent to all radio stations and networks. In 1946 a resolution was also adopted and sent to the stations and the networks. In the resolution the fundamentalists tried to apprise the radio industry of the differences between themselves and the Federal Council, and why it was that the latter could not rightfully claim to be the sole representative of Protestantism in America. The resolution, which was designed to assure 'the distinctively evangelical testimony . . . a voice on the air,'[31] stated:

One misconception is that American Protestantism is one unified religious group, whereas in fact there are two distinct kinds of Protestants in America today. Each adheres to a particular form of teaching – the one the antithesis of the other.

One group believes the Bible to be the infallible rule for belief and conduct whereas the other group does not.

We believe it could be demonstrated that the majority of American Protestants belong to the former group. Yet this group is not given time or representation on the radio, either by the networks or by individual radio stations, in proportion to their numerical strength.[32]

Understandings were reached under which the National Religious Broadcasters were able to develop cordial relations between the radio industry and themselves. They not only obtained protection for their broadcasting rights as a result of the establishment of an accredited and responsible broadcasting agency, but they also succeeded in persuading the networks to grant them a proportionate share of sustaining time, thus breaking the monopoly that the Federal Council had enjoyed in this area. Furthermore, fundamentalist programs were permitted to continue the purchase of radio time. Thus, the fundamentalists won the first round in their battle against the Federal Council to remain on the air and to propagate their doctrines.[33]

Apparently the rapidly expanding television industry had some effect upon the thinking of those connected with the broadcasting industry. As more television stations were introduced and made available for commercial programs, more time became available on the radio. This, plus the fact that America was experiencing a revival in religion, accounts for the decision of the National Broadcasting Company in April, 1956 to finally end its ban on selling time for religious broadcasts. At that time Billy Graham's 'Hour of Decision' was on the National Broadcasting Company network, while others began to transfer to its facilities. Donald Grey Barnhouse was given a contract in 1956 to broadcast his 'Bible Study Hour' on the National Broadcasting Company's network.[34]

Another phase of the controversy over radio evangelism began when the Broadcasting and Film Commission of the National Council of Churches renewed the drive started by the Federal Council of Churches to induce the radio industry, together with the infant television industry, to halt the sale of time for religious broadcasts and telecasts. A resolution was adopted by the Commission on March 6, 1956 requesting the two industries to allocate free time for nonpartisan religious broadcasts in the public interest. Furthermore, the Commission declared, such a policy would be a step toward the elimination of 'irresponsible racketeering religious broadcasts.'[35]

The fundamentalists responded immediately to this latest proposal, which was not much unlike the previous request of the Federal Council. Ralph Neighbour, a member of the National Religious Broadcasters, declared in Cleveland, Ohio during the convention of the National Association of Evangelicals: 'We are living in the last days - organized religion is attempting to captivate the peoples of the world.'[36] The National Religious Broadcasters immediately denounced the National Council's proposal and declared there were 20,000,000 Protestants whom the Broadcasting and Film Commission of the National Council of Churches does not represent. For that reason they asserted that the National Council could not rightfully claim all the free time allocated to the Protestants by the radio and television industry.[37]

Although the controversy was not settled, it appears that the radio industry had decided to ignore the recommendation of the National Council of Churches. The broadcasting companies found religious programs lucrative, which in part compensates for the tensions that have been created by competing religious factions. The National Religious Broadcasters commended the National Broadcasting Company for its new policy to make radio time available to all religious groups who are willing to pay for it. The fundamentalists were determined to maintain the existing policy as the only means of safeguarding freedom of speech and of religion on the radio and television facilities.[38]

A survey among fundamentalist broadcasters has shown that the attitude of aloofness on the part of the networks toward religious broadcasts has almost completely disappeared. This must be attributed in part to the revival of interest in religion. Theodore H. Epp, director of the 'Back to the Bible Hour' originating in Lincoln, Nebraska, reported that more people were listening to religious broadcasts than ever before. In 1948 Epp said he averaged 24,000 pieces of mail each month. In 1950 the volume of his mail reached 81,000 pieces each month. Many people wrote because they were alarmed over the campaign to restrict fundamentalist broadcasting. Becoming fearful the channels might be closed, people increased their support of their favorite programs to keep them on the air. Moreover, some people listened to and supported the various religious broadcasts because they were concerned over the seriousness of the threat of atomic warfare with Russia. Regardless what their reasons were, it is obvious the masses of Protestants supported the fundamentalists in the struggle for radio time for paid religious broadcasts, and they were willing to contribute toward its continuance.[39]

What has been the total effect of the expansion of interest in religious broadcasts? No survey has been conducted to determine the effects, but it can be assumed that much of the tithe money of Christians went into radio work. This has helped enhance interdenominationalism in America while at the same time increasing church attendance. However, the promotion of interdenominationalism explains why the Federal Council of Churches and the National Council of Churches had opposed religious broadcasting as conducted by the fundamentalists. The interdenominationalism which the fundamentalists encouraged was not ecumenical in any sense. Instead, the fundamentalists encouraged others of like mind in the various denominations to identify themselves with the fundamentalist movement. Many began to question the theology of the leaders of the National Council of Churches. Some observers are also sure that religious broadcasts had prepared the American mind for the present religious revival. This probably is true because revivals usually thrive when interdenominationalism is stressed and the approach to conversion is individualistic.[40]

Revival among American Youth
During the depression youth leaders in different parts of the United States sought new ways to attract young people to religion. Saturday nights became an important time for special youth rallies, for Bible study, chorus singing, and personal testimony meetings. Oscar T. Gillan organized the 'Detroit Voice of Christian Youth' in 1938. He later claimed this was the beginning of the 'Youth for Christ' movement. The printed circulars advertising the Detroit meetings contained the slogan: 'Voice of Christian Youth – Our Motto, Youth for Christ.'[41]

It was not until the war years, however, that the Saturday night plan for youth rallies reached mammoth proportions and spread sporadically across the United States. In 1940 Jack Wyrtzen, formerly an insurance salesman and dance-band musician, was encouraged by Percy Crawford, director of the 'Young Peoples' Church of the Air,' to start a radio program to help promote his 'Word of Life' rallies on Saturday nights in New York City. Wyrtzen's rallies began to draw large crowds as soon as he inaugurated his broadcasts. He first conducted his rallies in a small Tabernacle seating approximately two hundred persons. The Tabernacle was outgrown and Wyrtzen leased Carnegie Hall. Soon this was too small for the crowds. Eventually he conducted his rallies in the St. Nicholas boxing arena. On one occasion he leased Madison Square Garden for three nights against the advice of seasoned religious leaders. However, a crowd aggregating 67,000 persons contributed $ 62,000 to pay for the rental of the Garden. Wyrtzen heard of other similar rallies which occurred independently, causing him to remark that their spontaneity must be attributed to supernatural origin and not the work of man.[42]

On May 26, 1942 Roger Malsbary, a youth leader in Indianapolis, incorporated his movement under the name Youth for Christ. One of the first guest speakers was Torrey Johnson, who later helped organize the Chicagoland Youth for Christ. Johnson conducted his Youth for Christ rally in Orchestra Hall in Chicago on May 27, 1944. A victory rally attended by 30,000 persons was conducted in the fall of the same year. One tavern operator at first was delighted to see the crowd, but afterward he complained that it was the wrong kind of a crowd. They did not patronize him.[43]

Johnson called a group of interested persons together in January, 1945 to organize the Youth for Christ movement on a permanent basis to give the independent youth organizations an opportunity to be affiliated in an organized effort. The result of the meeting was the incorporation of the movement as Youth for Christ, International. Johnson said: 'We intend to send sparks to any part of the world to inspire the program of Youth for Christ, to start the ball rolling and then leave the work in the hands of resident groups.'[44] Johnson shared his dream with Billy Graham, who was serving as pastor of a small Baptist church in Western Springs, Illinois at that time. Graham became the first field representative of Youth for Christ, International, a post which was destined to start him on the road to evangelical fame. Graham and other youth leaders travelled extensively throughout the United States and in various foreign countries to speak and promote the new organization. They travelled so much that people called them 'Christian Gypsies.'[45]

Rolland Emerson Wolfe, rated as one of liberalism's outstanding contemporary biblical scholars,[46] said in his book, Men of Prophetic Fire, that one of the most significant aspects about the ministry of the Old Testament prophets was that most of them were young men who 'had been set on fire with a new spirit in the days of their youth.' 'Their contributions' he added, 'began as the product of youth's nobility, and the precedents they established were set by them as young men.'[47] The same thing might be said about the leaders of Youth for Christ. Most of them were young men who saw in their movement 'America's most promising avenues to spiritual revival, as well as one of the answers to the nation's growing problem of delinquency among the bobby-soxers and boogie-woogie boosters.'[48]

Mel Larsen, another youth leader, wrote a book entitled Young Men on Fire. In the book Larsen related Torrey Johnson's part in the Youth for Christ movement and also emphasized the part youth were playing in the revival of mass evangelism in America. It is not insignificant, for example, that Billy Graham, who developed as an appealing mass evangelist among youth, is a famous revivalist today. George Beverly Shea, baritone singer on Graham's crusade team, also came to the forefront as a result of his participation in Youth for Christ rallies.[49]

The Youth for Christ movement soon became known throughout the United States and in many places of the world, attesting to the influence and dynamic energy of its youthful leaders. By July, 1946 over 700 Youth for Christ centers were opened in the United States and in thirty-two foreign countries. The response in England was comparable to that in the United States. It was estimated that more than 1,000,000 young people attended the Saturday night rallies in the various Youth for Christ centers in the United States during the formative period of the organizations. Los Angeles averaged 2,000 in attendance, St. Louis leaders reported an average attendance of 2,500, and the Chicagoland Youth for Christ, apparently best attended averaged 3,000.[50]

Youth leaders connected with the Youth for Christ movement also attempted massive spectator-scale undertakings, conducting their meetings in large auditoriums and stadia requiring large sums of money for rental. The Chicagoland Youth for Christ, already assuming an annual budget of $ 85,000, sponsored a rally in Soldier's Field in May, 1945 which 65,000 attended. The fact that large sums of money were raised without anyone underwriting these efforts gave the Youth for Christ movement its super-natural character. It represented youth on the march without any denom-inational support or directions.[51]

The Youth for Christ Saturday night rallies were variously described as Christian vaudeville and Saturday night opera. Critics regarded them as trash and dispensaries of cheap music and mediocre sermons. The pattern in most instances was the same. Talented singers, soloists, duets, trios, quartets, and choirs, together with instrumentalists, ventriloquists, and magicians entertained the young people at Youth for Christ rallies. In some communities music derisively referred to as 'hill-billy' and country style was popularized and adapted to religious lyrics. Billy Weston, conductor of the St. Louis Youth Jubilee, became noted as a master-of-ceremonies because he kept his audiences in a jovial mood through his unique arrangements of old hymns, gospel songs, and choruses. Frequently he was advertised as the 'Fred Waring of Gospel Music.'[52] Finally, many vocalists on the Youth for Christ programs became important recording artists of the fundamentalist cause. In this sense the Youth for Christ movement also contributed to American musical culture.[53]

Anything that might appeal to youth and hold their attention, even though the device fostered mediocrity, was utilized to give youth a wholesome place to go on Saturday nights. Dating was encouraged between professing Christians, and many times visitors at the rallies were annoyed by the daters' disorderliness. Many dating youth whispered to each other, giggled, and in other ways detracted from the service, by their display of a lack of religious discipline.[54]

The Youth for Christ movement was not without its share of critics, fair and unfair. Rumors were spread, particularly during the war, that the movement was un-American, anti-labor, anti-Semitic, fascist, and communist in inspiration. In instances where separate rallies were conducted for negroes, they were also branded as segregationists.[55]

Many pastors objected, declaring that the fruit of the Youth for Christ movement was shallow conversions, which resulted from the diluted sermons; others were afraid the movement might emancipate the youth from ecclesiastical control or might foster informal religious worship because of the independent character of their rallies. Defenders of Youth for Christ answered these criticisms by stating that their primary objective was to obtain commitment to Christ. Thereafter, they said, it was the responsibility of the churches to instruct the converts substantially. The defenders also denied the second allegation, asserting that they encouraged young people to attend church regularly. Some thought that the movement represented a demand of young people in part for psychological expression, at a time when churches patronized adults who sought prestige and satisfaction for their ego. In this sense, it was claimed, Youth for Christ represented a democratic movement originating with the nation's youth on the one hand and the failure of the churches to meet the minimum needs of their youth on the other.[56]

Defenders also argued, whatever its shortcomings, that Youth for Christ contributed to American religious life and to the normal uplift of youth at a critical period in history. Young People from various areas of life were converted in the rallies and subsequently sent to the church of their own choice for nurture and service. Colorful conversions were reported, and they were interpreted as proof that God was somehow involved in the Youth for Christ movement. Night club singers, models, prostitutes, drunkards, tramps, and lonely servicemen were converted. Some of these people were invited to the meetings by young people, while others attended from curiosity.[57] One is reminded by these reports of notable conversions during the beginning of the Colonial revivals after Jonathan Edwards had reported and recorded his *Narratives of the Surprising Works of God*.[58]

Finally, the Youth for Christ movement contributed to the religious development of many by encouraging them to pray and to study their Bibles regularly. It also trained them as personal workers at youth rallies and in their churches. Many high school clubs were formed as a result and young people conducted daily prayer meetings before classes began every morning. Youth evangelism was in full swing. Many young people were also given an opportunity to speak at Youth for Christ meetings, and some of them displayed promise as public speakers. As a result many were recruited for the ministry. [59]

The revival in youth evangelism was also carried over into the nation's high schools. Early in 1940 the Miracle Book Club was formed to evangelize high school youth, to promote fellowship among them, and to help them counteract secular entertainment such as dancing. The club's theme, which explains its name, was 'Miracle book – the Bible.' In 1946 the club was incorporated as the Hi-C club and it formed a pattern for other clubs which were to be formed later. The Hi-C club movement originated in Chicago where it rapidly grew from its small beginnings in 1940 to sixty-two high school clubs. A varied program to keep youth interested was developed, i.e., recreation, Bible study, radio broadcasting opportunities, parties, and group singing. However, the primary purpose of the Hi-C club was evangelism. Most of its members carried Bibles to school under their arms for use in personal evangelism. Some of them became adept in instructing others in the doctrines of fundamentalism. Since everything depended upon personal evangelism, the club members were expected to memorize key verses from the Scriptures, enabling them to become effective soul winners. [60]

Other clubs rapidly formed in different parts of the United States. In 1944 the King's Teens was organized on the West Coast, while the Evangelism Fellowship, with clubs in New York, Long Island, and Boston was incorporated with headquarters in New York City. The American Soul Clinic of Huntington Park, California also formed clubs among high school youth on the West Coast. In 1951 the Tri-C club was organized by Louis Rhoden, the West Coast Regional Director of Youth for Christ, because he believed the high school was the greatest mission field in the world. Billy Graham told Rhoden that the seeds for a revival on the West Coast had been sown by high school students. [61]

How to explain the spontaneous rise of these high school clubs is difficult. However, one can safely assert that they were the result of a revival of fundamentalism among the nation's high school youth. In some instances sensitive youth were disturbed and desired moral encouragement. One said: 'You can help me! I'm sick of sin!' [62] A club leader explained the phenomena as a springing from spiritual hunger of the nation's youth. Another said: 'Young people are exhausted. They have been told of the theory of evolution but are asking 'So what! Where does it take us?' Discovering its inadequacy, they are searching for reality!'[63]

The high school clubs, like the Youth for Christ, were not without their share of criticism. In some areas the clubs were accused of being communist-inspired, although in no instance was this charge substantiated. The only similarity between the high school clubs, and the action of youth actually inspired by communism, was in the method of operation of both groups.

One leader of the high school movement said: 'Communists build their little units whose members must reach out to win more converts. How remarkable that the high school movement follows the 'cell pattern.' [64]

Fundamentalists said that the United States Supreme Court took the Bible out of the public schools as a result of its Illinois *ex rel*. McCollum *v*. Board of Education decision in 1948, but that the high school club movement restored it through its young people. [65] In some instances actual violations of the Supreme Court decision occurred, especially where principals, apparently in sympathy with the clubs, permitted them to use classrooms, corridors, auditoriums, and stadia for their meetings. However, where the school authorities upheld the Supreme Court, and the principle of separation of church and state, high school clubs were denied permission to use the facilities of the schools for their meetings. In any case clubs were formed and if it was necessary meetings were conducted in homes, churches, halls, vacant buildings, and parking lots. In Kansas City a high school club purchased a school bus as a meeting room. [66]

In practically all of the clubs the pattern of their programs was the same: prayer meetings before classes started in the morning, Bible study classes sometime during the day, student testimonials of the meaning of Christ to themselves, and personal evangelism. Sometimes club members singled out a popular athlete and concentrated upon him, hoping to bring about his conversion. If that happened, it was only a matter of time until others, inspired by the example of the athlete, were enticed to take the same step.[67]

The revival of fundamentalism among American youth also occurred after 1940 among college students. The Inter-Varsity Christian Fellowship sponsored meetings among college students. This Fellowship originated in Great Britain in the 1870's. In the late 1920's it spread to the British Commonwealths. But it was not until 1940 that the organization took root in the United States, when a headquarters was established in Chicago under the chairmanship of H. J. Taylor (president of Club Aluminium Company of Chicago), and C. Davis Wyerhaeuser (a Tacoma, Washington lumberman).[68]

Fundamentalist leaders were concerned because most American Colleges had abolished religious exercises on their campuses. They felt the time had come to reverse this trend and 'to fill an increasing need among college and university students.'[69] They also stated that 'as long as materialism, agnosticism, or liberalism is the accepted philosophy of life by many of our educators, someone must attempt to reach the student with the Gospel.'[70]

In 1940, the year the movement was established in the United States, there was only one university chapter which was affiliated with the Inter-Varsity Christian Fellowship. By extensive missionary effort leaders of the movement watched the Fellowship grow to 561 chapters by 1950. Students were given books, pamphlets, and other aids 'to withstand the subtle reasoning of . . . instructors.'[71] The fundamentalists were ready to engage the nation's intellectual leaders anew in a battle which had begun with the fundamentalist-modernist controversy fifty years before. The Inter-Varsity Christian Fellowships on the various campuses were also encouraged in 1950 because 'there seemed to be in most of the colleges and universities a disposition on the part of the average student to hear what Christians say.'[72] Part of this interest was attributed to 'the Korean war and the widespread perplexity caused by the peril of the atomic bomb.'[73] In this sense the revival of interest in fundamentalism among college students represented a search for absolute certainty. One lecturer, speaking on 'the quest of a peace of mind,' as he explained the situation in the United States in 1953, said:

We are flooded with prescriptions on how to escape from anxiety and the best-seller lists burgeon with guides to the Shangri-La of ease and serenity. The national code word seems to be 'relax.' We have virtually a national movement to evade any personal responsibilities which may, God forbid, affect the blood pressure or agitate the colon.[74]

Fundamentalists probably agree with this lecturer in his explanation of the escapism which was existent in 1953. His conclusion also tallied with the fundamentalists when he said:

We are building vast defenses to protect ourselves against new and terrifying enemies. Billions are poured out for ships and guns and planes and atomic weapons. But without faith that our lives have ultimate meaning all of this strength lacks heart and will and stamina. With such faith we build a defense in depth and such a defense is impregnable.[75]

In practically all of the Inter-Varsity Christian Fellowship groups on various campuses the pattern of their programs was the same: prayer meetings, Bible study, student testimonies, and personal evangelism. Campus leaders were usually sought out and every effort was made to convert them. If this happened, it was only a matter of time before others were impressed and probably encouraged to do the same. Conversions among engineering students, students with high academic standing, and students with Unitarian backgrounds made good news. The fundamentalists always took delight in the capitulation of intellectuals to the gospel. From 1949 to 1950, a total of twelve months, approximately 2,000 students were converted as a result of the activities of the Inter-Varsity Christian Fellowships on various college campuses. [76]

In 1951 the Inter-Varsity Christian Fellowship of Canada concentrated on a similar program in the 1,300 accredited training schools of this country. Consequently, in 1948 the Nurses Christian Fellowship became an affiliate of the Inter-Varsity Christian Fellowship. No reliable statistics are available, but it can be stated that many nurses were converted to fundamentalism and many of them were recruited as fundamentalist missionaries and church workers.[77]

In summary, it will be remembered that the Federal Council and the National Council sought to restrict the fundamentalists on the air. It was charged that the fundamentalists gave the public a distorted and one-sided view of the religious thinking in America by their monopoly of the available radio and television time. Undoubtedly this was true. However, in their struggle with the Federal Council and the National Council up to 1960, the fundamentalists were victorious. This indicates among other things that public opinion and the American tradition of freedom of speech and religion favored the fundamentalists. Furthermore, the developments in radio and television evangelism, in addition to other new techniques to reach the nation's youth, combined to make the fundamentalists a significant force in American religious life. The masses of people, in their uncertainty, apparently wanted to hear what the fundamentalists had to say.

CHAPTER SIX

Fundamentalist Education, Scholarship, and Literature

The Bible Institute

Immediately after the beginning of the fundamentalist controversy a generation or more ago the adherents of the oldtime religion recognized the need for establishing more schools, in addition to existing Bible Institutes and Colleges, to overcome the losses they had incurred as a result of being disinherited by schools which came under liberal influences. Many existing educational institutions in the United States were influenced by that type of educational philosophy which regarded the Bible as no different from any other form of great literature. Therefore, the fundamentalists did what they could to keep some schools loyal to their tradition, and they succeeded in some instances. However, their successes were meager. So they resorted to the device of organizing their own schools with the Bible as the central textbook. This gave rise to the Bible Institute movement.[1]

At first the growth of Bible Institutes was slow. Up to 1900 only nine Bible Institutes had been organized. Between 1900 and 1930, during the initial resistance of the fundamentalists against modernism, forty-nine such schools were organized. After that period, presumably because the fundamentalists had been awakened by the issues which were magnified by the Scopes trial, Bible Institutes began to spawn in every section of the United States. No part of the United States escaped the impact of their establishment. From 1930 to 1940 thirty-five Bible Institutes were founded, and from 1940 to 1950 sixty more were added. This made the two decades from 1930 to 1950 one of the most active and productive periods in fundamentalist education. Ninety-five schools had been established during the period from 1930 to 1950, almost doubling those established up to 1930.[2]

The growth of the Bible Institute was so rapid that there was some concern over the possibility of mediocrity in post-high school education. Some people began to refer to the spawning fundamentalist schools as 'chicken-coop colleges;' perhaps they wanted to create the impression these schools were hatched rather than planned. Many 'chicken-coop colleges' disappeared because of financial plight. But despite such discontinuances approximately two hundred schools were still functioning in the United States and Canada in 1955. James DeForest Murch compared the 'chicken-coop college' movement with the log colleges which arose after the American Revolution. He stated that although some of the new schools have disappeared, those which survived have revealed that fundamentalism is being restored in American education and the balance of power in religion is shifting back again.[3]

The student of American history is aware that religious controversy tended to engender the growth of educational institutions. The log college movement and the new 'chicken-coop colleges' were both the result of the demand to perpetuate the old-time religion. The spread of higher education in America before the Civil War to a large extent was also the result of the extraordinary growth of the same religious tradition. As a result of the fundamentalist-modernist controversy, with similar developments in education, a cycle of history was repeated. Apparently it is impossible to eliminate the older tradition from the American religious and educational scene.[4]

The original purpose of the Bible Institute was to provide opportunities for lay people to obtain specialized knowledge in the English Bible, thereby enabling them to participate in the work of the church and in personal evangelism. Many graduates of the Bible Institutes returned to their own churches to serve as Sunday School teachers, youth leaders, and as leaders in various departments of the local church, but most important of all, as personal evangelists. Little or no capacity of critical judgment in research and scholarship was required of Bible Institute students. Therefore, most Bible Institutes admitted their applicants regardless of prior academic preparation.[5]

Eventually Bible Institutes gained added importance, particularly after the issues between the fundamentalists and the modernists became clearly defined. Bible Institutes now began to train missionaries, pastors, evangelists, and gospel musicians, to mention only the most important specialties of Christian service. The Bible Institute became the citadel of the old-time religion where students during their formative years became 'set' before they were exposed to liberal education. There they were taught to defend the Bible as the Word of God 'against all attacks of modern infidelity.'[6]

In all Bible Institutes the principal textbook was the English Bible, and to understand it much time was required. Although other types of schools offered courses in religion, none offered extensive Bible-study courses. Most fundamentalist educators regarded all other courses to be secondary in importance and supplementary to the courses in the English Bible. Thus the Bible Institute became a school of specialization in one book. Even where liberal arts and sciences were introduced, the Bible still remained the core of the Bible Institute curriculum and all other subjects were integrated by it.[7]

Bible Institutes followed the more progressive methods in education in their clinical application of the gospel. One of the most important features of Bible Institute training was its practical work assignments, often referred to as 'learning by doing.' One graduation requirement was that each student conduct some type of Christian service each semester. This requirement was usually fulfilled by participation in street meetings, hospital visitation, meetings in jails, rescue missions, churches, and Sunday School classes. The practical work assignments were designed primarily to prepare students to become aggressive personal evangelists. Most of the important modern evangelists were trained in this manner, Billy Graham being the most notable example.[8]

To develop proficiency in personal evangelism Bible Institute students enrolled in at least one course in personal evangelism in which instruction directed students how to 'bring sinners to Christ.'[9] A major part of personal evangelism courses consisted of memorization of key verses from the Bible, usually those which supported the fundamentalist thesis of moral depravity and the doctrine of salvation by faith in Jesus Christ. Instruction also consisted in the selection and distribution of gospel tracts. Wherever Bible Institute students went they distributed tracts to people on the streets, in public conveyances, and in churches. Some people received tracts through the mails. Since World War II these activities have been increased, and there is evidence from educators that personal evangelism is more common today than ten years ago.[10] Practical work assignments have helped develop a generation of aggressive personal evangelists. This in turn has helped create the type of atmosphere which permits present revivalism to flourish.[11]

Originally applicants were admitted into Bible Institutes without regard to academic preparation, since little or no capacity for critical judgment in research and scholarship was required. Students were required to retain only what was given them in the classes to obtain a diploma. Rote memory was important. The primary requirement for admission, therefore, was a statement from the applicant on the following points: (1) whether he has been a Christian for at least one year, (2) whether he has been an active member of an evangelical church, and (3) whether he has been a zealous church worker or personal evangelist. Occasionally, applicants had to state they had 'led someone to Christ.'[12] These requirements assured the Bible Institutes of a relatively conformist student body zealously committed to the task of personal evangelism and defense of fundamentalist doctrine. This reinforced the revivalist atmosphere in schools where none but the fully committed students felt at ease.[14]

Since the end of World War II most older Bible Institutes with larger student bodies became more selective in their admission policies because of over-crowded conditions. As the demand for Bible Institute training increased, standards were raised. Almost all Bible Institutes now require a high school diploma from applicants in addition to the three requirements which were outlined in the preceding paragraph. The statement from the catalog of the Moody Bible Institute (1952-1953) illustrates the trend in upgrading ad-mission requirements in most Bible Institutes:

Those selected for Institute training as leaders in Christian service are chosen on the basis of spirituality, evangelistic zeal, scholastic ability and health. Applicants should possess qualities of character which evidence a future usefulness of the Institute family. For this reason candidates for admission are required to give evidence of approved Christian character, having accepted the Lord Jesus Christ at least one year before application, with a sincere desire to win others to Him. Membership in an evangelical church is also required.[14]

Fundamentalist Education Comes of Age

Most Bible Institutes developed independently. There was no comprehensive plan to make them homogeneous, except that most of them were patterned after some other Bible Institute. The only unifying factor in the Bible Institute movement was the orthodox instruction in the Bible and its derivative doc-trines. Gradually some of the Bible Institutes began to refine and expand their instructional programs by including liberal arts courses which, in some degree, gave them a collegiate character. This addition of liberal arts courses, al-though limited in quantity to the total curriculum, gave rise to the Bible Col-lege. This was an indication that fundamentalist education was coming of age.[15]

Another indication that fundamentalist education was maturing was the increased stress on the importance of accreditation for fundamentalist schools. Fundamentalist educators and students alike wanted their schools to have the respect ordinarily associated with accreditation. Another reason for this demand for accreditation was that many students contemplated further study after graduation. Therefore, uniformity in credit for Bible Institute courses had to be established.[16]

The first steps toward the establishment of a professional accrediting agency for Bible Schools were taken in 1946.[17] Howard E. Ferrin, president of Providence Bible Institute and chairman of the Bible Institute Division of the Commission on Education of the National Association of Evangelicals, invited other fundamentalist educators to a meeting in Minneapolis to explore the peculiar problems facing the Bible Schools. Twenty-eight schools sent representatives to the meeting. They unanimously agreed that Bible Institute training occupied 'a distinct area in the field of Christian education and should continue to do so.'[18] They also stated that Bible Institutes could 'best serve the evangelical cause by remaining distinctively biblical,' and that the college age was probably the most strategic period to establish fundamentalist youth in their faith.[19] After considering the importance of their schools, these fundamentalist educators decided the time had arrived to establish some standard for evaluating and transferring credit earned in their schools.[20]

The Minneapolis meeting ended fruitfully. The North American Association of Bible Institutes and Bible Colleges was formed and committees were chosen to prepare a constitution and to establish appropriate standards for course credit. Ferrin was recognized for his outstanding leadership in the field of fundamentalist education, by his selection as president of the new provisional organization. Safara A. Witmer, president of Fort Wayne Bible Institute, was chosen secretary.[21]

The accreditation fever seemed to spread. Others in the fundamentalist school movement also recognized its value. On January 29-31, 1947, the presidents and deans from several fundamentalist schools (the Bible Institute of Los Angeles, the National Bible Institute of New York City, Moody Bible Institute of Chicago, Providence Bible Institute, Denver Bible College, Philadelphia School of the Bible, and Kansas City Bible College) met at Winona Lake, Indiana to consider organizing a collegiate-grade accrediting agency and the formation of plans to gain recognition for their schools and courses of study from other colleges, seminaries, and state boards of education.[22]

Like the Minneapolis meeting in 1947 of other fundamentalist educators, the Winona Lake meeting was also fruitful. A provisional organization was formed, to be known as the American Association of Bible Schools: The Accrediting Agency of Bible Institutes and Bible Colleges. Samuel Sutherland of the Bible Institute of Los Angeles, also known as Biola, was made president and Terrelle B. Crum of Providence Bible Institute was chosen secretary. The delegates also set the date for a constitutional convention for October, 1947. During their deliberations the delegates avoided a serious breach between separatists and inclusivists by rejecting an attempt to get the new agency to affiliate officially with the National Association of Evangelicals. Neutral schools, like Biola, Moody Bible Institute, Philadelphia Bible Institute, and the separatist school, National Bible Institute, persuaded the various representatives at the meeting that the new association should remain unaffiliated with either the American Council or the National Association of Evangelicals.[23]

With two accrediting associations for Bible Schools the situation was scarcely improved and tended to be confusing and complicated instead. Various fundamentalist leaders recognized this at once and immediately took steps to have the two associations merge into one organization. Approximately forty schools with a combined enrollment of over 12,000 students sent representatives to Winona Lake for a meeting in October, 1947. There both groups fortunately agreed on a merger resulting in the formation of a single agency – the Accrediting Association of Bible Institutes and Bible Colleges. This name was shortened in 1958 to the Accrediting Association of Bible Colleges, and for the purposes of brevity it is known as the AABC. To satisfy the demands of the various schools two divisions were formed within the AABC: the collegiate division, patterned according to the academic requirements of liberal arts colleges; and the intermediate or sub-college division for schools unable to meet the more rigid standards of the collegiate division.[24]

The collegiate division provided for the Bible College and the Bible Institute. The curriculum of the Bible College, requiring a minimum of 120 semester hours of study for the bachelor's degree, provided for a limited amount of general education courses usually found in regular liberal arts colleges. But in method and spirit the Bible College was left untouched. It remained essentially in the tradition of the Bible Institute in which its course of study included the direct study of the English Bible, doctrine or systematic theology, and training in personal evangelism through practical work. It also differed from liberal arts colleges in that its primary purpose was to offer fields of specializations related to the ministry: theology, Christian education, missions, sacred music, Biblical languages, and other similar programs. Even the general education courses were integrated with Bible study having little to do with scholarly criticism. The general education courses were included to supplement the study of the Bible, not to create any doubt in it. Even the music courses were taught as a medium to teach Bible doctrine and propagate the gospel.[25] Of course, the general education courses were designed to prepare an individual to think logically and provide for specialization after graduation. However, most fundamentalist educators agreed that in a 'Christian college every course should be taught from the Christian point of view.'[26]

The study of the Bible was basic in the Bible College and Bible Institute. A minimum of forty semester hours in the direct study of the Bible and ten hours of systematic theology was established by the AABC as the graduation requirement for the Bible College. The Bible Institute provided a shorter program of study. In the collegiate division ninety semester hours of direct Bible study was established as the minimum requirement for a diploma. In the intermediate division two classes of Bible Institutes were provided for: one operating on a schedule of three years and the other on a schedule of two years to complete the requirements for a diploma. A minimum of thirty semester hours of direct study of the Bible and ten hours of systematic theology was established as the graduation requirement for a diploma from the former schools. A minimum of twenty semester hours of direct study of the Bible and six hours in systematic theology was established as the graduation requirement for a diploma from the schools on a schedule of two years.[27]

In their demand for the Bible as the core of all education, it should be noted that the fundamentalists were extremely conservative. The conservatives tend to look to the past for an answer to educational problems. Frank E. Gaebelein, chairman of the Committee on the Philosophy and Practice of Christian Education of the National Association of Evangelicals, commenting on the Harvard report on higher education in 1945,[28] wrote:

The diffusion resulting from specialization in higher education, the divorce of American culture from evangelical origins, the absence of a 'single generally accepted philosophy of education,' and the resultant differences in point of view have produced a wholesome reaction. Educators are rethinking their aims and purposes. Philosophy of education is of first-rate importance as the search is being made for some clear, coherent meaning to higher education.[29]

At this point Gaebelein stated the philosophy of fundamentalist education as established by the AABC in their Bible Schools:

The unifying philosophy is the Biblical view. It allows for breadth of cultural studies in the humanities and has room for both social and natural sciences. It seeks to orient the student theistically in the important areas of human knowledge. It seeks to co-ordinate history and science with revealed truth and thus bridge the gap between secular and sacred learning. It is concerned with our American heritage, but it traces that heritage to its historical roots in the Protestant Reformation. In a word, general education in the Bible college makes for orientation, integration, and unity.[30]

During the first year of its existence the AABC examined thirty-six schools and of that number accredited twelve in the collegiate division. Later membership in AABC increased rapidly, and today includes almost all of the larger Bible Schools in its membership. In 1947 the association was encouraged when it was accorded official recognition by the United States Office of Education as the sole accrediting agency for Bible Schools. Soon the AABC was also accorded recognition by other governmental agencies such as the Department of Justice, the Veterans' Administration, and various state boards of education. The National Association of Evangelicals also approved it. Finally, the AABC was accepted as a constituent member of the American Council of Education and the Council on Cooperation in Teacher Education.[31] The recognition of the AABC by these various agencies gave it and fundamentalist education some type of respectability which had previously been lacking.

To avoid confusion, Terrelle B. Crum, secretary of the AABC since 1947, defined the area of accreditation and the meaning of the terms peculiar to the new organization:

As officially defined today the field of the Bible Institute or Bible College (these are synonymous terms) is undergraduate 'Bible' in analogy to the graduate field 'theology' of the seminaries. The field is more inclusive than 'religious education', embracing the entire concept of undergraduate higher education which is Bible centered and Bible permeated.[32]

It is expected that programs will include general education and professional training for the various forms of Christian service, but a major in every curriculum is the Bible and theology ... (Finally), Christian liberal arts colleges are outside the scope of this Accrediting Association and fall within the jurisdiction of the regional accrediting associations.[33]

63539

Other Changes in Fundamentalist Schools

The effect of the accrediting association upon the Bible School movement was noticed almost immediately. The minimal entrance requirement in most of the schools was raised to include graduation from high school. Actually, this requirement ended the first era of the Bible School movement. The Bible Schools evolved from lay training centers to professional institutions. With the new entrance requirements these schools began to close their doors to those who lacked a high school diploma. The AABC established the requirement that not more than five percent of a school's total enrollment be admitted without a high school diploma.[34]

The educational qualifications of instructors in Bible Schools also came under scrutiny. Prior to the formation of AABC, instructors were generally chosen because of their agreement with the purposes of the Bible School movement. The academic requirement of the instructors was secondary. This in part represented the survival of anti-intellectualism which prevailed during the earlier part of the history of fundamentalism. As the Bible Schools graduated more and more students many of them became instructors in their alma maters. This inbreeding served to re-inforce the Bible School movement and helped maintain its rigid orthodoxy. However, with accreditation came a demand for qualified instructors with regular academic degrees in addition to their orthodox status. This in part, represents the evolution of the Bible School movement from anti-intellectualism to an appreciation of the value of intellectual competency. It means that new leadership has been raised and the Bible School movement has matured more precisely.[35]

The *Manual* of the AABC restated the original requirement of its instructors, which was established by tradition, that they have the proper Christian character and experience for the position they intended to fill. They are expected to sign a doctrinal statement of the employing school at the time of their appointment. Some schools require that this be also done annually. The *Manual* also stated 'to better preserve the genius of the Bible Institute movement, it is desirable for a considerable number of teachers to have had Bible Institute training.'[36]

In addition, instructors are now expected to have taken the first degree beyond the undergraduate degree (usually a master's) as a minimum educational requirement for a position. The only exception to this regulation is that the teachers may be employed who are eminently qualified in other ways. However, no requirement was established with regard to earned doctor's degrees. Presumably there is still a shortage of qualified teachers for positions in fundamentalist schools. The only logical explanation of this is that fundamentalist scholarship is only now beginning to shake off the shackles of anti-intellectualism which persisted for at least a generation.[47] The Dean of women at Moody Bible Institute of Chicago said:

There is a dearth of intellectually trained leaders in the Christian world today. Trained minds are necessary to maintain scholarship, and Christian scholarship is necessary to the effective propagation of the fundamentals of the faith.[38]

Another fundamentalist said: 'Because we are anti-intellectual we find ourselves with no university, no scientifically accepted textbooks, no positive approach to the problems of the day.'[39] Thus, at a time when the Bible School movement was ready for them, trained leaders were hard to find.

One of the most important developments in the Bible School movement in recent years has been the increased emphasis on degree programs. Although degrees had been granted to graduates of Bible Colleges for some time, it was not until the formation of the AABC that they have received added importance and value. This is because degrees in Bible Schools have been standardized by the regulations of the new accrediting association. And with the addition of general education courses in the Bible School curriculum, the training leading to degrees has come to be regarded as equivalent of other types of professional preparation such as nursing, teaching, and business administration. Schools like Biola, Providence-Barrington Bible College, Nyack, Fort Wayne Bible College, and several others have established degree programs of a terminal nature leading to bachelors' degrees in the following predominant fields: missions, religious or Christian education, Bible, sacred music, and elementary education. Some schools offer a Bachelor of Theology degree representing five years of study.[40]

All of these developments, no doubt, are having some impact upon American religious and educational thought. Since teacher training for positions in the public schools has been inaugurated in fundamentalist school curricula it is likely that fundamentalist influence will be noted in schools as well as in churches. Since the fundamentalists oppose humanism as the basis for an educational philosophy, the latter will probably have to defend itself more vigorously in the future. As the AABC clarifies its objections still more, and as more leaders are trained in its schools, the fundamentalists will undoubtedly become more vocal in public education.[41]

Another indication of the importance of the Bible School movement is shown in the increased enrollment in many Bible Institutes and Bible Colleges. Moody Bible Institute was one of the first schools to show a definite trend upward in enrollment among men and women students. In 1951 Gaebelein reported that the total enrollment in all fundamentalist schools, accredited and non-accredited, was approximately 41,834. The total enrollment in schools accredited by the AABC was well over 10,000. Although no degrees were offered, Moody Bible Institute still has the highest enrollment of all Bible Schools, which in 1956 was over 1,000. Biola was second with 734, Nyack third with 560, and Providence-Barringron Bible College was fourth with 502.[42] All of the other accredited schools reported enrollments of less than 500.[43] Since 1886 Moody Bible Institute has graduated over 56,000 men and women for Christian service. Of this number approximately 3,600 have entered into some type of foreign missionary service, while the rest have remained in the United States to influence American religious thought.[44] One can be reasonably safe in concluding that the growth of the Bible School movement during the past twenty years, and the upsurge in enrollment since the end of World War II, attests to a resurgence of fundamentalism in America.

Fundamentalist Colleges and Seminaries
Nothing has been said in this study about fundamentalist colleges and seminaries. Since they represent no major change in standard procedure from regular colleges and seminaries, it will not be necessary to deal with these schools at any length except to say that all of them are typically fundamentalist and are guided by practically the same educational principle. All fundamentalist colleges and seminaries are agreed that the Bible is the integrating and unifying principle of all education and that whatever the Bible says is the truth. For example, the catalogue of Gordon College, Beverly Farms, Massachusetts, contained this statement:

Believing that God has revealed himself in nature and in man, the College seeks to discover through a study of the natural sciences, social sciences, and humanities just what this revelation is. But it is recognized that such knowledge lacks coherence without some integrating factor. Gordon makes the Holy Scriptures the correlating revelation, particularly as they portray Jesus Christ in His sovereign creative, redemptive and sustaining work.[45]

An article published in the *United Evangelical Action* in 1949 stated that

there were approximately 400 Christian colleges in the United States adhering to the fundamentalist statement of faith. It is impossible to verify the
accuracy of this statement since the schools were not mentioned so they could
be checked. Furthermore, there is no single educational association in which
colleges with a fundamentalist statement of faith have been grouped. The
tone of the article led one to believe the fundamentalist viewpoint was very
strong in higher education today.[46] Another report published in 1948 was
equally optimistic. At that time a symposium was conducted by several
fundamentalist educators and from their discussions it was learned that of
seventy schools surveyed adhering to fundamentalist principles the total
enrollment in 1929 was 13,244. By 1940 a boom in fundamentalist education
was noted and at that time the enrollment in these seventy schools had been
doubled. From 1940 to 1948 the enrollment in these schools doubled again,
reaching 52,746. The conclusion drawn from this increased enrollment was
that in less than ten years Christian colleges once again emerged as a potent
force in American education and Christianity.[47]

   There is no separate accrediting association for fundamentalist colleges and
seminaries, as they do not fall within the scope of the AABC. Matters of
accreditation for Christian Colleges are taken care of by the regular regional
associations for colleges and secondary schools, while the American Association of Theological Schools has jurisdiction for accreditation of seminaries
in the United States.[48] There are no restrictions placed by the various
accrediting associations upon Christian colleges and seminaries because of
their theological belief. If a fundamentalist college or seminary meets the
requirements for accreditation, it is eligible to apply for appropriate recognition. Some fundamentalist colleges have been accredited, although the
number is very small. Probably most fundamentalist schools would willingly
be accredited if they could meet the requirements of their appropriate
regional educational association.[49]

   One notable exception to this is Bob Jones University, Greenville, South Carolina, one of the largest fundamentalist schools in the United States. Bob Jones,
Sr., founder of the school and chairman of the Board of Trustees, made the following declaration to explain why Bob Jones University refuses to become a
member of the Southern Association of Colleges and Secondary Schools, which
is the appropriate accrediting agency in the area where the school is located:

*We have something in the administrative policies of our university that, as
far as we can observe, no other institution has. This something is essential to*

the success of the school and the carrying out of this purpose for which *the institution was founded. We sincerely believe that we can render better service spiritually and even educationally without holding organic membership in an association.*

We wish to make it emphatically clear that the only reason we do not apply for membership in the Southern Association is that we do not wish to take any chance of having our administrative policies controlled or even influenced *by an educational association or any group anywhere in the world.*[50]

The administration itself has characterized Bob Jones University as the 'world's most unusual university.' Films produced by the school are called Unusual Films, and the call letters of the radio station which the school operates on a semi-commercial basis are WMUU, in keeping with the unusual distinction the administration desires to perpetuate. Perhaps no single phrase can explain the school better than this one. The school is unusual in the novel way it has combined fundamentalism and culture. Bob Jones, Jr., president of the school, has largely been responsible for the emphasis on dramatics, particularly Shakespeare's plays, which are produced by the students to illustrate fundamentalist doctrinal points. The university also emphasizes art and music in accordance with the policy of the school to promote 'Art without Bohemianism.'[51]

The university is unusual in other and more controversial ways. Bob Jones, Sr., who described himself as an old-fashioned preacher, has been characterized by others, particularly his biographer Donald E. Hoke, as a 'benevolent autocrat.'[52] This is because Jones arranged for an administration to rule with a firm hand. The university is administered in the fashion of a self-contained and self-sufficient mill town with company stores, homes, health facilities, and social welfare program. Bob Jones, Jr., son of the founder, makes practically all the appointments for the university, obviously to maintain the dynasty his father has established. Only those having the 'Spiritual slant of Bob Jones University' are hired for any position, whether it be for menial tasks or as a member of the faculty.[53] Salaries of university employees include a small cash allowance each month, a bonus at the end of the year, room and board in the school commons, hospital care in the school's infirmary, and a life insurance policy.[54] Although most fundamentalists have been outspoken critics of socialism, the Joneses have applied it as a matter of religious conviction in the operation of their unusual university. The older Bob Jones wrote:

Bob Jones University does not rank its faculty in a financial way nor does it standardize teachers' salaries. The Southern Association (of Colleges and Secondary Schools) bases teachers' salary requirements on rank, degrees, and experience. Bob Jones University bases its salaries on the needs of the teachers.[55]

Theodore C. Mercer, former registrar and assistant to the president (now president of William Jennings Bryan University, Dayton, Tennessee), revealed that he was one of the highest paid employees of Bob Jones University. Yet he and his wife received a joint salary of $ 160 per month for their services to the school. Room and board charged to them at $ 110 per month. Thus, since the last item was considered as part of their salary, it was estimated that Mercer and his wife jointly earned $ 260 per month. Single employees received from $ 75 to $ 100 in cash each month together with room and board. Younger single persons shared their rooms with two or three persons, while the older single employees had single rooms to themselves.[56]

This unusual arrangement to determine salaries of faculty members caused the school some unhappy moments, particularly since the method employed by the university conflicts with the established pattern of the various regional educational associations. However, Bob Jones, Sr., justified the school's salary plan on the grounds that it works. In other words, it is a pragmatic solution to the needs of the university.[57]

The elder Jones frequently was called upon to give lengthy explanations and reasons why the school had never been accredited. This matter was important enough to be included in the school's catalogue, which stated:

Bob Jones University, on the basis of its financial income, its equipment, its academic standards, and the educational background and degrees of its faculty, could qualify for membership in any educational association, regional or national.[58]

However, some fundamentalist educators questioned the accuracy of this statement. Hudson T. Armerding, Dean at Gordon College, one of a number of fundamentalist educators interested in the establishment of responsible scholarship and administrative procedures in fundamentalist schools, wrote a letter to Bob Jones, Jr., in which he called the statement misleading. He also outlined his reasons for believing Bob Jones University would have difficulty qualifying for membership in the New England Association of Colleges and Secondary Schools. He wrote:

In the statement of minimum requirements for an acceptable senior college or university, the Association outlines its qualifications with respect to the faculty of an institution making application. One of these is that heads of departments should have a Doctor's degree or a corresponding professional or technical education or attainment. In a conversation with representatives of the Association, I have learned that they also expect a substantial percentage of the other members of the faculty to have earned a Doctor's degree. From the catalog, it would appear that your institution lists only ten faculty members with an earned doctorate, and of these, four earned this degree at your school. From my experience, I know this ratio of earned doctorates to the number of department heads in particular, and to the number of faculty in general, would be considered by the New England Association to be a rather serious deficiency.

The Association also indicates what the ratio of the number of students to the number of faculty members above the grade of graduate assistants should be. Their requirement is that the ratio should not exceed fifteen to one. With approximately one hundred faculty members in your institution qualifying for consideration in this respect, your faculty-student ratio would appear to be thirty to one, or twice what the New England Association would require. Even if your graduate assistant were counted, it would seem that the faculty-student ratio at your institution would be twenty to one, or still in excess of the standards set by the New England Association.

Another important area in which the New England Association has sought to exercise rather strict control is that of the library. I note in your catalog that you have a collection of approximately 45,000 volumes, with a few thousand other volumes available to the students from the private collections of members of your staff. The combined libraries of our College and Divinity School now total approximately 38,000 volumes, and yet the New England Association has found occasion to question the adequacy of our resources in this area. Since we have little less than 500 students in all aspects of our program, it would seem reasonable to suppose that the Association would seriously question the adequacy of a library the size of yours to meet the needs of a student body of 3,000. Moreover, the fact that you have identified your institution as a university would make the question of the adequacy of your library a still more critical one, since the strength of your collection in a considerable number of fields would be brought under scrutiny.[59]

Bob Jones, Jr., replied to Armerding in a resentful manner, indicating among other things his dislike for this intrusion of another educator in the affairs of Bob Jones University. Jones wrote:

This is in reply to your letter of June 1
    First; we are too busy here at Bob Jones University trying to train approximately three thousand young people for Christian service to spend our time in looking for possible errors in the catalogues of other educational institutions. Then, too, we naturally take for granted that statements made in catalogs, especially catalogs of Christian institutions, are truthful statements.
    Second; Bob Jones University is probably the most individualistic educational institution in the world. I can see how a man who is connected with another institution that is more or less individualistic, but has only one-sixth the enrollment of Bob Jones University, might not altogether understand the inside academic workings of our school.
    When we bring out our next catalog, we will try to clarify the statement that you have questioned so that even the most technically minded, the envious, and the most lacking in imagination may have a better understanding of what we mean. Since our students come from all states and from twenty-five foreign countries, we are, of course, familiar with the standards of your New England Association, as well as all other regional associations.[60]

Shortly after Bob Jones University moved to Greenville in 1947 from Cleveland, Tennessee where it was formerly located, it requested that the South Carolina State Board of Education certify its teacher education program. The State Board refused to give the university the recognition it sought. However, the State Board raised several questions about the operation of the university, 'mainly faculty salaries, the unusual system of faculty tenure, and faculty loads, matters over which Dr. Jones exercised a personal control.'[61] Furthermore, the investigating committee found 'certain aspects of the instructional program including parts of the library collection, and the science setup as regards to space, equipment' and other details inadequate.[62] Many of the committee findings show how accurately Armerding appraised the situation at Bob Jones University. With respect to the science department, which was referred to as primitive, Malcom Yost (a practicing attorney in Cleveland, Ohio and a trustee of the university) said that one of the reasons the school was refused the recognition it sought was because it refused to shelve books on evolution.[63] Although the university advertised that 'it is interested in students who have brains in their heads,' it apparently was afraid to expose their brains to certain books, preferring to shield them instead in order to keep the 'old-time religion' in their hearts, and a desire in their souls to do the will of God.'[64] As a consequence of this experience with the State Board, Bob Jones, Sr. referred to the educational associations as 'educational trusts.'[65]

A sensation was created on the university campus when Theodore C. Mercer was summarily discharged as registrar and assistant to the president on July 15, 1953. The reasons given for his dismissal were: his popularity with the students, leading a faculty revolt against the administration, and the selection by his pregnant wife of a doctor unacceptable to the administration. That same year something of the nature of a faculty revolt occurred resulting in the summary discharge or resignation of approximately seventy employees. This indicated that the administrative policies were not pleasing to everybody.[66]

The Christian Day School Movement

During the past decade a new movement in education began to have widespread acceptance among the fundamentalists as an alternative to public school education, with which many fundamentalist parents were dissatisfied. The rapid rise of the Christian day school movement saw enrollment rise to over 1,000,000 during this period. The rapidity of its growth, together with the existence of other private schools in the United States, indicated that probably for the first time since the Civil War public school education was being seriously challenged.[67] The National Association of Christian Schools, the organization operating the Christian day school program, was organized in 1947 through the initial efforts of the National Association of Evangelicals to provide elementary and secondary school education for children of fundamentalist parents.[68]

Several reasons can be given to explain the growth of the Christian day school movement which came into existence immediately following World War II. For a long time before World War II the educational theories of John

110   *Fundamentalist education, scholarship, and literature*

Dewey, commonly known as progressive education, had been under constant attack. Following the war when fear affected the judgment of the American people, largely as an aftermath of the war and the postwar threat of attack from Russia, the attack against progressive education in the American schools was increased in various parts of the United States, more notably in Englewood (New Jersy), Arlington (Virginia), and Pasadena (California). In fact, some people were concerned that what the schools faced was 'little less than a nationally-directed conspiracy.'[69] Allen A. Zoll, founder of the American Patriots (now defunct and at one time on the United States Attorney General's list as a fascist organization), Gerald L. K. Smith, noted anti-Semite, and a large fundamentalist faction became virulent antagonists in the battle waged against the public schools. This was nothing new for the fundamentalists; their battle against modern education, which began before the twenties and was magnified by the Scopes trial in 1925, has never abated.[70]

However, Zoll was the single figure during the postwar period who captured the nation's attention in his organized campaign against the public schools through the National Council for American Education, which he also helped organize. Zoll's organized campaign, which undoubtedly influenced the fundamentalists, reached its zenith in 1951. After three years of service as Superintendent of Pasadena Schools, Willard Goslin, reputed to be one of the leading school administrators in the United States, was forced to resign after the people were stampeded into demanding his resignation.[71] Wherever the campaigns against the schools were waged the pattern of attack were identical. Sweeping accusations were made charging school administrators, teachers, and the National Education Association with using the public schools to implant communist and socialist ideas in the minds of the children, as a plot to sabotage free enterprise and American democracy. The progressive theory of education was blamed for the postwar epidemic of juvenile delinquency, while 'the 3 'R's' were once more glorified as the end-all of education.'[72] Also any attempt on the part of the teachers to instill a desire for international understanding in children was labelled socialistic. Complaints were made that the principles of the United Nations Educational, Scientific, and Cultural Organization was being taught to them.[73]

Fundamentalist parents expressed their general dissatisfaction over the public school curriculum. They had been taught through propaganda against the public schools to believe the public schools were not only moving away from religion and the educational tradition of the original settlers of this country, but that the curriculum was inadequate to cope with problems of a moral nature which were at the base of juvenile delinquency and adult criminality. They were persuaded to believe delinquency could be quickly decreased only where education had a religious perspective and disciplinarian methods were employed. This was more practical for character building than progressive education, which encouraged self-expression with a minimum of restraint and supervision by the teachers. Children, like adults, could not be expected to develop properly without Christian guidance because they too are affected by the Fall.[74]

Wilbur M. Smith, professor of English Bible at Fuller Theological Seminary in Pasadena, California, at the risk of being classified an obscurantist, criticized public education for the drift of religion from theism and supernaturalism to a religion of democracy based on humanism and naturalism.[75] Other fundamentalists said that Christian education was the crutch needed to help pupils when they met the theory of evolution for the first time. Public education was also criticized because other activities were offered which fundamentalists charged were harmful and demoralizing, such as instruction in dancing and showing of movies.[76]

There were some fundamentalists who defended public education. Frank E. Gaebelein and Harold C. Ockenga were the two most prominent fundamentalist leaders to do so. Gaebelein said:

The place of public education in America is secure. So essential is it to our democracy that without a national system of public schools America could not for a single generation continue free.[77]

Ockenga likewise referred to the American public school system as 'the bulwark of democracy.'[78] He also stated that American public schools were neutral in matters of religion and could be nothing else under the Constitution. He did not accept the radical statements of some fundamentalists that teachers in public schools were generally anti-Christian. Furthermore, he said, there was no reproach to secular education since it is neither religious nor anti-religious.[79]

Some fundamentalists waged a campaign to remove certain textbooks from the public schools because they were allegedly Marxist and atheistic propaganda designed to wreck American democracy and destroy faith in supernaturalism. Mark Fakkema, director of the National Association of Christian Schools, prodded the National Association of Evangelicals to prepare a resolution requesting the House Un-American Activities Committee to investigate subversion in textbooks.[80] Fundamentalist parents were also urged by others to campaign actively for elimination of certain textbooks from the public schools. The attack was centered around books which criticized the United States and those which taught evolution. Any book which alluded to the Genesis account of creation as a myth was extremely objectionable to the fundamentalists. Some of the books placed on the fundamentalist Index were: *Exploring Biology of Man*; Mavor, *General Biology*, Anabel Williams-Ellis, *A Child's Story of the World*; Washburne, *The Story of the Earth*; Harold Rugg and Louise Krueger, *The First Book of the Earth*.[81]

In another important instance the fundamentalists waged a campaign to halt the teaching of the Old Testament telecourse conducted from September 21, 1954 to January 18, 1955 by the Western Reserve University over television station WEWS of Cleveland, Ohio. Because the instructor of the course, Rolland E. Wolfe (Harkness Professor of Biblical Literature at Western Reserve University) did not declare the Bible to be the Word of God and for some other objectionable statements in his lectures he was attacked by orthodox Jews, Roman Catholics, and fundamentalists. The first two desisted from their attacks after hearing an explanation of the nature of Wolfe's lectures from university officials. However, Wolfe stated that 'from beginning to end the Fundamentalists were the nasty ones.'[82] They flooded the mails with insulting letters charging Wolfe with following the communist line to destroy faith in the Bible. Some people sent gospel tracts with their letters, ostensibly to convert Wolfe. The Metropolitan Fundamentalist Ministers' Fellowship of Cleveland wrote a letter to the manager of the television station protesting the lectures as 'unscientific, faith destroying teaching so utterly contrary to recognized historic-Christianity.'[83] They demanded the telecourses be discontinued unless they were granted free television time 'to reply and defend our Historic Christian Faith.'[84]

The fundamentalists among others were disturbed by a far-reaching decision of the United States Supreme Court in 1948. The decision followed the suit of Mrs. Vashti McCollum instigated against the Champaign, Illinois Board of Education protesting its released-time religious program. In her petition to the United States Supreme Court, after losing in the lower courts, Mrs. McCollum contended her son had been subjected to ridicule because of his non-attendance in the released-time religious education classes. She was supported in her suit by the Ethical Society, Unitarians, Baptists, Lutherans, Jewish Federation, Chicago Action Council, and the American Civil Liberties Union. The Supreme Court handed down an 8-1 decision on March 8, 1948 in which the majority ruled that released-time classes, as conducted by the Champaign Board of Education on public property, aided the establishment of religion and therefore they are unconstitutional.[85]

Immediately a storm of protest was heard across the land from those who had been adversely affected by the decision. The decision was a serious blow to some fundamentalists, who had hoped to bring religion to the public schools through the released-time program. Many of them regarded the decision of the Supreme Court as the final step toward the complete secularization of American public education and the eventual paganization of America. But the decision did not disturb the Roman Catholics, Lutherans, Seventh Day Adventists, and the Reformed churches, since they were operating day schools of their own. The fundamentalists were in a dilemma because of the inadequacy of their own day school system to meet the religious needs of their children, and there seemed to be no way to circumvent the First Amendment to the Constitution and the decision of the Supreme Court. [86]

However, many fundamentalists appraised the situation realistically, and accepted it as a practical one. Desirable as religious instruction in the public schools might have been, many fundamentalists recognized the danger in its continuance in the light of the demands of the Roman Catholics for public funds for textbooks and bus transportation for their parochial school children. The 1947 decision of the United States Supreme Court, upholding the legality of a New Jersey law to allow public school buses to transport private and parochial school children as a service to the parents, was still something to consider seriously. Should the fundamentalists insist on using public school property, the Roman Catholics would have more reason to make their demands. After careful consideration of these recent developments many fundamentalists accepted the McCollum decision, and it proved an impetus to speed the establishment of fundamentalist Christian day schools.[87]

The rapid growth of the Christian day school movement can also be attributed to other factors. During the postwar period the nation remained relatively prosperous. Parents, therefore, had more money to give toward the support of private schools. Because of the increased birth rate, overcrowding and shortage of teachers occurred in public schools and some fundamentalist parents decided to establish private schools to alleviate this condition. The motivation to do this can also be attributed to the propaganda that had been released against the public schools. Parents were persuaded to believe the public schools had been downgraded academically and that standards of achievement were higher in Christian day schools. Finally, the revival in religion which occurred during the past decade may have had an impact upon the development of these schools.[88]

The Christian day schools grew 'with the rapidity of a grassroots movement.'[89] Mark Fakkema said the sudden upsurge in the establishment of Christian day schools was the occasion for and not the result of the establishment of the National Association of Christian Schools. At first parents tried to enroll their children in Christian schools which had been operating for a long time, such as the Lutheran and Reformed church schools. The leaders of the schools in the Reformed tradition, or the National Union of Christian Schools, became concerned over the rapid rise of enrollment in their schools of non-Reformed children. Because they wanted to preserve their Reformed traditions, they asked the National Association of Evangelicals in April, 1947 to consider the establishment of an organization to meet the educational needs of the fundamentalists. The National Association of Evangelicals acted promptly and on May 13, 1947 the National Association of Christian Schools was established on the same doctrinal basis as the National Association of Evangelicals.[90] One of its publications stated:

In the nature of the case, the doctrinal basis of this affiliate is identical with that of the National Association of Evangelicals and its intended scope embraces all evangelical groups which can subscribe to its doctrinal basis.[91]

Reliable statistics were not available at the time of this study to give a clear indication of the numerical growth of the Christian day school movement. However, something of the nature of the enormous growth of all non-public schools, which include the Roman Catholics, Lutherans, Seventh Day Adventists, Reformed, and others, is shown from the following statistics. In 1930 nine out of every 100 pupils attended non-public schools. In 1952 thirteen out of every 100 pupils were in non-public schools. Between 1945 and 1951 public school enrollment increased fourteen percent while non-public schools increased thirty-six percent.[92]

In Table V the number of schools affiliated with the National Association of Christian Schools for the school year 1954-1955, together with their location by states and total enrollment, are shown. Of the one hundred twenty-three schools affiliated with the National Association of Christian Schools over one hundred had started since 1948. The latest report given in June, 1957 shows that one hundred forty-four schools with an enrollment of 13,000 pupils were affiliated with the National Association of Christian Schools.

Thirty-five of these forty-four schools were in California, indicating the tremendous advance made by fundamentalists in that state. Although the Christian day school movement is not strong in every state, there is reason to believe from the developments of the past decade that it is beginning to gain momentum.[93]

The Renaissance of Fundamentalist Scholarship
For several years fundamentalism failed to produce an outstanding thinker and proliferated no scholarly literature which won recognition beyond their own circles. Generally, fundamentalists were ignored in any serious theological debate. Since World War II, however, the tide has been reversed. A group of young fundamentalist scholars desiring to be called new evangelicals rather than fundamentalists, most of their coterie hold earned doctorates from reputable universities and seminaries in the United States and Europe, began expounding a revised version of fundamentalist theology. The new evangelicals, or neo-evangelicals, as they are also called, were determined to preserve the *fundamentals* without resorting to the tactics employed by their elders in their defense of Protestant theological orthodoxy.[94] Rather they 'are endeavoring to disentangle the core of concern for unqualified theological orthodoxy from the more objectionable traits heretofore seemed inseparable from fundamentalism.'[95]

These neo-evangelical scholars, most of whom are instructors on the faculties of Fuller Theological Seminary in Pasadena, California Baptist Theological Seminary in Covina, Northern Baptist Theological Seminary in Chicago, Gordon Divinity School near Boston, Westminister Theological Seminary in Philadelphia, and Wheaton College in Illinois, have proliferated a body of erudite literature demonstrating that they are not only articulate but that they can also deal responsibly with opposing theologies from the standpoint of their own presuppositions.[96] Fundamentalists with doctorates in science organized the American Scientific Affiliation in 1941 and publish their own *Journal* 'to study those topics germane to the conviction that the frameworks of scientific knowledge and a conservative Christian faith are compatible.'[97]

In an article he prepared for *The Christian Century*, Arnold W. Hearn, instructor in the philosophy of religion and systematic theology at Union Theological Seminary in New York City, wrote that neo-evangelical literature reveals a new flexibility developing among them in their restatement of Protestant orthodoxy and that in it neo-evangelicalism also demonstrates 'a capacity to make their case in terms more sensitive to the integrity of the modern mind.'[98] Hearn also observed that the publications of neo-evangelical scholars 'reveal thought which (1) has a comprehensive theological concern, (2) is abreast of developments in philosophy and theology, (3) endeavors to deal honestly with the findings of natural science, (4) manifests an interest in social ethics, and (5) is striving to attain a more moralistic approach to literature and the arts.'[99]

Neo-evangelicals have made impressive gains during the past decade, and this is reflected in their high morale. The rise of a new interest in biblical theology during the postwar period has enhanced their prestige among other theological thinkers. There are evidences that neo-orthodox and other Protestant groups in America are rapidly approaching a position where there is enough in common between them and the neo-evangelicals to engage them in an exchange of ideas.[100]

Changes reflecting a new mood in science and the deflation of the liberal philosophy of religion within recent years have boosted neo-evangelical morale. Some scientists have abandoned the reductionistic view of nature and admit the possibility of the existence of another order. Neo-evangelical scholars accept this change in scientific thought as an opportunity to reiterate that God does interlope the natural order and once more a rational defense can be proposed for special revelation and the miracles, such as the virgin birth and the resurrection.[101]

Neo-orthodoxy, assuredly now more accommodative toward neo-evangelicalism than toward the older fundamentalism, recognizes special revelation and the uniqueness of the biblical witness, although it rejects neo-evangelicalism's doctrine of infallible propositional revelation. God's Word, according to neo-orthodoxy, is not an objective, verbal record. It is the living Word revealing God who never appears as a thing or object to be studied. Despite this difference in neo-orthodoxy's biblical alternative, neo-evangelical scholars believe the current resurgence in biblical theology provides a propitious opportunity for their invasion into the territory formerly dominated by liberal theological thought.[102] Carl F. H. Henry, one of neo-evangelicalism's most prolific writers, optimistically declared that 'evangelical theology has nothing to fear, and much to gain, from aligning itself with the current plea for a return to biblical theology' because 'today's increasing stress on doctrines essential to biblical Christianity coincides in many respects with the doctrinal emphases of the fundamentalist controversy.'[103]

The growing list of publications including journal articles, essays, expositories, and books is not only impressive but it also portrays the range of neo-evangelical thought. *Indicia* of the trends within neo-evangelicalism are easily traced in two recent publications. In *Contemporary Evangelical Thought*, published in 1957, neo-evangelical scholars deal with Christian ethics, Christian education, biblical revelation, philosophy and religion, ecumenicity, evangelism, preaching, science, and philosophy of history. *In Revelation and the Bible: Contemporary Evangelical Thought*, published in 1958, neo-evangelical scholars in the United States, England, Scotland, Holland, France, South Africa, and Australia combined their energies to write essays dealing primarily with a rational defense of biblical revelation. They also offered their views on biblical inspiration, clarified their methodology on biblical interpretation, and presented their explanations of the source of textual errors found in the Bible.[104]

In assessing the fortunes of Christianity during the twentieth century, neo-evangelical scholars observed that liberal thought had deflated fundamentalism's theological authority, which rested on the doctrine of plenary inspiration and biblical inerrancy. Consequently, relying upon their training in archaeology and philology neo-evangelical scholars committed themselves to a searching review of their own position and devoted themselves to a program of critical biblical scholarship to determine the precise text of the Scriptures in order to find new answers to refute the liberal view that the Bible is a humanly contrived document marred by textual errors, contradictory statements, pseudo-assigned authorships, and scientifically untenable judgments about material and organic origins and the antiquity of man. They also committed themselves to the task of correcting the misconceptions held by nonfundamentalists regarding their views on the transmission of revelation. They also disavowed the identification of verbal inspiration with mechanical-dictation theories, which teach that the biblical writers were mere automatons transcribing God's communication of Himself and His purposes while the Holy Spirit dictated to them. They also disowned the linking of inerrancy with crass literalism.[105]

In their essays in *Revelation and the Bible*, neo-evangelical scholars asserted that only the original manuscripts of the Scriptures, now lost, were inerrant and that no particular existent translation of the Bible, such as the King James Version and the recent Revised Standard Version is more authentic than any other. They stated that God permitted the original manuscripts to become lost because God knew men would worship them as other relics attributed to a divine source are frequently worshiped. Although existent

translations are corruptions of copyists, God guarded the scribes and preserved the Bible from the type of error which would have changed his thought
and damaged his plan of salvation. Neo-evangelical scholars also explained
that the Bible, depending upon its style, must be read as prose and poetry; and
the interpretation of the Bible, depending upon its allegorical, literal, or
typological speech, must be in accord with the natural meaning of the text
and the idiomatic usages of the biblical writers.[106]

Nothing in neo-evangelical literature reveals any departure from the
doctrine of biblical inerrancy. It is perhaps correct to state that they reasserted
the doctrine of biblical inerrancy while attempting to add intellectual
respectability to it. The following summary constructed from the statements
of the essayists in *Revelation and the Bible* probably correctly represents
their combined view. The Bible in its original manuscripts is the absolute,
normative, inerrant, and complete verbalized revelation of God written in the
style of prose and poetry, in allegorical, literal, and typological speech, and in
the language and idiom of Providentially selected men, who through the
inspiration of the Holy Spirit were rendered the organs of God for the
infallible revelation of Himself, His thought, His will, and His plan of
redemption. It is the objective source of knowledge about God, the basis of
Christian doctrine, and the final, complete rule for Christian thought and
action.

Revisions of the older fundamentalist views, which involved them in a
clash with science over the origin of life and the antiquity of man, were also
suggested by neo-evangelical scholars, who accepted evolution as a reasonable
explanation of divine activity not in conflict with the Bible. Although in
agreement that evolution is here to stay, Bernard Ramm, a member of the
faculty of the California Baptist Theological Seminary, and Edward John
Carnell, a member of the faculty of Fuller Theological Seminary, did not
capitulate completely to the developmental views of naturalism. Instead they
proposed their own theories to harmonize the evolutionary hypothesis with
the Bible.[107]

In his book *The Christian View of Science and Scriptures*, published in
1954, Ramm espouses a theory he calls 'progressive creationism which teaches
that over the millions of years of geological history God has been fiatly
creating higher and higher forms of life.'[108] Accordingly, there is a purposeful
ordering of life by a Personal Intelligence which, more than naturalistic
explanations, most satisfactorily accounts for man's distinct origin and high
intelligence. Ramm believes that evolution simply actualizes anteriorly to

creation the master forms in the mind of God. In seeking a harmony of the geologic record and the days of the book of Genesis, Ramm enunciated a concept he calls concordism, which considers the days of the first chapter of the book of Genesis not as twenty-four hours in duration but as indefinite but successive periods of time, during which God through a series of creative acts brought 'the universe through various stages from chaos to man.' Ramm also declares that no date for the antiquity of man can be established from the biblical record, consequently his revisions in fundamentalist thought opens the way toward a harmonious relationship between anthropology and the Bible.[109]

Carnell formulated a theory he calls 'threshold evolution' which he declares 'can accommodate both the gaps which paleontology reveals to exist between the orders, and the development of multitudinous 'species' within these orders.' He asserts that the original unit of created life is not the species of science but the 'kind' of graded life in the book of Genesis, such as plant life, beasts, and man. Carnell specifically repudiates total evolution, insisting that science cannot show that one type of graded life or kind ever evolves from another. Because it lacks the facts to work with, science only speaks of missing links and mutations to close the gaps in total evolution. Accordingly, Carnell insists, neo-evangelicals can accept evolution and scrap the doctrine of the 'fixity of species' without jeopardizing their major premise that the original unit of life ordered by divine fiat remains fixed. He concludes that as an alternative theory threshold evolution can adequately explain all the known facts of science, and it enables neo-evangelicalism to continue believing man is one of the original kinds, the result of fiat creation and consequently unrelated genetically to any lower grades of life.[110]

Because neo-evangelical scholars criticized the separatist fundamentalists for their discordant tactics and for their lack of concern for respectable scholarship, they aroused their ire and precipitated a new controversy within organized fundamentalism. Incensed separatist leaders protested vehemently against the statements in magazine articles which were made by Sherman Roddy, Carl F. H. Henry, Edward John Carnell, Vernon Grounds, Harold Ockenga, and Bernard Ramm in which they rebuked the fundamentalists for their pugnacity, their intellectual bankruptcy, and their separatist policy. Carl McIntire, Bob Jones, Sr., Harvey Springer, Robert Ketcham, John R. Rice, and others who clung to the name 'fundamentalist' responded with a flood of literature in which they excoriated the neo-evangelical scholars and ridiculed them as mind-worshippers who 'cannot stand the stigma of not being classified among the scholars.'[111] Neo-evangelicals were also castigated as subversionists within fundamentalism preparing for a subtle retreat to modernism. John R. Rice charged that neo-evangelicals had compromised the historic *fundamentals* and warned that their movement constituted ' a bridgehead by which contacts may be made by modernists to get fundamentalists to come over to the modernists.'[112]

John F. Walvoord, scholarly president of the Dallas Theological Seminary, was also disturbed because the neo-evangelical scholars had abandoned the term 'fundamentalist.' He sympathized with neo-evangelicalism's desire to escape the odium surrounding the term 'fundamentalism,' but he argued that little can be gained and much lost by fleeing to the term 'evangelical.' He does not agree that neo-evangelicalism intends to compromise the historic *fundamentals*, but he is afraid that ambiguity surrounds the term they have chosen to identify their movement. 'In modern literature,' Walvoord wrote, 'the term *fundamentalist* carried with it clear, historical and theological meaning. While the term *evangelical* lends itself to manipulation by the modern liberal confusing both laity and clergy.'[113]

The Growth of Fundamentalist Publishing

Religious publication expanded tremendously during the period of postwar revival of religious enthusiasm in the United States. The impact of religious interest was particularly observed in the growth of orthodox journals and newspapers such as *His*, *Christian Life*, *Eternity*, *United Evangelical Action*, *Christian Beacon*, *The Sword of the Lord*, *Youth for Christ Magazine*, and several others which are published for popular consumption. Meanwhile, the neo-evangelical concern for sound scholarship was reflected in the strengthening of existing scholarly orthodox journals, such as *Bibliotheca Sacra*, and the appearance of new journals, such as *Christianity Today*, *Gordon Review*, and the *Journal* of the American Scientific Affiliation.

Besides its impact on orthodox journalism, the postwar interest in religion was also reflected in the growth of several orthodox book publishing firms in various parts of the United States. The most important publishers primarily engaged in the publication of orthodox theological books are Loizeaux Brothers in New York City; Channel Press in Great Neck, New York; Fleming H. Revell in Westwood, New Jersey; Christian Beacon Press in Collingswood, New Jersey; Dunham Publishing Company in Findlay, Ohio; Moody Press in Chicago; Cowman Publications Incorporated in Los Angeles; and seven Grand Rapids, Michigan houses, Wm. B. Eerdmans Publishing

Company, Zondervan Publishing House, Baker Book House, Kregel Publications, Gospel Folio Press, Grand Rapids International Publishers, and the Society for Reformed Publications.[114]

Eerdmans, Zondervan, and Baker, which have made Grand Rapids the center of orthodox publishing, started as bookstores selling used and rare orthodox books which the traditional Eastern publishers neglected and allowed to go out of print. As booksellers these firms gained a familiarity with the demands of the public for orthodox religious books. They decided the demand for certain out-of-print books was sufficient for a venture into a profitable reprint business. Aided by the new process of offset printing, these firms began to reprint the neglected orthodox titles which were in great demand, in most instances without payment of royalties because copyrights had elapsed.[115]

The postwar expansion of and increased enrolment in fundamentalist grade schools, Bible Institutes, colleges, and seminaries also created a demand for orthodox textbooks. New titles in sufficient quantity and quality to satisfy this demand were unavailable for the most part because fundamentalist scholarship had lagged and almost completely evaporated during the preceding thirty or forty years. This paucity in fundamentalist literature forced the Grand Rapids publishers to fill their lists by reprinting neglected books which had been produced by recognized nineteenth and early twentieth century orthodox textbook authors. During the last decade, however, the tide changed and the Grand Rapids publishers, already in the forefront of religious book publishing, were able to add new titles to their lists which were proliferated by neo-evangelical scholars. Although they still reprint old books, these firms and all other orthodox publishers are constantly adding new titles of neo-evangelical literature to their annual lists.[116] Commenting on these developments in orthodox publishing, Carl F. H. Henry states that 'viewed in proper perspective, the postwar theological reprint bonanza must be regarded as only a necessary preliminary action in the developing evangelical movement to face the world with a respectable, scholarly literature.'[117]

The Concern for Social Action

Because of neo-evangelicalism's influence on fundamentalist social action, the story of its development will be included here, although it might fit more appropriately elsewhere in this study. The immediate effect of the renaissance of fundamentalist erudition was an uneasy conscience among neo-evangelical scholars concerning the state of fundamentalism's social policy. In its reaction against liberalism's social gospel, fundamentalism lost interest in humanitarian

122   *Fundamentalist education, scholarship, and literature*

endeavors and permitted the concern for the application of the gospel in social welfare to fade and evaporate. In fact, fundamentalism made the inevitability of social decline a part of its creed. Social disintegration became for the fundamentalists a sign of the end of the age, an inescapable prelude, they said, to the second advent of Christ. Neo-evangelical scholars distressfully observed that a majority of fundamentalist clergymen, during the postwar threat of cultural disintegration and of nuclear annihilation, were almost completely silent about serious social problems, but instead inveighed almost exclusively on individual vices. Regarding this state of fundamentalist social policy as extremely inconsistent with Christian commitment, neo-evangelical scholars began to plead for the application of the gospel in the more constructive spheres of social welfare. This is one of the most pertinent developments within fundamentalism since World War II. These developments have already restored, appreciable enough, a measure of respectability to those adhering to biblical Christianity.[118]

Carl F. H. Henry's book *The Uneasy Conscience of Modern Fundamentalism*, published in 1947, reflects the acceptance of a growing bloc of neo-evangelical scholars and 'leaders that Christianity makes imperative the declaration of the social relevance of biblical religion and ethics in all spheres of life.'[119] The question raised by neo-evangelicalism in this connection was whether moderns left unguided by biblical ethical prescriptions can through purely intellectual and relativistic assumptions find sufficient basis for the ethical life. Their own answer to this question is that these are not enough and that the enlightened mind aided only by revelation was the most certain basis for the ethical life and social action.[120]

At the time of its formation, the National Association of Evangelicals not only placed renewed emphasis on the primacy of biblical theology but also focused its attention on the relevancy of the gospel in humanitarian efforts. The new Association promptly organized committees on varied social services which included programs of war relief in Europe and Korea. Committees were also organized to consider political problems, management-labor relations, and race issues. In the area of management-labor relations industrial chaplaincies were established and a Christian Labor Association, already functioning under the auspices of the Christian Reformed Church, became novel evangelical experiments in social action. Some people, however, expressed concern that the spreading industrial chaplaincy program, which was inaugurated in the plants of the fundamentalist industrialist R. G. LeTourneau, is apt to become the device by which management may keep its employees docile while exploiting them through sub-standard wages. Union leaders also suspect that industrial chaplains in non-union shops operate as buffers for management to subtly promote its own policies.[121]

Frequently, fundamentalists have been accused of perpetuating racial segregation by quoting from the book of Genesis, claiming that God, having predestined the Negroes as the sons of Ham to an inferior social status in the white community, was the original segregationist.[122] Neo-evangelical leaders were annoyed by this antiquated Biblical defense of segregation. Consequently, the panelists on the Forum on Social Action in 1951, three years before the United States Supreme Court made its memorable decision on school desegregation, discussed the race issue and conceded that segregation is not lawfully Christian and 'evangelicals are obliged to press the case against segregation simultaneously with evangelism.'[123]

Most utterances on the race issue by neo-evangelical leaders subsequent to the Supreme Court decision point to a moderate position on the problem. They urge that integrationists proceed cautiously without spreading inflammable propaganda, which already has worsened race relations in the United States.[124] Carl F. H. Henry suggested that moderates can take a stand on the issue 'by protesting race prejudice and disapproving forced segregation,' thereby detaching themselves from radical reconstructionism.[125]

Although their attack on social problems within a biblical framework has not advanced notably, neo-evangelical leaders are heartened by the operation of their own welfare organizations, such as the World Relief Commission and the World Vision organization, which provides assistance to distressed victims torn by political and social unrest. The World Relief Commission grew out of the War Relief Commission, which had been founded under the auspices of the National Association of Evangelicals in 1945, to provide assistance to refugees and other war victims in Europe and Asia. Under the direction of Bob Pierce (a former war correspondent during the United Nations police action in Korea) World Vision combines evangelism and social welfare in its program centered in Asia. Its services include provisions for health care, education, and an adoption program for homeless oriental children.[126] In 1950 the Evangelical Welfare Agency was granted a charter by the State of Illinois to provide for the care of and adoption services for children assigned to it by the courts in Illinois.[127]

Although the American Council of Christian Churches opposes many of the social welfare programs endorsed by the National Association of Evangelicals and by the neo-evangelicals, its leaders have not remained indifferent to

124   *Fundamentalist education, scholarship, and literature*

human suffering. Through its International Christian Relief Center, the American Council joined other fundamentalists in a program to provide assistance to distressed people in many parts of the world. A recent example is the aid given to Chileans following the disastrous earthquake in 1960. Other state and local organizations associated with the American Council are also engaged in humanitarian endeavors, providing camps and other facilities for American youth and rest homes for infirm and aged people in the United States.[128]

The combined efforts of the National Association of Evangelicals and the American Council of Christian Churches in the area of social welfare thus far has not been very impressive. However, these efforts reveal that fundamentalists have awakened to their responsibility in the practical application of the gospel in the alleviation of human suffering. Fundamentalist leaders declare that while there is still much that has been left untouched and much that must be done in the area of social welfare before their uneasy conscience can be assuaged, 'their critics cannot justifiably accuse them of quiescence in this field.'[129]

TABLE V

LOCATION OF NACS SCHOOLS BY STATES AND THEIR ENROLLMENT
1954–1955 *

State	Number of Schools	Enrollment
Arizona	2	217
California	32	4,842
Florida	6	390
Georgia	1	55
Idaho	1	—
Illinois	6	687
Indiana	3	217
Iowa	3	332
Kansas	4	346
Kentucky	5	706
Massachusetts	4	199
Michigan	2	162
Minnesota	1	122
Mississippi	1	42
Missouri	3	102
Nebraska	1	56
New Hampshire	1	9
New Jersey	6	350
New York	5	370
North Carolina	2	138
North Dakota	1	16
Ohio	1	48
Oklahoma	1	83
Oregon	7	611
Pennsylvania	8	598
South Carolina	1	55
South Dakota	2	—
Tennessee	1	464
Texas	2	264
Virginia	4	289
Washington	5	399
Wisconsin	1	18
TOTAL	123	12,187

* *Christian School Directory* for 1954–1955, p. 3.

CHAPTER SEVEN

Billy Graham and the Resurgence of Revivalism

The first chapter of this study suggests that religious fundamentalism in American Protestant Christianity has its roots in apostolic times, medieval-Reformation theology, and American revivalism. Therefore, although its name is of recent origin, fundamentalism must not be regarded as an aberration in Protestantism. In fact, the kind of individualism which the Reformation encouraged, and revivalism in America solidified, is one of the main characteristics of fundamentalism. The frontier, which nourished rugged individualism, was gone before 1900 when revivalism began to decline. The change from a strictly rural to a complex urban society brought with it uncertainty and insecurity in some instances. As a consequence, religious conformity was demanded and stress was placed not on personal sin but on alleviation of social maladies, as in the social gospel. These conditions and developments, in addition to the new intellectual currents such as evolution in science and higher criticism in Biblical study, set the stage for the fundamentalist-modernist controversy which, although its intensity varied at times, has never ended.[1]

Laissez-faire capitalism and evangelicalism came to fruition almost simultaneously in America, and for that reason both seemed inextricably bound together. Billy Sunday, whose professional evangelistic career reached its peak during the period 1908–1918, apparently sought to rescue laissez-faire capitalism and evangelicalism. William G. McLoughlin, Jr., Sunday's most recent biographer, believed this accounts for his hostility to modernism in theology and the social gospel, which presumably abetted economic liberalism and challenged the relevancy of laissez-faire capitalism to the twentieth century. Despite the assistance he received from the wealthy and middle-classes, Sunday's revivals proved inadequate. McLoughlin said that Sunday had not only 'failed to win the large numbers of new converts to Christianity, which the term generally implies', but his revivals also proved that 'high-pressure mass evangelism was not the way to solve either the churches' or nation's problems.'[2] After 1919 the churches began to abandon revivalism and fundamentalist theology. This situation continued until the resurgence of revivalism after World War II.[3]

From about 1927 onward church membership began to grow in the United States at a faster rate than the nation's population. During the period from 1927 to 1952 church membership expanded 59.8 percent while the nation's population advanced 28.6 percent. The greatest growth in church membership occurred four years after the end of World War II, as evidenced not only in church membership but also by a boom in church construction and the rapid rise in sales of Bibles and books on religious subjects. Book trade journals reported that Bible sales in 1949 reached 4,727,626 copies. In 1950 Bible sales suddenly leaped to 6,250,370 copies. At mid-century most observers agreed the nation was in the throes of a religious revival. Every denomination in the United States had been affected. None were left untouched.[4]

Several explanations for this phenomenal spread of religious interest were offered. In 1947 the editor of *Life* said:

Materialism and science worship are in full retreat, eminent scientists leading the chase. Millikan proclaims that 'mechanistic philosophy is bankrupt.' The trend is toward God ... or rather, it is away from His enemies. It has become as fashionable and easy to laugh at the blindness of ethical relativism with C. S. Lewis, the English wit, as it used to be to laugh with H. L. Mencken at the blindness of the Bible belt.[5]

A Presbyterian minister in New York City said:

I feel very definitely there's a heart-hunger; people are bewildered, confused, feeling frustrated. They've seen the failure of something, of a philosophy, that was pretty well engrained in them; the idea of the inevitability of human progress.

They've seen that shattered, because it's been shown now that it is at least conceivable that our civilization might come to an end in our lifetime-civilization as we know it.

Every circumstance that envisions the future brings with it a sense of dread. So, the sense of human failure is driving people to reach out to something greater and higher that may save the race.[6]

Perhaps more than anything else, the postwar revival occurred because people felt insecure. They were afraid of death and wanted to be saved from it. One observer said that the popularity of the book, *The Search for Bridey Murphy*, in 1956 explains the true source of the present religious revival, for the 'interest in Bridey Murphy is an outward reach for a spiritual world of some sort' where life continues even after death.[7] Harvey Wish, professor of history at Western Reserve University, summarized the reasons for the religious revival as a feeling of insecurity 'in the midst of wars, dictators, and lethal weapons.'[8]

Evangelist Billy Graham

William Franklin Graham, Jr., more familiarly known as Evangelist Billy Graham, was born on September 9, 1917 in Charlotte, South Carolina. Most of his life was spent in the country under the influence of fundamentalist parents. Graham's parents nurtured him in an undiluted atmosphere not much unlike that which Jonathan Edwards and George Whitefield had helped create during the colonial period of American history. Graham referred to himself as an average country boy who liked a good time driving fast cars, especially 'hot rods,' and he enjoyed the company of girls. In school he seldom studied, preferring to disturb others by his rowdy behavior. He enjoyed sports, especially baseball. At the age of sixteen his parents urged him to attend a revival campaign conducted by Evangelist Mordecai Ham, who was noted for his rapid and fiery delivery. Graham and his friend, Grady Wilson, joined the choir during the campaign. Even though the two were secluded from the pointed gestures of the evangelist, both were converted before the campaign had concluded. Graham reported that after he made the decision to become a Christian all was sweetness and joy, because he was 'born again.'[9] Graham's conversion did not cause any drastic change in his life. After graduating from high school he enrolled in Bob Jones College in Cleveland, Tennessee, in 1936. But he was not ready for the rigid fundamentalist atmosphere of the college where social life was regulated and regimented by President Bob Jones, Sr., a revivalist preacher and a stern taskmaster. Graham was disappointed when he discovered the college did not participate in intercollegiate sports, but instead required long hours of study, particularly in the Bible. Before his first semester had progressed very far, Graham discovered his study habits were poor, his classroom work was deplorable, and he was failing. At the end of his first semester he withdrew from Bob Jones College and later enrolled in the Florida Bible Institute (now Trinity College, of

Clearwater, Florida). His study habits and classroom work did not improve until he met Miss Emily Cavanaugh, with whom he immediately fell in love. She discovered that Graham had no earnest intention to study and told him she intended to marry someone who would become a servant of God and who would amount to more than he seemed destined to become. She announced that she had no further interest in his company and walked away.[10]

Graham became desolate after receiving Miss Cavanaugh's rebuff. But after stomping over the school golf course and shedding many tears, he decided he would devote his life in service to God. He began to practice speaking aloud along a river bank, using a cypress stump for a pulpit, and alligators and fish as his audience. John Minder, dean of the Bible Institute and pastor of a Tampa church, was impressed with Graham's new earnestness and asked him to supply for him when he was absent from his Tampa church. This was an opportunity Graham wanted, but he became frightened with the thought of appearing before a human audience. Nevertheless, he began his pulpit career, preparing sermons in the homiletical pattern of famous evangelists and concluding them with an altar call. When Minder returned after an absence he discovered Graham had started a revival in his church.[11]

After he graduated from the Florida Bible Institute, Graham enrolled in Wheaton (Illinois) College, another fundamentalist school, but one with accredited standing and probably having the highest academic standing of any school of its kind. At Wheaton, Graham met and courted Ruth Bell, daughter of a southern Presbyterian missionary serving in China. Graham had improved his study habits before he met Miss Bell and this time his protestations of love were reciprocated. In fact, Miss Bell was convinced that Graham would become a successful evangelist and gladly consented to become his wife. In 1941, two years before he graduated from Wheaton where he majored in anthropology, Graham was ordained in Florida as a Baptist minister.[12]

Graham became pastor of the Village Baptist Church with eighty-five members in Western Springs, Illinois (a suburb of Chicago). While serving there his philosophy began to crystalize. Graham said:

I became convinced that it is the absence of the knowledge of God, and man's refusal to obey Him that lay at the root of every problem that besets us. It is man's confusion about God's plan that has the world in chaos.[13]

Within two years after becoming pastor of the Village Baptist Church, Graham's fame as a capable preacher began to spread, particularly after Torrey Johnson, pastor of the Midwest Bible Church of Chicago, turned over his radio broadcast to him. Graham's voice was heard over an area of eighteen states, the distance the transmitter carried. He said that it was during this period he discovered the secret of revivalist preaching – the Bible. He said, 'I made the Bible the keystone of every sermon I preached.'[14] Graham was elated when mail from his radio audience began to flow into his office like a flood. In many of the envelopes he received financial contributions to maintain his broadcasts, and commendations for his sermons and for the songs of George Beverly Shea, Graham's baritone soloist.[15]

Torrey Johnson was impressed with Graham as a preacher and shared with him his dream of establishing the Youth for Christ, International to specialize in mass youth evangelism. Graham saw in this a new opportunity, and so he resigned as pastor of the Village Baptist Church in 1945 to become the first field representative of Youth for Christ, International. That summer Graham preached his first sermon before a massive youth audience in Orchestra Hall in Chicago. His duties as field representative required much travelling. Within the next twelve months he covered 100,000 miles organizing Youth for Christ groups. At Asheville, North Carolina he met Cliff Barrows, whose ability as a song leader attracted him. Graham asked him to join him and Shea in conducting revivals among the nation's youth. Graham not only gained valuable experience as a speaker during this period but he also built an evangelistic team to help him conduct his revival meetings. There were after that numerous requests from various churches for their services.[16]

The Rebirth of Mass Evangelism

Graham's efforts were relatively obscure and in no way unusual until 1949. In that year he and his team, Shea, Barrows, and Grady Wilson, undertook a mass revival in Los Angeles, which they called the Greater Los Angeles Crusade, in a tent seating 6,000 people. In this undertaking seven hundred churches and their ministers were enlisted to support it. Graham was announced as 'America's Sensational Evangelist' supported by 'Glorious Music.'[17] Despite the co-operation of a greater proportion of Los Angeles churches the revivalist wondered if they had not undertaken a task much too big for them. The meetings proved to be nothing extraordinary. Other evangelists had equal if not better success.[18]

Near the end of the third week, the time planned for the crusade, Graham and his team began to look for visible signs which might help them to decide whether the crusade should end or be extended. On the final Sunday night of the crusade a contingent of newspaper correspondents with their photographers converged upon the scene and greeted Graham when he arrived for the service. Graham was pleased but he did not grasp the significance of their presence until later, when it was learned that William Randolph Hearst had sent a telegram to his editors consisting of two words: 'Puff Graham.' Graham's meeting was given front page newspaper coverage, and he was convinced that he had benefited from an act of Providence.[19]

As the crusade entered the fourth week, Graham was convinced that a new phase of his evangelistic career had begun. He had come to Los Angeles unheralded but now his name was becoming familiar wherever newspapers were read. He also believed he had received a new anointing for his work. Before five days of his extended crusade had passed, three well-known persons in the Los Angeles area, Stuart Hamblen, Jim Vaus, and Louis Zamperini, were converted and interest in Billy Graham increased accordingly.[20]

Hamblen, a guitarist who called himself 'the singing cowboy with a thousand songs,' was a minister's son. He was more familiarly known as a radio entertainer and master of ceremonies on the 'Stuart Hamblen and His Lucky Stars' radio program, which he had conducted for twenty-one years. Hamblen was also a race-horse enthusiast. One year his famous horse El Lobo won a $50,000 stake at Santa Anita. Hamblen met Graham at a private prayer meeting and followed this by attending one of the meetings at the Los Angeles Crusade. He was impressed by Graham's sincerity and simplicity. One night after spending several restless hours Hamblen telephoned Graham that he was troubled. Graham invited him to his hotel room where at approximately 3:30 A.M. Hamblen was converted on his knees beside the evangelist. Hamblen promised Graham he would reform by giving up night clubs, gambling, drinking, and his connection with horse races. The following morning Hamblen told his radio audience what had happened. On his car radio Jim Vaus heard Hamblen's program, which was sponsored by a cigarette company. He was astonished to hear Hamblen say:

Folks, smoking won't do you any good at all! In fact, you might just as well quit. But if you've already got the habit, well, buy your cigarettes from my sponsor. But if you aren't smoking now, there's no use in starting.[21]

Louis Zamperini, a Roman Catholic, was a former University of Southern California and Olympic track star. As an airman during World War II his plane crashed in the sea and he had floated forty-seven days on a raft. The Japanese found him and took him as their captive. After his release he returned to the United States as a war hero. At the time of the Los Angeles Crusade Zamperini was experiencing marital difficulties. He attended one of Graham's meetings and after hearing a sermon on hell's fire and brimstone he was immediately converted.[22]

The newspapers mentioned the conversions of Hamblen and Zamperini. At least one more surprise awaited the Los Angeles news reporters, who were hungry for more sensational developments. The day after Hamblen's conversion Vaus, an electronics expert and a wire-tapper for Mickey Cohen (notorious race-track gambler), attended Graham's crusade from curiosity. Vaus, whose father was a minister, had a prison record for armed robbery and a military prison for the theft of electronic equipment from the Army. He had also been a student at the Bible Institute of Los Angeles but he was asked to leave because he pilfered money from the school's mail. Mickey Cohen hired Vaus as protection against the wire-tapping activities of the police. While in the service of Cohen he perfected an electronic gadget which enabled Cohen's gambling syndicate to plug into the Continental Wire Service carrying information from the race tracks. The device Vaus perfected delayed the teletypewriters long enough after the winners at the race track were posted to allow Cohen's stationed henchmen time to place bets on the winning horse before the bookmaker received the final race results.[23]

Vaus was restless after he had heard Hamblen relate his conversion experience over the radio. This, coupled with reports of other conversions at Graham's crusade, aroused his curiosity. He and his wife Alice went to the tent together that evening to hear the evangelist. Vaus watched Graham as he moved about the platform, noted his youthful appearance, his height, and was struck by the authority in his voice. Vaus had heard the same message before, but this time it seemed to be more convincing. He hesitated when the altar call was given, then suddenly decided to go forward and knelt in the sawdust as a repentant sinner. His wife immediately rose from her seat and followed him. While Vaus was kneeling a reporter from the *Los Angeles Times* recognized him and quickly took a photograph. The next day the newspaper electrified its readers when it announced: 'Wire-Tapper Vaus Hits Sawdust Trail.'[24]

After his conversion Vaus immediately sought to make restitution for his past crimes and to sever his connection from Cohen and his syndicate. He confessed the theft of expensive electronic equipment and on his own initiative he appeared before the Los Angeles County Grand Jury where he confessed he had perjured himself in previous testimony. His confession cleared one policeman facing imprisonment on the perjured testimony. Those from whom he had stolen forgave him and the Grand Jury, obviously convinced of the sincerity of his conversion, never indicted him. Vaus asked Graham and Barrows to go with him to explain to Cohen what had happened and to sever his association with the gambling syndicate. Apparently Cohen was impressed by Vaus' testimony, and said: 'I want you to promise me that you'll never come back to this sort of life. Quit for good.'[25] Vaus turned from a life of crime to become active in missionary service. He and others formed the Missionary Communication Service to provide missionaries with transmitters, receivers, and generators to enable them to propagate the gospel.[26]

Before the Los Angeles Crusade concluded it had been extended from the original three to eight weeks. Approximately 350,000 attended, partly because of the widespread publicity in newspapers and the sensational conversions of Hamblen, Zamperini, Vaus, and many others. An estimated 3,000 were converted. The crusade was compared with Sunday's revival in Los Angeles a generation before. First Mate Bob of the Haven of Rest, a fundamentalist organization, said that Graham's crusade was the greatest in the history of Southern California. Many other observers agreed that Graham had become the phenomenon of the mid-century.[27]

The fundamentalists rejoiced because the old-fashioned religion was still powerful enough to capture the attention of the masses in the United States. Many fundamentalist leaders began to write articles explaining what had happened and the reason for the success of revivalism. They were jubilant because they were certain that religious liberalism had been halted, and believed fundamentalism was on the threshold of better days, national and international in scope.[28]

The Youth for Christ, Inter-Varsity Christian Fellowship, the High School Clubs, and various adult organizations, such as the Gideons and Christian Businessmen Committees, were also credited with being partially responsible for the revival, because they had continued to conduct evangelistic meetings since the thirties. Furthermore, by mid-century the fundamentalists had been fully organized and had developed an integrated system of education, which helped strengthen the revivalist tradition and provide the personnel to carry it on. Finally, there never was any relaxation in promoting the revivalist tradition despite the reverses the fundamentalists had experienced. They published the facts of their faith in tracts, brochures, magazines, and books, and their many radio broadcasts undoubtedly had had influence. The way seemed to be prepared for Billy Graham.[29]

Mass Evangelism Spreads
After the close of the Los Angeles Crusade, Billy Graham accepted an invitation from the Park Street Congregational Church in Boston to conduct a campaign there for nine days. Graham and his team began the Boston meetings on December 30, 1949 with a capacity audience of 1,200, and several hundred were turned away. The next day the officials of the church and pastor Harold Ockenga, perceiving from the results of the first night what might happen, rented Mechanics Hall which had 6,000 seats. Newspapermen reported the developments on the front pages of Boston papers. On New Year's Eve, when most people usually celebrate the passing of the old year in other ways, Graham and his team conducted a religious service before another capacity audience. Thus, a one-church campaign had precipitated a city-wide revival in less than twenty-four hours.[30]

The inevitable result of the publicity which the newspapers gave the revival was that many people talked about its suddenness. Others came from various parts of New England to see and hear Graham, 'the handsome, youthful, dynamic, fearless prophet', who preached the old-fashioned gospel and captivated his audience.[31]

Since no plans had been made beforehand for an extended campaign, fundamentalists in Boston had to improvise seating requirements if the campaign was to continue the full nine days. When Mechanics Hall was not in use, the meetings were conducted there. At other times the Opera House was rented. The final meeting was conducted in the Boston Garden which had 16,000 seats. Approximately 10,000 who sought to enter could not be accommodated. One newsman wrote that he could not understand what he had seen, but he was positive that nothing of this nature had ever happened in Boston during his time as a reporter.[32] Graham was also moved by the suddenness of the Boston revival, and his faith in mass evangelism was given additional support. 'In Boston God's guidance was evident,' he commented, 'and I became wholly convinced He meant for me to keep on winning souls.'[33]

The results of the Los Angeles and Boston revivals indicated that the people in the United States were interested in religion. Were the people in the

interior equally concerned? Graham's next meeting was in Columbia, South
Carolina, a city of approximately 100,000 people. The campaign ran for six
weeks during February and March, 1950. The meetings were conducted in the
Municipal Auditorium which had 3,500 seats, but its capacity was far too
small for the people who wanted to attend. Early in the campaign Kirby
Higbe, pitcher for the New York Giants, was converted. State Senators,
together with Governor J. Strom Thurmond, attended the meetings, and the
latter called Graham's Columbia campaign the greatest religious movement
in South Carolina during his lifetime. The final meeting of the campaign was
conducted on March 12 in the South Carolina University football stadium,
which had 40,000 seats. The highway patrol reported that after all the seats
and standing space were filled, other thousands who tried to get in the stadium
were turned away. On that day approximately 2,000 persons came to the
altar after Graham had concluded his sermon and had given them the invitation to accept Christ as Saviour.[34] James Brynes, former Secretary of
State during the administration of President Harry S. Truman said: 'I've
been with statesmen, presidents, and Kings, but this is the most thrilling
moment of my life.'[35]

Fundamentalist leaders admitted that much of the success Graham enjoyed
was attributable to the cooperation of newspapers, magazines, and radio
stations which constantly made announcements of the attendance and
presented daily reports of the number of conversions. Graham credited his
success to God rather than any human manipulation of the masses. He was
convinced that God had laid His hand upon him, and had given him a
special anointing for the work of an evangelist.[36]

After the Columbia campaign Graham and his team toured New England
and then returned to Boston on April 19-22, to be greeted again by capacity
crowds. On April 24, Graham concluded his visit to Boston with an open air
meeting on the commons where George Whitefield had stood and had
spoken to large crowds in 1740 on essentially the same themes. When Graham
rose to speak he faced approximately 50,000 people from various towns,
villages, and cities in New England.[37]

It became apparent after these early outbursts of religious excitement
connected with Graham's meetings in 1949-1950 that he could expect their
recurrences elsewhere. One writer commented that Graham had 'plenty
of fire and a brand of gab,' and that these talents explained his popular
appeal.[38]

Fundamentalist leaders were certain that the hour they had longed for had finally arrived and that God had chosen Graham for their purposes.[39] He was fast becoming the symbol of a rethinking of religion in America. By 1957, the Gallup Poll indicated that fifty-nine percent of the populace were favorably impressed by Graham, because they believed he was a great preacher doing constructive work for God. Only twelve percent looked at his work with disfavor.[40] Many people were convinced that God had a significant role in Graham's ministry. In addition, Graham sought to explain his success in these words: 'You can't explain me if you leave out the supernatural. I am a tool of God.'[41]

Graham kept busy conducting meetings in various cities of the United States and in Europe. Excited multitudes jostled each other as they pressed into large auditoriums to hear him preach. Between 1950 and 1954 almost every large city in the south had been stirred by his revivals. Graham was greeted by capacity crowds in Atlanta, Fort Worth, Shreveport, Memphis, Greensboro (North Carolina), Dallas, Houston, New Orleans, Portland, Seattle, Detroit, Washington and Pittsburgh. In 1956 he conducted three other campaigns in St. Louis, Louisville, and Richmond. He also made brief visits to other cities to speak before local ministers' groups, primarily to survey conditions with regard to the possibility of future revival campaigns and prospects for their success.[42]

Invitations to conduct meetings flooded Graham's headquarters constantly after 1950. This great demand for his service, coupled with his own growing awareness of his importance in the mid-century revivals, was a factor in the establishment of a new policy for his crusades. Graham notified those who invited him that two conditions must be met before he could consent to accept an invitation to conduct a crusade: (1) a majority of the local churches must invite him, and (2) all the finances must be handled by a committee composed of local businessmen.[43]

The practical advantages of this new policy were many. Its most important feature was that it assured success for Graham's crusades where a majority in the city cooperated toward that end. A campaign conducted under the auspices of a cooperating majority of local clergymen solved a major problem of establishing good-will and starting a campaign on a positive basis. Furthermore, Graham did not have to concern himself with criticisms emanating from the minority of non-cooperating clergymen. Finally, by placing the responsibility of raising money upon a local committee of businessmen, Graham not only had guarantees of solvency but he protected himself from the charge usually levelled against evangelists, namely, that they were mercenary. Following every crusade an audit was prepared and published in the local newspaper by the committee, revealing receipts and disbursements. This fiscal policy also eliminated the necessity of raising large sums of money *during* the crusade, a practice which had tended to detract from the solemnity and spontaneity of revivalism.[44]

Graham's Brief Visit to Europe

Billy Graham looked for new worlds to conquer after his successful crusades in the United States. In 1954 he went to England where he conducted a crusade lasting three months. Approximately 1,000 London churches sponsored the crusade which was conducted in Harringway Arena with a seating capacity of 12,000. Before his arrival in England the British press showed its hostility to Graham by calling him an 'unwelcome American export' with an 'outdated message' operating a 'gospel circus.'[45] The British Labor Party voiced their disapproval as a result of Graham's alleged criticism of British socialism. There was some talk of denying him a visa. Apparently Graham did not understand that socialism was not regarded with contempt in England as in America. Before he arrived in England, however, he corrected his statement by saying he meant that secularism, not socialism, was the great danger to the world today. The controversy surrounding him abated accordingly.[46]

Graham and the British clergy were overwhelmed by the results of the crusade. An estimated 2,000,000 people, many of them arriving in London on specially arranged commuter schedules, attended the meetings. The arena was filled to capacity every night except on three occasions when inclement weather prevented many from attending. On the afternoon of the crusade's final day, 65,000 people attended a meeting conducted in the White City football field. That same night all attendance records were broken, when 120,000 people were huddled together, standing and seated, to bring the crusade to an arousing conclusion. The final tabulation indicated that approximately 40,000 decisions to accept Christ had been made during the London crusade.[47] It is also significant to note that most newsmen had changed their attitude toward him, and meant it as praise when they called him the 'Hollywood version of John the Baptist.'[48]

During the next two years Graham confined his preaching campaigns, despite the language barrier, mostly on the Continent of Europe. He preached in Glasgow, and there was a return engagement in London lasting eight days. Within five months Graham had spoken to approximately 4,000,000 people, and recorded an estimated 100,000 decisions for Christ. His success in Europe increased his prestige immeasurably. He had weathered successfully a storm of controversy about his methods and his alleged statements about socialism, and he returned to the United States praised by foreign newsmen.[49]

Planning the New York Crusade

Plans were already in a formative stage for Graham's invasion of New York City, for a crusade which he recognized as the supreme challenge of his professional evangelist career. New York would perhaps test not only his ability but his popularity as well, even as Sunday in 1917 staked 'his fame and his genius in the attempt to reform the city known as the 'graveyard of evangelists'.[50]

When Graham and his wife arrived in New York several days before the crusade was to begin on May 15, 1957, he was greeted by a contingent of newsmen who detected the apprehensions which he felt because New York was a tough 'nut to crack.'[51] On the other hand, he was fortified by the knowledge that millions of people had promised to pray for him during the New York Crusade. He said that mass prayer would bring success in New York, because prayer was 'simply tremendous in its accumulated and accelerated working.' It was prayer that helped him 'penetrate the sin-hardened shells' of people in New York.[52] Believing that God was imminent in all of his previous crusades, Graham approached the New York Crusade with the confidence that results similar to other crusades would be guaranteed by God, and that he would be the vehicle through whom God would accomplish His ends. Graham frequently was heard to say that 'the difficult is easy when God is in it'.[53]

In planning the New York Crusade, Graham carefully considered the manifold social, racial, religious, economic, and political problems of the big city. Recognizing New York's character, Graham said: 'Humanly speaking New York is the most unlikely city in the world for successful evangelism,'[54] because Protestantism in New York was actually a 'submerged minority' (as Graham claimed) of less than ten percent of the total population. Cooperative action on the part of the ministers was accordingly made much easier. Graham observed that 'ministers who could not agree with us theologically or did not believe in our type of evangelism are willing to cooperate simply because there seems to be no other possible way for them to reach the conscience of this city.'[55]

Graham also explained that he and his team were 'approaching New York with a sense of mission.'[56] Because of its strategic situation at the junction between the old and the new world, he regarded his crusade as important as that of the Apostle Paul whose base of operation was Jerusalem. 'New York is our Jerusalem,' he said, 'like Jerusalem of old it is the hub where many conflicting social and religious ideologies meet.'[57] He added that New York was also the headquarters of the United Nations, which actually makes it a world capital. A spiritual awakening in New York could have tremendous impact on the entire world.'[58] Graham also shared the belief expressed by others that 'this crusade could possibly be God's last call to New York.' He said:

There is fear that if Russia ever decided to launch a sneak attack against the United States that New York would be the first on the list of targets. This terrifying thought gives us a sense of urgency and responsibility.[59]

Following the practices of Billy Sunday a generation ago, Graham adopted modern business methods to promote the New York Crusade. Jerry Beaven, Graham's chief organizer, perfected and executed the plans. He obtained the support of prominent financial leaders and the cooperation of approximately 1,500 churches and their ministers to make the New York Crusade one of the most efficiently organized and united campaigns in Graham's entire career. Roger Hull, executive vice president of the Mutual Life Insurance Company of New York, was selected as chairman of the New York Crusade sponsoring committee. George Champion, president of Chase Manhattan Bank, held the position of chairman for evangelism of the Protestant Council of New York, although he admitted he seldom attended church. Other prominent businessmen on the sponsoring committee were Howard E. Isham, treasurer of the United States Steel Corporation; Alexander C. Nagle, president of the First National Bank of the City of New York, and Edwin F. Chinlud, retired treasurer of R. H. Macy & Co., who was the treasurer of the crusade committee. By serving on the committee, these men said in effect, that big business was seriously interested in the principles for which Graham stood.[60]

The New York Crusade

Graham opened his New York Crusade on May 15 in Madison Square Garden, a few days after Ringling Brothers, and the Barnum and Bailey Circus, had ended a run of forty days. The odor of animal excrement was still present. Many people waited for hours in a line a block long to assure themselves of seats in the Garden, which had a capacity of 18,500. When Graham ascended the improvised pulpit he noticed that almost every seat had been occupied. The New York Crusade was off to a good start. The attendance on the second night dropped to approximately 13,000, but this did not disturb the evangelist. He said this was normal until more publicity was given and the news began to spread that 'people are finding God here.' [61] Attendance on the third night increased to 16,500. By the fifth night the Garden was filled to capacity and most observers surmised that the crusade would be successful. [62]

During the second week of the crusade the attendance had outgrown the capacity of the Garden. Approximately 2,000 people sat in the basement and heard the service over the public address system, while more than 2,000 remained outside. Graham gave the latter an opportunity to see and hear him, by arranging an abbreviated service on the street from an improvised platform before he entered the Garden for the regular service. Many people on the street responded to his invitation to make decisions to accept Christ. [63] Forty-three days after the campaign began, on June 26, the audience was told that the New York Crusade 'had outlasted and outdrawn any other attraction in the 30-year history of Madison Square Garden.' [64] They were also informed that approximately 739,000 had attended the meetings, and that 22,000 people had made decisions to accept Christ as Saviour. Thousands of them had been referred to various New York churches. The Marble Collegiate Church received more than 100 into its membership. [65]

Part of the success of the New York Crusade must be attributed to the precise planning which brought delegations from as far west as Texas to the meetings. [66] Opponents of mass evangelism declared that this amounted to 'engineering by consent,' but a pre-arranged audience was no true indication of the real impact Graham was having on New York. [67] Only a fraction of those who attended the meetings, approximately 6,000, had come as a part of a delegation at any one given night. Even had there been more, the fact that they came across the continent to hear an evangelist would indicate that there was a revival in religion in the United States. Hardened newsmen reported that New York had been deeply affected; people discussed religion as freely as some discussed baseball. [68]

Originally, the New York Crusade was to close on June 30. Within two weeks after the meetings began, however, the sponsoring committee decided there was sufficient interest to extend the Crusade to July 21. On July 20, the hottest day of the summer in New York, a special meeting was conducted in Yankee Stadium on what was to have been the climax of the crusade. Gamblers wagered Graham would not fill the stadium. People arrived by various means of transportation, a few from Australia by plane, to attend the meeting. The audience, estimated at approximately 100,000, was not only Graham's largest in the United States, but also the largest in the history of Yankee Stadium. Another 10,000 were turned away because every seat and permissible standing space was occupied. One observer said: 'It was also a triumphant justification of the announcement made by Graham headquarters the day before; the crusade at Madison Square Garden would be extended for three more weeks.' [69]

Vice-President Richard Nixon was present in Yankee Stadium. He spoke briefly and congratulated Graham for filling the stadium. Graham corrected Nixon by saying: 'I didn't fill the stadium, God did. No one is here by accident but by divine appointment. This shows what can be done when the churches co-operate to win souls for Jesus Christ.' [70] Earlier Graham had told newsmen that 'he never felt such 'power' in his preaching as he has felt during the Madison Square Garden Crusade' and that he knew 'the Holy Spirit' was present. [71] He also told them that even though the effects of the New York Crusade might not be felt immediately, the result would appear in due course. 'We hope to leave behind a few apostles,' Graham said, 'people ready to die for Christ. If we can do that, New York could be touched in the next ten years.' [72] On August 3, the New York Crusade was extended the third time to September 1. [73]

The interest in the crusade was indicated by the number of people who watched and heard Graham on television on Saturday nights beginning on June 1. The National Broadcasting Company, which carried the broadcasts over its network, reported that between 7,000,000 and 10,000,000 people watched the crusade over television. It was also reported from the crusade headquarters that many people were converted in their homes as a result of the telecasts. This encouraged the crusade sponsoring committee and was a factor in the extension of the telecasts beyond June 22. [74]

Graham's Crisis in New York
The New York Crusade was important for other reasons. Only a small number of people were aware, for example, that Graham was 'rapidly becoming one of the most controversial religious figures on the American scene.' One should be able to understand why non-fundamentalists were divided on Graham and his methods in evangelism, but it is difficult for most

people to understand why fundamentalists such as Carl McIntire, John R. Rice, and Bob Jones, Sr., resorted to a campaign of villification to discredit the New York revival before it started. The attacks by the representatives of the American Council served to magnify the essential division within the fundamentalist movement over the issue of separation. Graham was criticized because of his association with modernists, many of whom were represented on the sponsoring committee, and for rejecting the separatist position of the American Council in order to conduct the New York Crusade on a mass basis. Graham replied to his critics: 'I intend to go anywhere sponsored by anybody, to preach the gospel of Christ, if there are no strings attached to my message.' [75] This seemed reasonable to the inclusivist National Association of Evangelicals, which supported the New York Crusade, but the separatists objected, saying: 'Old-time Bible-believing fundamentalists insist that the Bible clearly forbids yoking up with unbelievers, even though one's motives may appear to be good.' [76]

New York leaders of the American Council were rebuffed by Graham when he rejected their invitation in 1951–1952 to conduct a crusade in New York City under their auspices on a separatist basis. When he announced that the Protestant Council of New York would sponsor him, the controversy concerning his fidelity to the fundamentalist cause began to rage and its fury spread rapidly. McIntire called the New York Crusade, 'a distinct defeat for the fundamentalists,' and a victory for modernism and apostasy. [77] Graham explained that he had rejected the separatists' invitation because there had been too much discord and disagreement among them and because their committee was not representative of all the churches in New York City, a requirement for a successful campaign. He wanted an ecumenical committee to sponsor his crusade, thus assuring the cooperation of a major part of Protestants in New York City. [78] In addition, Graham said he did not want to be known primarily as a fundamentalist because of the 'aura of bigotry and narrowness associated with the term.' [79] He preferred instead to be known as a constructionalist. [80] Graham took this position because he wished to avoid controversy, which he believed was one of the causes of the failure of the fundamentalists to make a greater impact upon the United States. He spurned the older fundamentalism with its slogan 'contend for the faith,' and adopted the constructionalist slogan of 'Ye must be born again.' Constructionalists believed that 'there was more to Christianity than being on the defensive all the time.' [81] Graham also avoided controversy because of his single desire to preach the gospel and to achieve many conversions.

To that end he said, 'I have patterned my preaching and my work a great deal after that of the late Dwight L. Moody, who was careful to avoid controversy or argument.' [82] He refused to reopen the sores left after the bitter fundamentalist controversy a generation before. But McIntire and Rice accused him of expediency because, they charged, he refused to attack the modernists for their sin of apostasy. [83]

Another factor in the controversy surrounding Graham was the latter's relationship with the neo-evangelical scholars mentioned earlier in this study. Although Graham, by his own admission, cannot be called an intellectual, he aligned himself with this new generation of fundamentalist intellectuals because of their interpretation of and more constructive approach in the dissemination of fundamentalist theology. The influence of neo-evangelicalism upon Graham can be noted in the latter's less literal attitude regarding theology than is customarily associated with fundamentalist evangelists. Graham believes in the existence of hell, for example, but without a literal fire. [84] John R. Rice noted the changes in Graham's interpretations and he also objected to Graham's association with the neo-evangelicals. Rice assailed Graham for compromising the gospel in order to avoid controversy, although earlier in Graham's career he had said:

Thank God for Billy Graham and members of his team. He is preaching the gospel of Jesus Christ in all its simplicity, authority, and power like Dwight L. Moody and Billy Sunday. He preaches a plain message leading to a definite point-repentance and faith in Christ. [85]

Because of Graham's new alliances, however, Rice, McIntire, Jones, and other separatists came to regard him as 'one of the spokesmen, and perhaps the principal spark plug of a great drift away from strict Bible fundamentalism and strict defense of the faith.' [86] Thus, the attack against Graham in New York must also be regarded as a campaign on the part of the separatists to destroy Billy Graham and to defeat the inclusivists and the new fundamentalist intelligentsia.

Liberalism's Criticism of Graham and the Fundamentalist Revival
Although there was general agreement on the quantity of the current religious interest in the United States, there were many who differed regarding its quality. Edward L. R. Elson, the Presbyterian minister in Washington, D. C., who baptized President Dwight D. Eisenhower the Sunday following

the latter's inauguration, said that there were evidences of a genuine religious revival in the United States.[87] Norman Vincent Peale, minister of Marble Collegiate Church in New York City, said that the United States was the most religious country in the world, and that the current religious revival was genuine.[88] Graham was more modest and cautious in his appraisal of the religious situation in the United States. He stated that America was headed toward a genuine religious revival and that this was reflected in the ease in which ministers gained the interest of the people today. But unless new church members become fully committed to their faith, he believed no genuine revival would come.[89]

Those rabidly opposed to revivalism as the proper method to recruit new members were apprehensive of Graham's final impact on the quality of church membership in the United States. In view of the higher incidence of various crimes among adults and juveniles, the president of the National Council said: 'Today in our country, it is a cause of worry that morality seems to be on a decline at the moment when there appears to be a religious boom.'[90] Others criticized the current revival because much of it was motivated by fear, selfishness, longing for security; they contended that it engendered a relatively immature religiosity.[91] Reinhold Niebuhr denounced the flight for security because it tended 'to depict religion as a mere means to a selfish end, and to make God appear the servant of man rather than vice versa.'[92]

The single objective in all of Graham's crusades was to get people to commit their lives to Christ as Saviour. Because of the nature of his theology an element of fear and a tone of urgency may be found in all of his sermons. Invariably he warned his audiences that hesitation to accept Christ might prove disastrous, because no person could know when death might strike. On the fifth night of the New York Crusade Graham told his audience that on the basis of certain statements in the Bible, as well as the word of contemporary scientists, the world's catastrophic end was within sight, and that this might be God's last call to the present generation before it was destroyed. 'The Iron Curtain countries are arming to the teeth,' he warned, 'and we in the West are arming to the teeth, and we are told that in a flash – in a moment – it is possible to destroy New York with a push button.'[93] It must be conceded, therefore, that the element of fear helped explain the success of Graham's New York crusade. To some it was one of the most objectionable aspects of the Graham crusade, because people were using 'God for their own purposes rather than to serve God and find His purposes.'[94] One of the most satirical remarks regarding the fundamentalist revival was made by

A. Powell Davies, minister of All Soul's (Unitarian) Church in Washington, D. C. He likened the appeal of evangelists to the hawking of a salesman on a medicine show. He wrote:

Try God, folks. He will clear away your troubles in a twinkling. Works for you while you sleep. Works for you all the time. Cures your worries instantly. Nothing for you to do, so inexpensive! Go to your corner church today, folks and get God! G-O-D, easy to pronounce, easy to remember, easy for you in every way. [95]

Churchmen in the National Council attacked Graham because he preached a 'narrow and divisive creed which the churches rejected a generation ago.' [96] Carl F. H. Henry stated:

Liberal Protestantism is critical of Dr. (Billy) Graham because of his success with New Testament evangelism in which it disbelieves and not because there is anything intrinsically harmful about a bulk response to Christian evangelism. If hundreds of converts nightly were led to Christ by Dr. Graham through personal counseling, rather than through mass evangelism, it would still criticize him. [97]

The National Council also opposed revivalism because of 'the rising tempo of a powerful evangelical drive developing independently of the churches.' [98] The emphasis upon personal evangelism represented a revival of frontier individualism in the churches, and the National Council saw it as a threat to ecumenicism and the centralizing tendency within the major Protestant denominations in the United States, which has been advancing rapidly since World War II. [99]

It was for these two reasons that both Graham and the Protestant Council of New York were criticized by the leaders in the National Council. The Protestant Council, however, was faced with a serious problem, for it had no speaker who could command the attention of the masses as Billy Graham. Most of their churches were in a deplorable condition, and although many on the Protestant Council did not approve of Graham's technique or his message, there seemed to be no alternative method to revive the Protestant churches without a mass movement as in revivalism. [100] One commentator stated: 'Some ministers wince at the content and others at the context but they unite in urging that any kind of religious event is better than no event at all.'[101] But the Protestant Council was criticized for opening 'an access to a channel of official church life which had previously been closed' to the fundamentalists.[102]

Another criticism of the current revival in the United States was that the American way of life has been confused with a supernatural kingdom. Since the end of World War II, a nationalist fervor dangerously close to chauvinism had gripped the people in the United States in the face of the threat of Russian attack upon them. Somehow religious orthodoxy has been associated with nationalism and the two have become joint factors in the struggle for existence in the mid-twentieth century. As a consequence various pressures have been exerted on Congress to enact legislation to promote Christian nationalism, to the alarm of those concerned with the civil and Constitutional right of agnostics, atheists, and others unable to subscribe to Christian tenets. A Christian Amendment Movement, which received support and encouragement from the National Association of Evangelicals, was organized in 1946 to promote national righteousness through legislative enactment by correcting the omission of reference to the Deity in the federal Constitution.[103]

The Christian Amendment Movement represents a revival of the National Reform Organization which proposed a Christian amendment to the Constitution in 1894 and in 1910.[104] When the National Reform Organization first proposed the amendment, Robert Ingersoll, the famous agnostic, immediately campaigned against it because confusion would follow its ratification. He proposed instead a complete secularization of the United States as more practical and more in line with American tradition. He said:

It is impossible to put God into the Constitution because there was no agreement on the Divinity which was to have the honor. Would it be the Deity of the Catholics, the Calvinists or the Puritans?[105]

The Christian Amendment Movement revived the proposed amendment of the National Reform Organization and in 1947 petitioned Congress to take the necessary action for its ratification. The first section of the proposed amendment read as follows: 'This nation devoutly recognizes the authority and law of Jesus Christ, Saviour and Ruler of nations, through whom are bestowed the blessings of Almighty God.'[106] Although each Congress since 1947 has been petitioned to consider the amendment, no action has been taken.[107]

Perhaps the seriousness of the proposal for a Christian Amendment can be estimated when one recalls the statement of a fundamentalist who wrote:

The only person who is not guaranteed liberty under our Constitution is an Atheist, for we are guaranteed liberty to 'worship God according to the dictates of our own consciences.' (Italics are inserted).[108]

This statement reveals the inherent danger of confusing the American way of life with a supernatural kingdom, as the critics of the current revival have pointed out. It also reveals the lack of understanding on the part of some people of the historical meaning of the Constitution of the United States with regard to the matter of civil rights and the principles of freedom of religion and speech.

There has been some legislation indicating a trend in the direction of a relaxation of the American principle of separation of church and state. Louis C. Rabaut, Democrat member of the House of Representatives from Michigan, presented a bill in Congress to amend the pledge of allegiance to the national banner by the inclusion of the phrase 'under God.'[109] When this measure was adopted in 1954 Rabaut said that American youth who repeat it in their classrooms will understand that 'democratic institutions presupposes a Supreme Being.'[110]

In 1954 an eight-cent postage stamp for international mail was printed with a picture of the Statue of Liberty with the motto 'In God We Trust' subscribed, in order that those behind the Iron Curtain might note the spiritual origin of the United States.[111] In 1956 the same slogan was adopted by Congress as a national motto for all coins and currency. Previously the motto had appeared only on a few coins. Senator Joseph O'Mahoney of Wyoming, who had presented a favorable report on the measure, said that 'E Pluribus Unum' was unsatisfactory as a national motto 'because few people know what it means.'[112] He argued that the new motto would 'be of great spiritual and psychological value to our country.'[113] Critics of the current revival of religion believe otherwise. They contend that legislative acts and proposals for Christian nationalism will lead to confusion and violation of individual Constitutional rights. Furthermore, it is doubtful if the mere mention of God or Christ in the Constitution, or exposure to any religious phrase or motto, can induce righteousness among the nation's millions.[114]

Notes

The full citation of each title used in this study is to be found on its first mention, with the exception of the following magazines and newspapers, which receive abbreviated citation throughout:

The Christian Beacon is abbreviated Beacon.
The Christian Century is abbreviated Century.
The Christian Register is abbreviated Register.
The Sword of the Lord is abbreviated Sword.
United Evangelical Action is abbreviated UEA.

CHAPTER I

[1] Kay Stillwell, 'C. S. Lewis Modern Christian Writer', His, January, 1957, p. 14; 'Tense Expectancy Grips U.S.', 'Christian Life', February, 1952, p. 75; Joseph T. Bayly, '56: This Year of Our Lord', His, January, 1956, pp. 1–4.

[2] Time, September 19, 1956, p. 76; Century, October 3, 1956, pp. 1124–1125.

[3] Virginia L. Grabill, 'Mencken from the Grave', Christianity Today, December 24, 1956, p. 17; Cleveland Plain Dealer, April 9, 1956, p. 37.

[4] James DeForest Murch, Co-operation Without Compromise (Grand Rapids: Wm. B. Eerdmans Publishing Co., 1956), pp. 113–116; E. C. Homrighausen, 'Billy Graham and the Protestant Predicament', Century, July 18, 1956, pp. 848–849; Time, July 23, 1956, p. 51.

[5] Notes from a speech delivered by William Ward Ayer in Cleveland, Ohio, April, 1956.

[6] J. M. Carroll in The Trail of Blood (Lexington, Kentucky: Byron-Page Printing Co., 1931), shows the unbroken descent of the Baptists from the time of Christ, which William Warren Sweet identified as Landmarkism in Religion in the Development of American Culture (New York: Charles Scribner's Sons 1952), p. 225.

[7] Notes from Ayer's speech.

[8] Edwin A. Burtt, Types of Religious Philosophy (New York: Harper & Brothers Publishers, 1951), pp. 149–159.

[9] George M. Stephenson, The Puritan Heritage (New York: The Macmillan Co., 1952), pp. 11–13; Arthur Cushman McGiffert, Protestant Thought Before Kant (New York: Charles Scribner's Sons, 1926), pp. 9–10; Jacob Blaauw, 'Needed: A New Reformation', Moody Monthly, July, 1947, p. 785.

[10] Notes from Ayer's speech.

[11] Eugene C. Bewekes, et al, Experience, Reason, and Faith: A Survey in Philosophy and

Religion (New York: Harper & Brothers Publishers, 1940), pp. 458–459; 463; Walter G. Muelder and Laurence Sears, *The Development of American Philosophy* (Boston: Houghton Mifflin Co., 1940), pp. 2–4.

[12] Stephenson, *op. cit.*, pp. 14–17.

[13] Josiah Combs, 'Language of the Southern Highlanders', *Publication of the Modern Language Association of America*, December, 1931, pp. 1302–1322; Lester V. Berrey, 'Southern Mountain Dialect', *American Speech*, February, 1940, pp. 45–54.

[14] 'Bible Burnings', *Beacon*, January 1, 1953, p. 1; *Denver Post*, November 30, 1952, p. 1.

[15] William Warren Sweet, *The American Churches: An Interpretation* (New York: Abingdon-Cokesbury Press, 1948), pp. 11–25.

[16] William Warren Sweet, *The Story of Religion in America* (New York: Harper & Brothers Publishers, 1939), pp. 185–186.

[17] William Warren Sweet, *Religion in the Development of American Culture*, p. 146.

[18] Joseph Tracy, *The Great Awakening: A History of the Revival of Religion in the Time of Edwards and Whitefield* (Boston: Tappan and Dennet, 1842), pp. 11–13.

[19] Thomas A. Schafer, 'Jonathan Edwards and Justification by Faith', *Church History*, December, 1951, pp. 55–57.

[20] Charles Hartshorn Maxson, *The Great Awaking in the Middle Colonies* (Chicago: The University of Chicago Press, 1920), pp. 139–151; Sweet, *Religion in the Development of American Culture*, p. 148; Sweet, *The Story of Religion in America*, pp. 184–200; William Warren Sweet, *Revivalism in America: Its Origin, Growth and Decline* (New York: Charles Scribner's Sons, 1944), p. 85.

[21] Tracy, *op. cit.*, pp. 39–46.

[22] Sweet, *Revivalism in America*, pp. 86–89; Jonathan Edwards, *Sinners in the Hands of An Angry God* (Louisville, Kentucky: Pentecostal Publishing Co., n. d.).

[23] Stephenson, *op. cit.*, pp. 56–57.

[24] Charles G. Finney, *Memoirs* (New York: A. S. Barnes & Co., 1876), p. 85.

[25] *Ibid*, p. 90.

[26] Carl Wittke, *We Who Built America* (New York: Prentice-Hall, Inc., 1939), pp. 477–482; Sweet, *Religion in the Development of American Culture*, pp. 282–311; Whitney R. Cross, *The Burned-Over District: The Social and Intellectual History of Enthusiastic Religion in Western New York, 1800–1850* (Ithaca, New York: Cornell University Press, 1950).

[27] Jan K. Van Baalan, *The Chaos of the Cults* (Grand Rapids: Wm. B. Eerdmans Publishing Co., 1942), pp. 18–38; 99–127; William Young, 'Demons Today?', *Moody Monthly*, May, 1956, pp. 20–21; 73; Sweet, *The Story of Religion in America*, pp. 404–405.

[28] Sweet, *Religion in the Development of American Culture*, pp. 305–311.

[29] John R. Rice, 'Coming Without Signs', *Sword*, October 14, 1955, p. 1; L. Sale-Harrison, 'The Combination of Nations and God's Great Prophetic Word', *Moody Monthly*, June, 1940, p. 549.

[30] V. Raymond Edman, 'From Luther to Barth', *Moody Monthly*, August, 1956, pp. 22–23; Bernard Ramm, *The Christian View of Science and Scripture* (Grand Rapids: Wm. B. Eerdmans Publishing Co., 1954), pp. 171–197; John H. Randall, Jr., *The Making of the Modern Mind* (Boston: Houghton Mifflin Co., 1940), pp. 485–489.

[31] Fredrick E. Mayer, *The Religious Bodies of America* (St. Louis: Concordia Publishing House, 1954), pp. 474–475.

[32] Ibid.

[33] Oswald T. Allis, The Unity of Isaiah: A Study in Prophecy (Philadelphia: The Presbyterian & Reformed Publishing Co., 1950), pp. 1–2; Rolland Emerson Wolfe, Men of Prophetic Fire (Boston: The Beacon Press, 1951), pp. 5–10; Phillips E. Osgood, Religion Without Magic (Boston: The Beacon Press, 1954), pp. 137–138.

[34] Irving E. Howard, 'The Origins of the Social Gospel', Faith and Freedom, May, 1952, pp. 3–7.

[35] Stewart G. Cole, The History of Fundamentalism (New York: Richard R. Smith, Inc., 1931), pp. 16–20; Sweet, The Story of Religion in America, pp. 523–524; 532–534.

[36] Richard Hofstadter, The Age of Reform: From Bryan to F.D.R. (New York: Alfred A. Knopf 1955), pp 7–11; Benjamin L. Masse, The Catholic Mind Through Fifty Years: 1903–1935 (New York: The American Press, 1953), pp. 493–498; Gaius Atkins, Religion in Our Times (New York: Round Table Press, 1932), pp. 40–55.

[37] Howard, op. cit., pp. 4–7.

[38] Ibid.

[39] Atkins, op. cit., p. 65; Carl F. H. Henry, The Uneasy Conscience of Modern Fundamentalism (Grand Rapids: Wm. B. Eerdmans Publishing Co., 1947), p. 49.

[40] Arnold S. Nash, ed., Protestant Thought in the Twentieth Century (New York: The Macmillan Co., 1951), pp. 6–7; Harry M. Buck, 'Biblical Criticism and the Christian Faith', The Journal of Bible and Religion, January, 1956, p. 21.

[41] 'Is Evangelical Theology Changing?', Christian Life, March, 1956, p. 18.

[42] Hofstadter, op. cit., pp. 7–11.

[43] 'Be Ever on Guard', King's Business, November, 1916, p. 982; Atkins, op. cit., p. 227.

[44] The term 'substitutionary atonement' as used by the fundamentalists refers to the redemptive work of Jesus Christ on the cross with the results accruing to the benefit of others who place their faith in Christ and accept His sacrifice as adequate satisfaction to the offended, infinite majesty of God. Another term usually used is vicarious atonement or sacrifice.

[45] Cole, op. cit., pp. 34–35; Atkins, op. cit., pp. 222–227.

[46] Atkins, op. cit., p. 227.

[47] Catalog of the Nyack Missionary Training Institute, 1952–1953, p. 14.

[48] Catalog of the Moody Bible Institute, 1952–1953, p. 12.

[49] Catalog of the Providence Bible Institute, 1952–1953, p. 19.

[50] Catalog of Gordon College, 1952–1953, p. 8; Catalog of Shelton College, 1951–1952, p. 6.

[51] Frank E. Gaebelein, Christian Education in A Democracy (New York: Oxford University Press, 1951), p. 157.

[52] Hubert Reynhout, Jr., 'A Comparative Study of Bible Institute Curriculums', (Unpublished Master's Thesis in the Department of Education, University of Michigan, Ann Arbor, 1947), p. 2.

[53] Norman F. Furniss, The Fundamentalist Controversy, 1918–1931 (New Haven: Yale University Press, 1954), pp. 117–188.

[54] Ibid., pp. 12–13.

[55] The Fundamentals: A Testimony to the Truth. Vols. 1–12 (Chicago: Testimony Publishing Co., n.d.), entire.

56 *Ibid.*, Vols. 1–10, entire.

57 Bernard F. Ramm wrote a comprehensive statement in the *UEA*, March 15, 1951, pp. 2 and 23, which not only explains what the fundamentalists were fighting for but also why odious connotation has surrounded their name: '*Fundamentalism* originally referred to the belief that there were certain great truths in Christianity, which, if changed, would dissolve Christianity . . . In the last forty years another movement has developed within historical fundamentalism that has given the term an odious connotation. Men with much zeal, enthusiasm, and conviction, yet lacking in education or cultural breadth, and many times highly individualistic, took to the stump to defend the faith. Many times they were dogmatic beyond evidence, or were intractable of disposition, or were obnoxiously anti-cultural, anti-scientific, and anti- educational. Hence, the term came to mean one who-was bigoted, an obscurantist, a fidest, a fighter, and anti-intellectual.'

58 Bob Jones, Sr., 'Why Bob Jones University Was Founded', *Christian Life*, June, 1950, p. 28.

59 'Is Evangelical Theology Changing?', *op. cit.*, p. 18.

60 *Ibid*; Charles Francis Potter, *The Preacher and I* (New York: Crown Publishers, Inc., 1951), p. 427.

61 Furniss, *op. cit.*, p. 14.

62 *Ibid.*, pp. 49–50; 66–68; 109–121; 125–126.

63 *Ibid.*, pp. 49–100.

64 *Ibid.*, p. 56.

65 'Fundamentalists are Always Fighting', *The Fundamentalist*, April, 16, 1956, p. 3.

66 Harold John Ockenga, 'Can Fundamentalism Win America?', *The Moody Student*, June 27, 1947, p. 2.

67 'Dr. Luther Peak Joins Southern Baptists', *Sword*, June 15, 1956, p. 1.

68 *Ibid.*

69 Luther Peak, 'Why We Left Fundamentalism', *Baptist Standard*, April 7, 1956, p. 7.

70 *Ibid.*

71 Furniss, *op. cit.*, pp. 131–136; 170–176.

72 *Ibid.*, pp. 139–141.

73 *Ibid.*, p. 177; Carl McIntire, 'J. Gresham Machen - January, 1937–1957', *Beacon*, January 10, 1957, p. 1.

74 Ralph Lord Roy, *The Apostles of Discord* (Boston: Beacon Press, 1953), pp. 344–350.

75 Statement by F. M. Kepner, personal interview.

76 Furniss, *op. cit.*, pp. 103–118.

77 'Why the Conservative Baptist Association' (pamphlet published by the Conservative Baptist Association, Chicago, 1951), p. 3; Glenwood Blackmore, 'Northern Baptists Face Grave Doctrinal Issue', *UEA*, June 15, 1946, pp. 10–16.

78 *Ibid.*

79 *Ibid.*; 'The Conservative Baptist Association of America: Its Mission (pamphlet published by the Association, n.d.), pp. 3–10.

80 Furniss, *op. cit.*, pp. 119–126; Roy, *op. cit.*, pp. 350–358.

81 *Ibid.*

82 Furniss, *op. cit.*, pp. 178–181.

83 *Ibid.*

84 Edman, *op. cit.*, pp. 113–116.

85 On the publication of fundamentalist literature see Cole, *op. cit.*, pp. 240–245. For a concise history of the Old Fashioned Revival Hour see the *Bulletin of Fuller Theological Seminary*, April-June, 1955, pp. 6–8.

CHAPTER II

1 Furniss, *op. cit.*, p. 181.

2 Francis L. Patton, *Fundamental Christianity* (New York: The Macmillan Co., 1926), pp. 247–250.

3 Frequently secessionist churches identified themselves by use of the phrase 'An Independent Fundamental Church'.

4 Statement by the Reverend Jack Murray in an address before the American Council of Christian Churches of Ohio at Findlay, Ohio, November 1, 1949.

5 'By This Shall All Men Know', *Christian Life*, March, 1951, p. 22.

6 See Chapter 3. The term 'ecclesiastical' is here used opprobriously; cf. James DeForest Murch, *The Growing Super-Church* (Cincinnati: National Association of Evangelicals, 1952), pp. 5–36; 'The Perils of Independency', *Christianity Today*, November 12, 1956, pp. 20–24.

7 Carl McIntire, *Twentieth Century Reformation* (Collingswood, New Jersey: Christian Beacon Press, 1946), pp. 180–181.

8 Donald E. Hoke, 'Gentle Fighter', *Sunday*, October, 1943, p. 24.

9 McIntire, *op. cit.*, p. 181.

10 'Which Council?', (pamphlet published by the American Council of Christian Churches, n.d.), p. 3.

11 *Ibid.*; Carl McIntire, *The Testimony of Separation* (Collingswood, New Jersey: Christian Beacon Press, 1952), p. 60.

12 The fundamentalists used the terms modernism and liberalism interchangeably. Liberalism is defined by them as a 'movement which rejects the authority of the Bible as the inerrant Word of God, tending to interpret it in the light of modern-day science and philosophy', and modernism is 'sometimes equated with liberalism . . .' 'Is Evangelical Theology Changing?', *loc. cit.*

13 'Constitution of the American Council of Christian Churches' (pamphlet published by the American Council of Christian Churches, n.d.), Article I, Section 2 (e).

14 McIntire, *Testimony of Separation*, p. 60.

15 *Newsweek*, September 29, 1941, p. 56; McIntire, *Twentieth Century Reformation*, p. 187.

16 Carl McIntire, 'The Shadow of the American Council of Christian Churches', *Beacon*, December 27, 1956, p. 4; McIntire, *Twentieth Century Reformation*, pp. 190–192.

17 McIntire, *Twentieth Century Reformation*, pp. 186, 196.

18 *Ibid.*, p. 196.

19 Murch, *Co-operation*, p. 51.

20 *Ibid.*; McIntire, *The Testimony of Separation*, pp. 3–11.

21 Murch, *Co-operation*, p. 53.

22 *Ibid.*; McIntire, *The Testimony of Separation*, pp. 3–11.

23 George L. Lord, 'Why the NAE is Succeeding', *UEA*, March 15, 1956, p. 5; Murch, *Co-operation*, pp. 52–53.

24 Murch, *Co-operation*, pp. 56–59.

25 Hoke, *op. cit.*, p. 24; Murch, *Co-operation*, p. 59.

26 Murch, *Co-operation*, pp. 59, 71; Ford, *loc. cit.*

27 Murch, *Co-operation*, pp. 60–63.

28 *Ibid.*, pp. 64–65.

29 'We Get Slapped', *UEA*, February 15, 1946, p. 2.

30 'Sectarianism Receives New Lease on Life', *Century*, May 19, 1943, p. 596.

31 Murch, *Co-operation*, pp. 65–66.

32 Ford, *loc. Cit.*

33 Murch, *Co-operation*, pp. 68–70.

34 James DeForest Murch, 'Fundamental Principles in Papal–U. S. Relations', *UEA*, March 1, 1946, pp. 4–5; Murch, *Co-operation*, pp. 69–70; Paul Blanshard, *American Freedom and Catholic Power* (Boston: Beacon Press, 1949), p. 41; Freeman Butts, *The American Tradition in Religion and Education* (Boston: Beacon Press, 1950).

35 'As Others See the NAE', *UEA*, March 1, 1947, p. 7; J. Elwin Wright, 'Growth of NAE is Modern Miracle', *UEA*, April 15, 1946, p. 5; Harold J. Ockenga, 'The 'Pentecostal' Bogey', *UEA*, February 15, 1947, pp. 12–13; 'N. A. E. Meets in Cleveland', *Century*, May 16, 1956, p. 622; Murch, *Co-operation*, p. 202.

36 'The Evangelical Year', *UEA*, January 1, 1957, p. 5.

37 John T. Nichol, 'The Role of the Pentecostal Movement in American Church History', *Gordon Review*, December, 1956, pp. 127–131; Sweet, *The Story of Religion in America*, pp. 505–506.

38 Nichol, *op. cit.*, p. 133.

39 McIntire, *The Testimony of Separation*, p. 61.

40 *Catalog of the National Bible Institute*, 1949–1950, p. 20.

41 McIntire, *Twentieth Century Reformation*, p. 203; McIntire, 'The Shadow of the American Council', *op. cit.*, p. 4.

42 'The Attack Upon Dr. McIntire', *Beacon*, July 12, 1956, p. 8; 'Associated Press Feature Writer Sends Story on McIntire to Paper,' *Ibid.*, p. 1.

43 Kenneth A. Horner, Jr., 'An Analysis of Problems in the Bible Presbyterian Church and Separation Movement' (mimeographed report by the author, May 17, 1956), pp. 7–8; 'A One-Man Denomination', *Free Press*, March 26, 1956, pp. 1–2; J. Oliver Buswell, Jr., 'An Open Letter to the 'Committee for True Presbyterianism', *The Bible Press*, July 22, 1955, p. 1; 'Buswell Released from Shelton', *Ibid.*, pp. 9–10.

44 J. Oliver Buswell, Jr., 'Recent Sad Meetings and Their Significance', *Bible Presbyterian Observer*, March, 1956, p. 9.

45 Horner, *op. cit.*, pp. 1–5; 'The Attack Upon Dr. McIntire', *loc. cit.*

46 Horner, *op. cit.*, pp. 7–9.

47 *Ibid.*

48 Robert G. Rayburn, 'American Council of Christian Churches—Its Statistics', *Bible Presbyterian Observer*, November, 1955, pp. 1–2.

49 'Constitution of the American Council of Christian Churches', Article I–II.

50 This ineligibility was transferred to the National Council, successors of the Federal Council, after it was organized in November, 1950.

51 'Constitution of the American Council of Christian Churches', Article I, Section 2 (e).

52 *Ibid.*, Section 3 (c).

53 Roy, *op. cit.*, p. 198.

54 This explains why the Methodist Evangelical Church is shown as member of both the National Association of Evangelicals and the American Council in Tables I and III.

55 Roy, *op. cit.*, pp. 197, 396. The American Episcopal Church (Evangelical) is not listed in Table III because it was expelled in 1945.

56 Stephen W. Paine, 'Separation'—Is Separating Evangelicals (Boston: Fellowship Press, 1951), pp. 23–24.

57 'The A.C.C.C. Situation', *Bible Presbyterian Observer*, December, 1955, p. 6; Rayburn, *op. cit.*, p.8.

58 Rayburn, *op. cit.*, p. 2.

59 *Ibid.*

60 *Ibid.*, pp. 1–2.

61 'Ketcham Explains ACCC Statistics', *The Free Press*, July 6, 1956, pp. 23–24.

62 Paine, *loc. cit.*

63 'The A.C.C.C. Situation', *op. cit.*, p. 8; Horner, *op. cit.*, p. 3; 'Buswell Released from Shelton College', *op. cit.*, p. 10.

64 Horner, *op. cit.*, p. 6.

65 'Bible Presbyterians Repudiate McIntire', *The Free Press*, July 6, 1956, p. 1; 'International Council of Christian Churches' (pamphlet published by the I.C.C.C., n.d.), entire.

66 'Bible Presbyterians Repudiate McIntire', *loc. cit.*; *Bulletin of Covenant College and Theological Seminary*, April, 1956, pp. 8, 10–11, 75.

67 Horner, *op. cit.*, p. 9; 'The Bible Presbyterian Church Association', *The Free Press*, July 6, 1956, p. 12.

68 *UEA*, August 1, 1957, p. 9.

69 Horner, *loc. cit.*

70 See the section on The fundamentalist controversy in this study above.

CHAPTER III

1 *Bulletin of the Los Angeles Baptist Theological Seminary*, June, 1949, p. 4.

2 Nash, *op. cit.*, p. 20.

3 *Ibid.*, pp. 130–131.

4 Fred I. Cairns, 'Every Crisis Produces Its Prophets of Doom', *What is This Neo-Orthodoxy?* (Boston: American Unitarian Association, 1948), p. 15; Louis Berkhof, *Recent Trends in Theology* (Grand Rapids: Wm. B. Eerdmans Publishing Co., 1944),p. 42.

5 Ernest H. Klotsche and J. Theodore Mueller, *The History of Christian Doctrine* (Philadelphia: Muhlenberg Press, 1945), p. 339.

6 Nash, *op. cit.*, pp. 114–115, 117.

7 *Ibid.*, pp. 117, 120.

8 Berkhof, *loc. cit.*

9 Klotsche and Mueller, *loc. cit.*; *Gordon Review*, February, 1955, p. 33.

10 Reinhold Niebuhr, *The Nature and Destiny of Man: A Christian Interpretation*, Vol. II, *Human Destiny* (New York: Charles Scribner's Sons, 1943), p. 178; Emil Brunner, *The Divine-Human Encounter* (Philadelphia: The Westminster Press, 1943), Chapter 2; Burtt, *op. cit.*, p. 396.

11 Niebuhr, *op. cit.*, p. 4.

12 *Ibid.*, p. 178; Klotsche and Mueller, *loc. cit.*

13 Charles W. Kegley and Robert W. Bretall, *Reinhold Niebuhr: His Religious, Social, and Political Thought*, Vol. II (The Library of Living Theology: New York: The Macmillan Co., 1956), pp. 198–199; Niebuhr, *op. cit.*, Vol I, *Human Nature* (New York: Charles Scribner's Sons, 1941), pp. 178–181; Berkhof, *op. cit.*, p. 44.

14 Walter M. Horton, *Christian Theology: An Ecumenical Approach* (New York: Harper & Brothers Publishers, 1955), p. 198; Nels F. S. Ferré, *The Christian Faith* (New York: Harper & Brothers Publishers, 1942), p. 109.

15 Horton, *op. cit.*, pp. 197–198; Ferré, *op. cit.*, pp. 106–110.

16 H. Richard Niebuhr, *Christ and Culture* (New York: Harper & Brothers, 1951), p. 28.

17 Ferré, *op. cit.*, p. 160.

18 Kegley and Bretall, *op. cit.*, p. 438.

19 David H. C. Read, *The Christian Faith* (New York: Charles Scribner's Sons, 1956), p. 84; Edmund Schlink, 'Christ—the Hope of the World', *Century*, August 25, 1954, p. 1003.

20 Ferré, *op. cit.*, pp. 177–178.

21 Reinhold Niebuhr, *op. cit.*, Vol. II, pp. 294–299; Charles M. Laymon, ed., *The International Lesson Annual* (Nashville: Abingdon Press, 1957), p. 137.

22 Walter G. Muelder, 'The Second Coming of Jesus', *Christian Advocate*, August 25, 1955 as photographically reproduced in the *Beacon*, September 27, 1955, p. 2.

23 Reinhold Niebuhr, *op. cit.*, Vol. II, p. 49.

24 Ferré, *op. cit.*, p. 178.

25 Horton, *op. cit.*, p. 32.

26 Nash, *op. cit.*, p. 120; Earl A. Loomis, Jr., 'Fundamentalism', *His*, April, 1948, pp. 7–8; Murch, *Co-operation*, pp. 210–211.

27 Stephen Paine, 'God's Word for God's World', *UEA*, May 1, 1950, p. 12; Nash, *op. cit.*

28 *Ibid.*, p. 12.

29 *Ibid.*

30 *Ibid.* The term neo-orthodoxy as used in this study is a comprehensive term which includes Christian realism. The use of the term neo-orthodoxy in this manner might not be philosophically correct, but most fundamentalists regard neo-orthodoxy and Christian realism as basically the same. Both mediate the problems of the Scriptures from the perspective of man and history, while fundamentalism mediates the problems of man and history from the perspective of the Scriptures. See Edward John Carnell, 'Can Billy Graham Slay the Giant?', *Christianity Today*, May 13, 1957, p. 3.

31 *New York Times*, August 21, 1948, p. 16.

32 'International', *Christian Life*, August, 1948, p. 10; Roy, *op. cit.*, p. 191. Roy stated that McIntire's strategy in holding meetings in the same place at the same time of those whom he opposed was 'a deliberate attempt to create confusion' and 'blatant attempts to harass the movement toward Protestant unity . . .'

[33] *New York Times*, August 21, 1948, p. 16.

[34] *Ibid.*, September 7, 1948, p. 23.

[35] Carl McIntire, *Modern Tower of Babel* (Collingswood, New Jersey: Christian Beacon Press, 1949), pp 224–234. McIntire identified his movement as the 'Twentieth Century Reformation' in his book by the same title.

[36] Roy, *op. cit.*, pp. 303–304; Erwin A. Gaede, 'The Federal Council of the Churches of Christ in America: The Evolution of Social Policy' (unpublished Master's Thesis, Department of Political Science, University of Wisconsin, 1951), p. 95.

[37] This item was taken from the footnote in Gaede, *loc. cit.*

[38] 'Mr. Pew and the Clergy', *Century*, February 22, 1956, pp. 229–231.

[39] *Ibid.*

[40] McIntire, *Modern Tower of Babel*, p. 227.

[41] *Ibid.*, pp. 230–231.

[42] *New York Times*, August 21, 1948, p. 16.

[43] McIntire, *Modern Tower of Babel*, p. 230.

[44] *Beacon*, November 18, 1948, p. 2 as quoted in Roy, *op. cit.*, p. 192.

[45] *New York Times*, September 3, 1948, p. 11.

[46] *Ibid.*, pp. 1, 11.

[47] *Ibid.*

[48] *Ibid.*

[49] *Ibid.*

[50] *Ibid.*, September 4, 1948, p. 16.

[51] *Ibid.*, October 30, 1948, p. 16.

[52] Harold E. Fey, 'The Amsterdam World Assembly of Churches', *Century*, October 6, 1948, pp. 1034–1035.

[53] *Ibid.*, p. 1035.

[54] *Ibid.*, p. 1039; John C. Bennett, 'Capitalism and Communism at Amsterdam', *Century*, December 15, 1948, p. 1364.

[55] *New York Times*, October 1, 1948, p. 24; Kegley and Bretall, *op. cit.* p. 73.

[56] E. Stanley Jones, *Is the Kingdom of God Realism?* (Nashville: Abingdon-Cokesbury Press, 1940), p. 88.

[57] *New York Times*, September 3, 1948, p. 11.

[58] Noel Smith, 'The National Council and the Revised S.V.' *Christian Victory*, March, 1956, p. 36.

[59] *New York Times*, September 3, 1948, p. 11.

[60] E. Schuyler English, 'World Prospect—The Ecumenical Movement', *Our Hope*, March, 1952, pp. 529–530.

[61] Horton, *op. cit.*, p. 2.

[62] 'Appraising Amsterdam', *Century*, September 29, 1948, p. 1000.

[63] James DeForest Murch, 'God's Church and Man's Design', *UEA*, April 1, 1949, p. 11.

[64] 'The Coming Great Church', *Beacon*, March 13, 1952, pp. 1, 8.

[65] Murch, 'God's Church and Man's Design', *loc. cit.*

[66] 'The Coming Great Church', *loc. cit.*

Notes: The resurgence of militant fundamentalism   157

[67] Stephen Nenoff, *Two Worlds: U.S.A.–U.S.S.R.* (Chicago: Midland Publishing Co., 1946), p. 243.

[68] McIntire, *Twentieth Century Reformation*, p. 99.

[69] Kegley and Bretall, *op. cit.*, p. 65; Fey, *op. cit.*, p. 1040; *New York Times*, September 3, 1948, p. 11; 'The Amsterdam Reports', *Century*, October 6, 1948, pp. 1051–1052; G. B. Wurth, 'Theological Climate in America', *Christianity Today*, February 18, 1957, p. 13; McIntire, *Modern Tower of Babel*, pp. 98–103.

[70] 'International Affairs—Christians in the Struggle for World Community', *The Christian Hope and the Task of the Church* (New York: Harper & Brothers Publishers, 1954), p. 12.

[71] Nenoff, *op. cit.*, p. 245.

[72] 'Spirit of Revival Marks Indianapolis Meeting', *UEA*, May 1, 1950, p. 5; 'The Bricker Amendment', *Western Voice*, June 15, 1955, p. 2.

[73] 'The Bricker Amendment', *loc. cit.*

[74] 'Spirit of Revival Marks Indianapolis Meeting', *loc. cit.*

[75] V. Raymond Edman, 'The Pathway to Peace', *The Christlife Magazine*, March, 1956, p. 7.

[76] *Ibid.*, p. 8.

[77] Millenialism is inextricably bound to the doctrine of Messianism, the belief that the goal of history is a state of blessedness, during which men will live in harmony under a divine sovereign seated on a physical, earthly throne for 1,000 years (millenium). Premillenialists teach there are two future resurrections, one of the righteous, another of the unrighteous, with 1,000 years separating them. The order of future events as taught by Premillenialists are essentially these: (1) the resurrection of saints, (2) the manifestation of anti-Christ and commencement of the Tribulation (Armageddon), (3) commencement of Christ's (Messiah's) millenial reign in Jerusalem in perfect justice with His saints and restored Israel, after Satan and his rebels have been bound and Armageddon ended by divine intervention, (4) the end of the millenium, after which Satan and his rebels are released and destroyed, and the final resurrection of the dead followed by the final judgment of the nations and people, and (5) the appearance of a new heaven and a new earth. Fredrick A. Tatford, 'The Second Company of Christ . . .', *Our Hope*, July, 1951, pp. 27–32; cf., George A. Smith, *The Book of Isaiah*, Vol. I (New York: A. C. Armstrong & Son, 1898), pp. 141–142; Albert Knudson, *The Religious Teaching of the Old Testament* (Nashville: Abingdon-Cokesbury Press, 1918), pp. 351–381; Charles P. Kent, *The Sermons*, Epistles and Apocalypses of Israel's Prophets (New York: Charles Scribner's Sons, 1910), p. 41.

[78] T. DeCourcy, 'Can the Jews Succeed in Palestine?', *Moody Monthly*, June, 1948, p. 724.

[79] This view is not held by the Jews. For a contrary opinion see Wilbur M. Smith, 'The Disappearance of the Messianic Hope in Contemporary Judaism', *Moody Monthly*, April, 1956, p. 26; 'Questions Asked a Rabbi', *American Judaism*, January, 1955, pp. 28–29.

[80] *Ibid.*

[81] C. S. Lewis, 'The World's Last Night', *His*, May, 1955, pp. 4, 23; Paul L. Arnold and Bernard Ramm (a symposium), 'Is Doctor Henry Right?', *UEA*, May 15, 1947, p. 5.

[82] McIntire, *Modern Tower of Babel*, pp. 5–6; Murch, Co-operation, p. 183; 'The United Nations A Tower of Babel', *The Defender Magazine*, July, 1953, p. 3; 'NAE Convention Resolutions', *UEA*, May 15, 1956, p. 7.

[83] James DeForest Murch, 'In the Pattern of Peaceful Coexistence', *UEA*, May 1, 1956, p. 9.

[84] Wilbur M. Smith, *The Increasing Peril* (Wheaton, Illinois: Van Kampen Press, 1947), pp. 9–11.

[85] *Ibid.*, p. 15.

[86] *Ibid.*, p. 12.

CHAPTER IV

[1] *New York Times*, November 26, 1950, p. 111; November 29, 1950, p. 44; November 30, 1950, p. 35; December 3, 1950, Sec. IV, p. 8.

[2] *Ibid.*, November 27, 1950, p. 27; 'Issues Joined', *Beacon*, November 30, 1950, p. 1; 'One Protestant Church', *Beacon*, July 6, 1950, p. 1.

[3] *Ibid.*

[4] 'Contending for the Faith', *Beacon*, November 30, 1950, p. 4.

[5] New York Times, November 27, 1950, p. 27; 'NCC', *Beacon*, November 30, 1950, p. 1.

[6] 'Cleveland', *Beacon*, September 21, 1950, p. 8.

[7] 'An Interpretive Report', *Beacon*, December 7, 1950, p. 8.

[8] *Ibid.*

[9] *Ibid.*

[10] *Ibid.*, p. 1.

[11] Murch, *The Growing Super-Church*, p. 5.

[12] *Ibid.*, entire.

[13] Carl McIntire, 'Imitating Rome', *Beacon*, December 14, 1950, p. 4; Verne P. Kaub, 'Super-Church is Born', *UEA*, January 1, 1951, p. 3.

[14] 'National Council Again', *Catholic Standard and Times*, December 15, 1950, as photographically reproduced in the *Beacon*, December 21, 1950, p. 8.

[15] Murch, *Co-operation*, p. 208.

[16] Murch, *The Growing Super-Church*, p. 36.

[17] Gaede, *op. cit.*, pp. 89–94; Roy, *op. cit.*, pp. 228–250; J. B. Matthews, 'Reds in Our Churches', *The American Mercury*, July, 1953, pp. 3, 13.

[18] John T. Flynn, *The Road Ahead: America's Creeping Revolution* (New York: The Devin-Adair Co., 1949), Chapter 10; Gaede, *op. cit.*; Arthur M. Schlesinger wrote in *The Age of Roosevelt: The Crisis of the Old Order, 1919–1933* (Boston: Houghton Mifflin Co., 1957), pp. 200–201 that Flynn said during the depression that capitalism was doomed unless the individual investor was replaced by 'investment pools, operating under government supervision'.

[19] Gaede, *op. cit.*, pp. 90–92; 'How Red is the Federal Council of Churches?' (Madison, Wisconsin: American Council of Christian Laymen, 4th printing, February, 1950).

[20] 'How Red is the Federal Council of Churches?'

[21] *Ibid.*

[22] Letter from Verne P. Kaub, March 10, 1950.

[23] Gaede, *op. cit.*, p. 92.

[24] *Ibid.*, p. 94.

[25] *Ibid.*, p. 95.

Notes: The aggravation of militant fundamentalism   159

²⁶ *Reader's Digest*, February, 1950, p. 138; 'Methodist Social Action Federation . . .', *Beacon*, February 23, 1950, p. 1; *Oklahoma City Times*, February 14, 1950, reproduced photographically in the *Beacon*, February 23, 1950, p. 4.

²⁷ Letter from Verne P. Kaub, March 10, 1950.

²⁸ *Ibid.*

²⁹ E. Stanley Jones, 'What the United Church Crusade Proved', *Century*, January 14, 1948, pp. 42–43.

³⁰ See the section on The Communist Issue, Chapter 4, in this study.

³¹ Pasadena *Independent*, December 1, 1950, p. 3 as photographically reproduced in the *Beacon*, December 1, 1950.

³² Reference to these two newspapers was made in the *Beacon*, December 1, 1950.

³³ Pasadena *Independent*, *loc. cit.*

³⁴ *Ibid.*

³⁵ Flynn, *op. cit.*, pp. 104–112.

³⁶ Pasadena *Independent*, *loc. cit.*

³⁷ *Ibid.*

³⁸ *Ibid.*

³⁹ *Congressional Record*, January 20, 1956, pp. 863–864 as quoted in *Western Voice*, February 29, 1950.

⁴⁰ Carl McIntire, 'Methodist Church Presents Socialist Propaganda as Kingdom of God', *Beacon*, October 5, 1950, pp. 1, 8.

⁴¹ *Ibid.*

⁴² 'Bishop Oxnam Blasts ACCC at Meeting in Pittsburgh', *Beacon*, February 21, 1952, pp. 1, 8.

⁴³ For titles of some of McIntire's publications see the *Beacon*, July 27, 1950, p. 7; December 17, 1953, p. 8.

⁴⁴ *New York Times*, March 10, 1953, pp. 1, 16; 'Probing Reds in Religion', *American*, May 30, 1953, p. 235; 'Investigation of Communist Clergy Occupies First Place in Religious and Secular News', *Beacon*, May 21, 1953, pp. 1, 8.

⁴⁵ 'ACCC Issues Statement on Important Current Problems', *Beacon*, May 14, 1953, p. 2.

⁴⁶ Philadelphia *Evening Bulletin*, June 26, 1953 as photographically reproduced in the *Beacon*, July 2, 1953, pp. 1, 8.

⁴⁷ 'Congressman Jackson Receives ACCC Petitions', *Beacon*, May 14, 1953, pp. 1, 8.

⁴⁸ *Ibid.*, p. 1.

⁴⁹ *Ibid.*, p. 8.

⁵⁰ Matthews, *loc. cit.* Arthur M. Schlesinger said Matthews was one of those during the depression who believed capitalism 'meant poverty and unemployment', 'imperialism and war', while communism 'meant jobs and security', 'freedom and peace'. See Schlesinger, *The Age of Roosevelt*, p. 22.

⁵¹ *New York Times*, July 3, 1953, pp. 1, 6; July 4, 1953, p. 4; July 8, 1953, p. 1.

⁵² *Ibid.*, July 7, 1953, p. 1; July 8, 1953, p. 1.

⁵³ *Ibid.*, July 7, 1953, p. 11.

⁵⁴ *Ibid.*, July 22, 1953, p. 1; 'Case of the Missing Clergy', *Register*, November, 1953, p. 14;

Bishop Oxnam and the Un-American Activities Committee (Boston: Beacon Press, 1953), pp. 28–29.

⁵⁵ Ralph Lord Roy, 'Mr. Protestant and the Inquisitors', *Register*, September, 1953, pp. 12–13; *Cleveland Press*, July 23, 1953, p. 14.

⁵⁶ *New York Times*, July 22, 1953, p. 4; Roy, 'Mr. Protestant', *loc. cit.*; 'Bishop Oxnam's Challenge', *Century*, August 5, 1953, pp. 886–887; *Bishop Oxnam and the Un-American Activities Committee*, pp. 14, 20–21.

⁵⁷ Roy, 'Mr. Protestant', *loc. cit.*; 'Bishop Oxnam's Challenge', *loc. cit.*; *Bishop Oxnam and the Un-American Activities Committee, loc. cit.*

⁵⁸ Donald Grey Barnhouse, 'Oxnam', *Eternity*, October, 1953, p. 8.

⁵⁹ 'Evangelicals Join Issue of Modernism and Communism in Churches With Oxnam in San Francisco Bay Area', *Beacon*, November 3, 1955, p. 1.

⁶⁰ Carl McIntire, *Servants of Apostasy* (Collingswood, New Jersey: Christian Beacon Press, 1955), p. 110; Ralph Lord Roy, 'Blueprint of Discord', *Century*, June 30, 1954, p. 782.

⁶¹ Roy, 'Blueprint of Discord', *loc. cit.*; 'ACCC to Meet at Fort Worth', *Western Voice*, February 29, 1954, p. 1.

⁶² *Beacon*, March 18, 1954, pp. 2, 4; McIntire, *Servants of Apostasy*, pp. 110–111; *Report on Civil Liberties: January 1951–June 1955* (New York: American Civil Liberties Union, 1953), p. 49.

⁶³ 'Attack Launched on Evanston Delegates', *Century*, March 17, 1954, p. 324.

⁶⁴ *Ibid.*

⁶⁵ McIntire, *Servants of Apostasy*, pp. 110–112.

⁶⁶ *Ibid.*, p. 113.

⁶⁷ Donald Grey Barnhouse, 'Hromadka . . . Red Stooge or Saint?', *Eternity*, September, 1954, pp. 6–7, 33.

⁶⁸ Carl McIntire, 'Barnhouse & Hromadka', *Beacon*, September 9, 1954, p. 4.

⁶⁹ Barnhouse, 'Hromadka', *op. cit.*, p. 7.

⁷⁰ McIntire, *Servants of Apostasy*, pp. 110–113.

⁷¹ *Ibid.*, p. 337.

⁷² E. J. P. Connor, 'The Revised Standard Version', *Beacon*, March 18, 1954, pp. 2–3.

⁷³ Peter Chew, 'The Great Bible Controversy', *Look*, February 10, 1953, p. 97.

⁷⁴ Murch, 'God's Word and the Church's Witness', *op. cit.*, p. 15; Connor, *loc. cit.*; 'Clergymen to Protest Revised Standard Version of Bible', *Beacon*, February 5, 1953, p. 8; 'The New Revised Standard Version', *Moody Monthly*, December 12, 1952, p. 269; 'The New Unholy Bible', *The Defender*, November, 1952, pp. 8–9.

⁷⁵ John Haverstick, 'Which Bible for You?', *Saturday Review of Literature*, November 10, 1956, p. 53.

⁷⁶ *Cleveland Press*, November 24, 1952, p. 15; Chew, *loc. cit.*

⁷⁷ *Cleveland Press*, December 1, 1952, p. 8; *Cleveland News*, December 1, 1952, p. 26.

⁷⁸ *Beacon*, November 20, 1952, December 25, 1952, January 22, 1953, and February 5, 1953.

⁷⁹ 'Clergymen to Protest Revised Version of the Bible', *op. cit.*, p. 3.

⁸⁰ Chew, *loc. cit.*

⁸¹ Connor, *loc. cit.*; Carl McIntire, *The New Bible* (pamphlet, Collingswood, New Jersey: Christian Beacon Press, n.d.), pp. 3–9.

82 'The New Unholy Bible', *loc. cit.*

83 *Ibid.*

84 'Clergymen to Protest Revised Standard Version of the Bible', *loc. cit.*

85 James DeForest Murch, 'The Way a Super-Church Works', *UEA*, November 15, 1952, pp. 8–9; 'NCC Bible Adopts Roman Catholic Lord's Prayer', *Beacon*, October 16, 1952, p. 1; 'Time' Likens NCC's Letter to Roman Catholic Hierarchy's Deliverances', *Beacon*, December 25, 1952, p. 8.

86 Paul Griffis, 'Let's Be Fair', *Christian Life*, March, 1953, p. 10.

CHAPTER V

1 Murch, *Co-operation*, p. 109.

2 *Ibid.*, p. 115.

3 *Ibid.*, p. 110.

4 'Christian Radio', *Christian Life*, August, 1948, p. 16.

5 'Christian Radio', *loc. cit.*; 'Radio Log of Evangelical Broadcasts', *Christian Life*, August, 1948, p. 17.

6 'Christian Commercial Stations', *Christian Life*, August, 1949, p. 14.

7 *Ibid*; Kenneth L. Wilson, 'The Religious World Has to Step Lively to Keep up with the Joneses', *Christian Herald*, June, 1951, p. 26.

8 'How Big is Gospel Radio?', *Christian Life*, January, 1954, pp. 24, 57, 86.

9 Paul A. Hopkins, 'Dr. Barnhouse Moves to N.B.C. Network July 1', *Eternity*, July, 1956, p. 6.

10 *Bulletin of Fuller Theological Seminary*, April-June, 1955, pp. 6–7.

11 *Ibid.*

12 *Ibid.*

13 *Ibid.*; Dorothy C. Haskins, *Christians You would Like to Know* (Grand Rapids: Zondervan Publishing House, 1954), pp. 18–19; 'Radio', *Christian Life*, July, 1949, p. 29.

14 Stanley High, *Billy Graham: The Personal Story of the Man, His Message, and His Mission* (New York: McGraw-Hill Book Co., 1956), pp. 160–166.

15 'Religious Hucksters', *Time*, July 30, 1956, p. 43.

16 *Ibid.*

17 *Ibid.*

18 'Broadcasting Affiliate Scorns National Council Stand', *Century*, May 16, 1956, p. 622; 'What Now for Gospel Radio?', *Sunday*, October, 1944, pp. 7–8; *Century*, June 20, 1956, p. 743.

19 Letter from Henry C. Geiger, June 4, 1956; 'That They Might Know Christ' (pamphlet published by the Children's Hour, n.d.).

20 'Crawford Makes History', *Christian Life*, November, 1949, p. 36; 'Seeing is Believing', *Christian Life*, April, 1950, p. 14; *Moody Alumni News*, November-December, 1956, p. 4; Paul A. Hopkins, 'Television', *Eternity*, October, 1955, pp. 6–7.

21 Noel Smith, 'Big Boy—Barnhouse', *Western Voice*, April 11, 1956, p. 2; Hopkins, 'Television', *loc. cit.*

22 Murch, *Co-operation*, p. 72.

23 *Ibid.*, p. 80.

[24] Donald Hoke, 'Now—A Gospel Radio Network', *Sunday*, March, 1944, p. 57.

[25] *Ibid.*; McIntire, *Twentieth Century Reformation*, pp. 58–59.

[26] Murch, *Co-operation*, pp. 74–75.

[27] Glenwood Blackmore, 'Shall the NCC Control Religious Broadcasting?', *UEA*, July 1, 1956, p. 6; 'American Council', *Christian Life & Times*, September, 1946, p. 23.

[28] Murch, *Co-operation*, pp. 75–78.

[29] *Ibid.*, p. 78.

[30] *Ibid.*

[31] *Ibid.*, p. 79.

[32] *Ibid.*

[33] *Ibid.*, pp. 79–81; Blackmore, 'Shall The NCC Control Religious Broadcasting?', *op. cit.*, pp. 5–6; Theodore Elsner, 'NRB—Ever Present Help in Evangelical Radio', *UEA*, March 1, 1949, p. 5.

[34] 'NBC Sells More Time for Religion', *UEA*, July 1, 1956, pp. 10–11; 'Evangelicals Fear Radio, TV Restrictions', *Moody Monthly*, June, 1956, pp. 5–6.

[35] *Century*, June 20, 1956, p. 743; 'Condemn Sale of Radio Time for Religious Use', *UEA*, April 1, 1956, p. 9; 'Broadcast Probe', *Christianity Today*, February 4, 1957, p. 30.

[36] Speech by Ralph Neighbour in Cleveland, Ohio during the convention of the National Association of Evangelicals, April, 1956.

[37] James DeForest Murch, 'Spiritual Unity in Action at Cleveland', *UEA*, May 15, 1956, p. 6.

[38] *Ibid.*; Blackmore, 'Shall The NCC Control Religious Broadcasting?', *loc. cit.*

[39] Russell T. Hitt, 'Whither Christian Radio?', *Christian Life*, August, 1950, pp. 13–14.

[40] *Ibid.*

[41] 'Youth for Christ', *Christian Life & Times*, September, 1946, p. 4.

[42] 'Youth Alone & Liked', *Sunday*, April, 1946, pp. 19–20, 54–57; Carl F. H. Henry, 'Accent on Youth', *Sunday*, January, 1945, p. 19.

[43] Henry, 'Accent on Youth', *loc. cit.*; 'The History of Youth for Christ', *Christian Life & Times*, July, 1946, p. 61.

[44] *Ibid.*; High, *op. cit.*, pp. 140–143.

[45] High, *loc. cit.*

[46] 'People You Know', *The Ohio Universalist*, April, 1956, p. 3.

[47] Wolfe, *op. cit.*, pp. 4–5.

[48] Henry, 'Accent on Youth', *op. cit.*, p. 18.

[49] Mel Larsen, *Young Man on Fire: The Story of Torrey Johnson and Youth for Christ* (Chicago: Youth for Christ Publications, 1945); 'The History of Youth for Christ', *op. cit.*, p. 59.

[50] 'The History of Youth for Christ', *op. cit.*, pp. 61, 63, 69–70; Henry, 'Accent on Youth', *op. cit.*, pp. 19, 48–49; 'Youth Alone & Liked', *op. cit.*, p. 21; 'Behind the Scenes at a Youth for Christ Meeting', *Sunday*, September, 1946, p. 43.

[51] *Ibid.*

[52] 'Weston on Hand', *Western Voice*, May 16, 1956, p. 1.

[53] 'The History of Youth for Christ', *op. cit.*, pp. 58–59, 65; Henry, 'Accent on Youth',

op. cit., pp. 18, 20, 22; High, op. cit. p. 140. Fundamentalist vocalists, such as Bev. Shea, 'Redd' Harper, star in Billy Graham's evangelistic films, Bill Carle, former New York star on Broadway, Stuart Hamblen, and others who appeared on Youth for Christ programs became gospel music recording artists. Shea and Hamblen were also popular in other than fundamentalist circles. Hamblen composed several gospel songs which became 'hit' tunes. Millions of copies of his songs and records were sold. *Christian Life*, May, 1955, p. 69.

54 *Ibid.*

55 'The History of Youth for Christ', op. cit., pp. 67–68; Jack Hamilton, *Youth for Christ High School Bible Club Directors' Manual* (Wheaton, Illinois: Youth for Christ International, n.d.), pp. 4–5; 'What and Why of Youth for Christ' (pamphlet published by Youth for Christ International, n.d.), pp. 3–8; Henry, 'Accent on Youth', op. cit., p. 20.

56 'History of Youth for Christ', loc. cit.; Hamilton, loc. cit.; 'What and Why of Youth for Christ', pp. 3–8; Henry, 'Accent on Youth', loc. cit.

57 'What and Why of Youth for Christ', loc. cit.; 'The History of Youth for Christ', op. cit., p. 63.

58 Vernon Louis Parrington, *Main Currents in American Thought*, Vol. I, *1620–1800: The Colonial Mind* (New York: Harcourt, Brace and Co., 1930), p. 160.

59 'Youth for Christ Hi-School Clubs' (pamphlet published by Youth for Christ International, n.d.); Henry, 'Accent on Youth', op. cit., pp. 48–49.

60 'So You're Going to be a Hi-C Leader', (mimeographed manual, n.d.), entire.

61 'Teen-Agers on the Rampage', *Christian Life*, February, 1954, pp. 20–21.

62 Leslie B. Flynn, 'These Teen-Agers Are Not Delinquents', *Christian Life*, November, 1951, p. 72.

63 *Ibid.*

64 *Ibid.*, p. 80.

65 *Ibid.*, p. 77; Carl Brent Swisher, *American Constitutional Development* (Boston: Houghton Mifflin Co., 1954), p. 1030.

66 Flynn, 'These Teen-Agers Are Not Delinquents', op. cit., pp. 21–22.

67 *Ibid.*, p. 79; Dorothy Haskins, 'Youth Ablaze', *Power*, March 16, 1952, p. 2.

68 From a report distributed by the Inter-Varsity Christian Fellowship, 1950.

69 *Ibid.*, p. 19.

70 *Ibid.*

71 *Ibid.*, p. 15.

72 Inter-Varsity Christian Fellowship Annual Report, 1950, p. 15.

73 *Ibid.*, p. 16.

74 *Cleveland Plain Dealer*, February 12, 1953, p. 6.

75 *Ibid.*

76 'One Campus and One God', *His*, May, 1946, p. 20; Robert Oerter, 'College Students Want Christ', *Moody Monthly*, September, 1943, p. 45; 'Christianity on the Campus', *Moody Monthly*, December, 1941, p. 207.

77 Inter-Varsity Christian Fellowship Annual Report, 1950, p. 14.

CHAPTER VI
1 See Chapter 1.

2 Reynhout, op. cit., p. 24; 'Bible Institutes and Colleges' (typed report of the Accrediting

Association of Bible Institutes and Bible Colleges, n.d.), p. 2. These two sources show different statistics for the period covered. Since the latter reference was the latest its statistics were chosen.

³ *Ibid.*; James DeForest Murch, 'Revolution in Education', *UEA*, July 1, 1947, p. 14; *Manual of the Accrediting Association of Bible Institutes and Bible Colleges* (Providence, R.I., 1955), p. 3.

⁴ See Chapter 1.

⁵ 'Who's Who of Christian Education', *Christian Life*, June, 1952, pp. 19–20; Reynhout, *op. cit.*, p. 3.

⁶ *The Catalog of the Simpson Bible Institute, 1951–1952*, p. 11; *The Catalog of the Northwestern Schools, 1949–1950*, p. 30; William A. Mierop, 'The Place and Purpose of Bible Institutes', *Christian Life & Times*, September, 1947, pp. 30–31; Clarence Mason, 'Why Choose Bible School?', *Sunday*, April, 1948, pp. 39–40.

⁷ Gaebelein, *op. cit.*, pp. 158–159.

⁸ Mitchell, Curtis, 'I Was Born Again', *The American Weekly*, January 16, 1955, p. 6.

⁹ This is the term frequently used in connection with personal evangelism.

¹⁰ Statement by Emerson Shuck, Dean at Bowling Green State University, Bowling Green, Ohio, 1956.

¹¹ *Catalog of Moody Bible Institute of Chicago, 1952–1953*, p. 40.

¹² See footnote 9.

¹³ Gaebelein, *op. cit.*; Reynhout, *op. cit.*, pp. 15–18.

¹⁴ *Catalog of the Moody Bible Institute of Chicago, 1952–1953*, p. 13.

¹⁵ *Catalog of the Philadelphia Bible Institute, 1951–1952*, p. 24.

¹⁶ Gaebelein, *op. cit.*, pp. 171–172.

¹⁷ Hereafter the term will refer to both Bible Institutes and Bible Colleges.

¹⁸ Gaebelein, *op. cit.*, p. 172.

¹⁹ *Ibid.*, pp. 172–173.

²⁰ *Ibid.*

²¹ Reynhout, *op. cit.*, pp. 32–33.

²² *Ibid.*

²³ 'Bible Institutes Organize', *Christian Life & Times*, May, 1947, p. 68.

²⁴ Gaebelein, *loc. cit.*; S. A. Witmer, *The Bible College Story: Education with Dimension* (Manhasset, New York, 1962), p. 249.

²⁵ *Ibid.*, pp. 161, 176–177; 'Case for Christian Education', *Christian Life*, June, 1952, p. 26; *Manual of the AABIBC*, pp. 5–14.

²⁶ Voskuyl, Roger, 'Who Should Go to College?', *Sunday*, April, 1948, p. 78.

²⁷ Mimeographed form from the AABIBC; Wallace Emerson, 'Christian Education Today', *Christian Life*, September, 1948, p. 47.

²⁸ The Harvard Report of 1945 (General Education in a Free Society) was one of two reports in American higher education which was made to discover a unifying philosophy in education.

²⁹ Gaebelein, *op. cit.*, p. 177.

³⁰ *Ibid.*, p. 178; 'Christian Education', *King's Business*, June, 1956, p. 9.

³¹ Gaebelein, *op. cit.*, p. 174; *Manual of the AABIBC*, pp. 3–4; *Education Directory:*

Part 3, *Higher Education* (U.S. Office of Education, 1956–1957), p. 6; *Higher Education*, Part IV, *Education Association* (U.S. Office of Education, 1955–1956), p. 2.

32 Terrelle B. Crum, 'Bible Institutes and Colleges' (typed statement, n.d.), pp. 2–3.

33 *Manual of the AABIBC*, p. 5.

34 *Ibid.*, pp. 15–21.

35 *Ibid.*, pp. 15–17; Reynhout, *op. cit.*, pp. 15–21.

36 *Manual of the AABIBC*, p. 15.

37 *Ibid.*, pp. 15–16.

38 Angelyn G. Dantuma, 'The Christian and Education', *The Moody Student*, November 9, 1945; p. 2.

39 'So Why do They Laugh at Us?', *The Moody Student*, March 21, 1947, p. 2.

40 Much of this data was taken from the various catalogs of the schools mentioned; also from the mimeographed statement on requirements of the AABIBC, 1949, p. 3.

41 *Catalog of Providence-Barrington Bible College*, 1956–1957, p. 69.

42 'Enrollment of Men Reaches New High', *The Moody Student*, January 17, 1947, p. 1; Gaebelein, *op. cit.*, p. 170; *Lovejoy's College Guide* (New York: Simon and Schuster, 1956–1957).

43 *Ibid.*

44 'God's Chosen from the Ends of the Earth', (pamphlet published by the Moody Bible Institute of Chicago, n.d.).

45 See the catalogue for 1956–1957, p. 4.

46 'The Evangelical Year', *UEA*, January 1, 1949, p. 11.

47 Harry J. Albus, 'Christian Education Today', *Christian Life*, September, 1948, pp. 26, 46.

48 *Education Directory*, Part 3, *Higher Education*, pp. 6–7.

49 See the manuals of the various regional accrediting associations in the United States.

50 Bob Jones, 'Why Bob Jones University Was Founded ... Why It Does Not Hold Membership in a Regional Educational Association' (pamphlet published by the author, n.d.), pp. 6–7.

51 'World's Most Unusual', *Time*, June 16, 1952, p. 74; Donald E. Hoke, 'The Unusual Dr. Bob', *Christian Life*, February, 1953, pp. 24–26, 92–93.

52 Hoke, 'The Unusual Dr. Bob', *op. cit.*, pp. 24–25; 'A Modern Miracle in Christian Education', *UEA*, July 1, 1947, p. 7.

53 Letter from Bob Jones, Sr., August 27, 1956.

54 Theodore C. Mercer, 'An Additional Statement to the Alumni and Board of Trustees of Bob Jones University' (pamphlet published by the author, August, 1953), pp. 14–15.

55 Pamphlet written by Bob Jones, Sr. explaining the operation of Bob Jones University, n.d., p. 7.

56 Mercer, *op. cit.*, pp. 14–16.

57 Letter from Bob Jones, Sr., August 27, 1956.

58 *Catalog of Bob Jones University*, 1951–1953, p. 24.

59 Letter from Hudson T. Armerding to Bob Jones, Sr., June 1, 1953.

60 Letter from Bob Jones, Sr. to Hudson T. Armerding, June 5, 1953.

61 Mercer, *op. cit.*, p. 12.

[62] Ibid.

[63] Telephone conversation with Malcom Yost, May 29, 1957.

[64] See Bob Jones University advertisement in Christian Life, June, 1956, inside cover.

[65] Mercer, op. cit., p. 10.

[66] Ibid., entire.

[67] Blanshard, op. cit., p. 24.

[68] Murch, Co-operation, pp. 91–92; 'For Such A Time As This' (pamphlet published by the National Association of Christian Schools, n.d.), pp. 2–4.

[69] Norman D. Fletcher, 'Conspiracy Against Our Schools', Register, January, 1952, p. 16; Arthur D. Morse, 'Who's Trying to Ruin Our Schools?', McCall's, September, 1951, p. 27.

[70] Fletcher, op. cit., pp. 15–16; see Chapter I of this study.

[71] Morse, op. cit., pp. 26, 102–108.

[72] Louis H. Gerteis, 'How We Fought the Zoll Forces', Register, January, 1952, p. 8.

[73] Ibid.; William E. Drake, The American School in Transition (New York: Prentice-Hall, Inc., 1955), pp. 481–482.

[74] Russell T. Hitt, 'Treason in Our Textbooks', Christian Life, April, 1950, pp. 10–12; Evangelical School Movement (published by the National Association of Christian Schools, 1952), pp. 3–4.

[75] Smith, The Increasing Peril, p. 36.

[76] 'Is The Christian Day School a Crutch?', Western Voice, July 10, 1956, p. 2; 'Christian Schools', September, 1953, p. 1.

[77] Gaebelein, op. cit., p. 99.

[78] Harold C. Ockenga, 'What Cardinal Spellman Wants in Our Schools', UEA, October 1, 1949, p. 9.

[79] Ibid.

[80] Hitt, 'Treason in Our Textbooks', op. cit., p. 12; Fletcher, loc. cit.; Morse, op. cit., p. 94.

[81] Hitt, 'Treason in Our Textbooks', loc. cit.; see also letters to the editor in Christian Life, May, 1950, p. 14; Cora A. Reno, 'Students Beware', Christian Life, January, 1951, pp. 17, 55.

[82] Letter from Rolland E. Wolfe, April 2, 1957.

[83] Letter to WEWS, Cleveland, Ohio, October 12, 1954.

[84] Ibid.; Other letters cited in this paragraph were from: Betty Jane Winchell, November 30, 1954; January 8, 1955; May 23, 1955; George Rudolph, December 3, 1954; Elsie Lindrose, October 5, 1954; and those written in reply by Rolland E. Wolfe to: George Rudolph, December 14, 1954; Rev. Donald E. Woodby, December 18, 1954.

[85] Drake, op. cit., p. 500; Swisher, op. cit., pp. 1030–32; in released-time programs instruction in religion is given during reserved time during school hours. In the McCollum complaint use of school property for this purpose was challenged; see Gaebelein, op. cit., pp. 82–83.

[86] 'The Evangelical Year', loc. cit.; Ockenga, 'What Cardinal Spellman Wants', op. cit., pp. 8–11.

[87] 'The Evangelical Year', loc. cit.; Ockenga, 'What Cardinal Spellman Wants', op. cit., p. 6; Drake, op. cit., pp. 492–493; Swisher, op. cit., pp. 1029–1030.

88 'Why Johnny Goes to Christian School', *Christian Life*, June, 1957, pp. 12–31; 'Where Christian Schools Mushroom, '*Christian Life*, June, 1957, pp. 17–18.

89 Gaebelein, *op. cit.*, p. 105.

90 'For Such a Time as This', pp. 1–4; *Evangelical Christian Day School Movement* (Chicago: National Association of Christian Schools, 1952), pp. 3–4.

91 'For Such a Time as This', p. 3.

92 *Christian Day School Directory for the School Year 1954–1955* (Chicago: National Association of Christian Schools), pp. 2–11; 'Christian Schools', *Christian Life*, June, 1956, p. 15; 'Who's Who of Christian Education', *op. cit.*, p. 29; 'Third NACS Anniversary' (pamphlet published by the National Association of Christian Schools, 1950), p. 2; Gaebelein, *op. cit.*, p. 105; *Evangelical School Movement*, pp. 3, 5.

93 *Ibid.*

94 Arnold W. Hearn, 'Fundamentalist Renascence', *Century*, April 30, 1958, pp. 528–530; Ernest Pickering, 'New Evangelicalism', *Sword*, April 24, 1959, pp. 1–4; Sherman Roddy, 'Fundamentalists and Ecumenicity', *Century*, October 1, 1958, pp. 1109–1110; Carl F. H. Henry, 'Dare We Renew the Controversy?', *Christianity Today*, June 24, 1957, pp. 23–26; Edward John Carnell, 'Post-Fundamentalist Faith', *Century*, August 26, 1959, p. 971; Vernon Grounds, 'The Nature of Evangelicalism', *Eternity*, February, 1956, pp. 42–43; *Christian Life*, March, 1956, pp. 18–19; John F. Walvoord, 'What's Right About Fundamentalism?', *Eternity*, June, 1957, pp. 6–7, 34–35.

95 Hearn, *op. cit.*, p. 528.

96 *Ibid.*

97 *Journal* of the American Scientific Affiliation, inside cover of any issue.

98 Hearn, *loc. cit.*

99 *Ibid.*, p. 529.

100 *Ibid.*, pp. 528–530; William Hordern, *A. Layman's Guide to Protestant Theology* (New York: The Macmillan Co., 1955), pp. 75–77; Roddy, *loc. cit.*

101 Henry, 'Dare We Renew The Controversy', *Ibid.*, July 22, 1957, p. 24; John Dillenberger, 'Science and Theology Today', *Century*, June 17, 1959, p. 722; Edward John Carnell, *An Introduction to Christian Apologetics* (Grand Rapids: Wm. B. Eerdmans Publishing Co., 1952), pp. 229–242–275.

102 Henry, 'Dare We Renew The Controversy', *Ibid.*, July 18, 1957, pp. 15–18; July 22, 1957, pp. 23–26.

103 *Ibid.*

104 See books edited by Carl F. H. Henry, *Contemporary Evangelical Thought* (Great Neck, New York: Channel Press, 1957) and *Revelation and the Bible: Contemporary Evangelical Thought* (Grand Rapids: Baker Book House, 1958).

105 Henry, *Revelation and the Bible*, entire; Hordern, *op. cit.*, pp. 63–67; William Hordern, *The Case for a New Reformation Theology* (Philadelphia: The Westminster Press, 1959), pp. 55–67; Bernard Ramm, 'Are We Obscurantists?', *Christianity Today*, February 18, 1957, pp. 14–15; George Eldon Ladd, 'RSV Appraisal: New Testament', *Christianity Today*, July 8, 1957, pp. 7–8.

106 Hordern, *New Reformation Theology*, p. 58; Henry, *Revelation and the Bible*, pp. 70–78, 222–223.

107 Carnell, *Apologetics*, pp. 236 ff.; Ramm, *The Christian View of Science and Scripture*, pp. 17 ff., 265 ff., 306–307; Henry, *Contemporary Evangelical Thought*, pp. 250–269.

[108] Ramm, *The Christian View of Science and Scripture*, p. 256.

[109] *Ibid.*; Hordern, *New Reformation Theology*, p. 60.

[110] Carnell, *Apologetics*, pp. 236 ff.

[111] John R. Rice, 'Don't Be Fooled', *The A.G.C. 'Reporter'*, September, 1958, p. 2.

[112] *Ibid.*, p. 10; Henry, 'Dare We Renew The Controversy?', *Ibid.*, June 24, 1957, p. 26.

[113] Walvoord, 'What's Right About Fundamentalism?', *op. cit.*, p. 35.

[114] *Christianity Today*, May 13, 1957, p. 4; May 27, 1957, pp. 20–21; February 17, 1958, pp. 20–21.

[115] *Ibid.*

[116] *Ibid.*

[117] *Ibid.*, February 17, 1958, p. 20.

[118] Henry, *The Uneasy Conscience of Modern Fundamentalism*, entire; Carl F. H. Henry, 'Perspective for Social Action', *Christianity Today*, January 19, 1959, p. 10.

[119] Henry, 'Perspective for Social Action', *op. cit.*, p. 11.

[120] Carnell, *Apologetics*, pp. 166, 231–233.

[121] Murch, *Co-operation*, pp. 165 ff.; Clair M. Cook, 'Industrial Chaplains', *Century*, August 31, 1955, pp. 992–994.

[122] Murch, *Co-operation*, p. 165.

[123] *Ibid.*, pp. 165–166.

[124] *Ibid.*; E. Earle Ellis, 'Segregation and the Kingdom of God', *Christianity Today*, March 18, 1957, p. 7; Carl F. H. Henry, 'Race Tensions and Social Change', *Christianity Today*, January 19, 1959, p. 22.

[125] Henry, 'Race Tensions', *loc. cit.*

[126] Murch, *Co-operation*, p. 167; *World Vision Magazine*, any issue; Portland *Sunday Oregonian*, April 29, 1956, Rotogravure section.

[127] Murch, *Co-operation*, pp. 166–167.

[128] *Beacon*, September 8, 1960, p. 8.

[129] Murch, *Co-operation*, p. 168.

CHAPTER VII

[1] Besides the information in Chapter I of this study, see also William G. Mc Loughlin, Jr., *Billy Sunday Was His Name* (Chicago: University of Chicago Press, 1955, pp. 293–297).

[2] Mc Loughlin, *op. cit.*, pp. 295–297.

[3] *Ibid.*

[4] *Cleveland Press*, May 8, 1952, p. 49; May 19, 1952, p. 15.

[5] 'The Road to Revival', editorial, *Life*, April 5, 1947, p. 36.

[6] *Cleveland Press*, May 19, 1952, p. 15.

[7] Simon Stylites, 'Meet Bridey Murphy', *Century*, June 6, 1956, p. 692.

[8] Harvey Wish, *Contemporary America* (New York: Harper & Brothers Publisher, 1955).

[9] Mitchell, *op. cit.*; High, *op. cit.*, p. 72; 'The New Evangelist', *Time*, October 25, 1954, p. 55.

[10] *Ibid.*; *Cleveland News*, September 8, 1954, p. 7.

11 Mitchell, *op. cit.*, p. 9; *Cleveland News*, *loc. cit.*; High, *op. cit.*, p. 83.

12 *Ibid.*

13 'The New Evangelist', *loc. cit.*; High, *op. cit.*, p. 110.

14 Mitchell, *op. cit.*, p. 14.

15 *Ibid.*; High, *op. cit.*, pp. 138–139.

16 High, *op. cit.*, pp. 140–143; Mitchell, *op. cit.*, January 23, 1955, pp. 15–16.

17 'The New Evangelist', *op. cit.*, p. 56.

18 High, *op. cit.*, p. 147.

19 *Ibid.*, pp. 147–150; Mitchell, *op. cit.*, January 23, 1955, pp. 16–17.

20 *Ibid.*

21 Jim Vaus, *Why I Quit Syndicated Crime* (Wheaton, Illinois: Van Kampen Press, 1955); High, *op. cit.*, p. 149; Haskins, *Christians You Would Like to Know*, pp. 42–46.

22 Vaus, *op. cit.*, p. 55; Haskins, *Christians You Would Like to Know*, pp. 82–89.

23 Haskins, *Christians You Would Like to Know*, pp. 77–78; Vaus, *op. cit.*, pp. 53–54.

24 Haskins, *Christians You Would Like to Know*, pp. 79–80; Vaus, *op. cit.*, pp. 61–62.

25 Vaus, *op. cit.*, pp. 70, 73–84.

26 Haskins, *Christians You Would Like to Know*, pp. 80–81.

27 *Ibid.*, p. 24; Dorothy Haskins, 'California Revival', *Christian Life*, January, 1950, pp. 30–31; 'Revival Fires in Los Angeles', *Christian Life*, December 1949, p. 28; 'A Change of Heart', *Christian Life*, April, 1950, p. 26; Harold J. Ockenga, 'America's Revival is Breaking', *Christian Life*, March, 1950, p. 20; William W. Gothard, '4 Minutes to 12', *Christian Life*, January, 1950, p. 13.

28 Ockenga, 'America's Revival is Breaking', *loc. cit.*; Gothard, *loc. cit.*

29 See the previous discussions in this study which indicate the truth of the statements in this paragraph.

30 Mitchell, *op. cit.*, January 30, 1955, p. 10; Harold J. Ockenga, 'Boston Stirred by Revival', *UEA*, January 15, 1950, p. 4.

31 *Ibid.*; Robert C. Van Kampen, 'I Was In Boston', *Christian Life*, March, 1950, pp. 21–22.

32 *Ibid.*; Ockenga, 'Boston Stirred by Revival', *op. cit.*, p. 4.

33 Mitchell, *op. cit.*, January 30, 1955, p. 10.

34 Donald Hoke, 'South Carolina Revival', *UEA*, April 1, 1950, pp. 5,18; 'Graham Revival Stirs South', *Christian Life*, April, 1950, p. 25.

35 'Graham Reports 7,300 Decisions', *Christian Life*, May, 1950, p. 34.

36 Hoke, 'South Carolina Revival', *loc. cit.*

37 '50,000 Hear Graham', *Christian Life*, June 1950, p. 43; Van Kampen, *op. cit.*, p. 22.

38 *Variety*, November 8, 1950, quoted in *Christian Life*, January, 1951, p. 8.

39 Howard W. Ferrin, 'Revival and Evangelism', *UEA*, March, 1, 1950, p. 10.

40 *Cleveland Plain Dealer*, June 2, 1957, Section A, p. 9.

41 *Time*, October 25, 1954, p. 55.

42 *UEA*, November 1, 1950, pp. 14–15.

43 Mitchell, *op. cit.*, January 30, 1955, p. 10.

44 High, *op. cit.*, pp. 151–160. Graham adopted much of the methods employed by Billy Sunday in his revivals. See Mc Loughlin, *op. cit.*, p. 20.

[45] *Cleveland Press*, March 1, 1954, p. 33; High, *op. cit.*, pp. 171, 183.

[46] George Burnham, *Billy Graham: A Mission Accomplished* (Westwood, New Jersey: Fleming H. Revell Co., 1955), pp. 15–16; oral report of the London Crusade made by Paul E. Rees, member of the Graham team, made in Cleveland, Ohio, April 28, 1954.

[47] High, *op. cit.*, pp. 170–171.

[48] *Time*, May 31, 1954, pp. 58–59.

[49] *Ibid.*; Burnham, *op. cit.*, pp. 21–22, 91–100, 120–141, 157–158; *Cleveland Press*, April 7, 1955, p. 14; *Cleveland Plain Dealer*, May 1, 1955, Section B, p. 4.

[50] Mc Loughlin, *op. cit.*, p. xvii.

[51] *New York Times*, May 19, 1957, Section E, p. 11.

[52] Armin Gesswein, 'Billy Graham's Big Secret', *Christian Life*, March, 1957, pp. 19–20.

[53] Edward John Carnell, 'Can Billy Slay the Giant?' *op. cit.*, p. 4; Billy Graham, 'Why I Must Go to New York', *Christian Life*, February, 1957, p. 17.

[54] Graham, *loc. cit.*

[55] *Ibid.*, pp. 17–18.

[56] *Ibid.*, p. 17.

[57] *Ibid.*

[58] Billy Graham, 'Why We Must Go to New York' (pamphlet published by the Billy Graham Evangelistic Association, 1957), pp. 3–4.

[59] Graham, 'Why I Must Go To New York', *loc. cit.*

[60] *Newsweek*, May 20, 1957, p. 68; Frank Gaebelein, 'This is How We Are Preparing for the Crusade', *Christian Life*, May, 1957, pp. 11–12; *UEA*, May 15, 1957, p. 14; *Cleveland Press*, May 20, 1957, p. 26.

[61] *New York Herald-Tribune*, June 10, 1957, Sec. II, p. 1.

[62] *New York Times*, May 19, 1957, Sec. E, p. 11.

[63] *Ibid.*, May 25, 1957, p. 1; *New York Herald-Tribune*, May 25, 1957, p. 6; *Cleveland Press*, May 25, 1957, p. 6.

[64] *Ibid.*, June 27, 1957, p. 48.

[65] *Cleveland Plain Dealer*, June 27, 1957, p. 20.

[66] 'Graham in the Garden', *Century*, May 15, 1957, p. 614.

[67] *Ibid.*; 'Mass Conversion', *Century*, May 29, 1957, p. 678.

[68] *New York Times*, May 19, 1957, Sec. E, p. 11; *Cleveland Plain Dealer*, May 30, 1957, p. 35.

[69] *Time*, July 29, 1957, p. 48.

[70] Statement by Billy Graham over television, July 20, 1957.

[71] *Cleveland Press*, June 8, 1957, p. 2.

[72] *New York Herald-Tribune*, June 10, 1957, Sec. II, p. 1.

[73] *Cleveland Plain Dealer*, August 4, 1957, Sec. A, p. 10.

[74] *Cleveland Press*, June 3, 1957, p. 20; statement by Billy Graham over television, June 22, 1957.

[75] John R. Rice, 'Billy Graham's New York Crusade', *Sword*, April 19, 1957, p. 1.

[76] *Ibid.*, p. 2.

[77] 'About Billy Graham', *Beacon*, April 11, 1957, p. 1; *Beacon*, April 25, 1957, p. 3.

78 *Beacon*, April 25, 1957, p. 3.

79 'Is Evangelical Theology Changing?', *op. cit.*, p. 16; 'Is Evangelical Christianity Changing?', *King's Business*, January, 1957, p. 23.

80 'Is Evangelical Theology Changing?', *loc. cit.*

81 *Ibid.*

82 *UEA*, May 15, 1957, p. 4.

83 Rice, 'Billy Graham's New York Crusade', *loc. cit.*; 'Goliath and Graham', *Beacon*, May 30, 1957, p. 8.

84 High, *op. cit.*, p. 69.

85 Burnham, *op. cit.*, p. 69.

86 John R. Rice, 'Billy Graham Openly Repudiates Fundamentalism', *Sword*, May 17, 1957, p. 2.

87 *Cleveland Press*, November 2, 1955, p. 32.

88 *Ibid.; UEA*, October 15, 1956, p. 8; 'U.S. Religious Interest Quickens', *Christian Life*, June, 1956, pp. 20–23.

89 'Billy Graham on Evangelism', *Christian Life*, January, 1951, p. 11.

90 Eugene C. Blake, 'Is the Religious Boom a Spiritual Bust?', *Look*, September 20, 1955, p. 30; *Cleveland Plain Dealer*, April 9, 1956, final edition, p. 37.

91 William Hordern, 'America's Religious Revival—Asset or Liability?', *The Messenger*, June 18, 1957, pp. 14–15.

92 *Cleveland Press*, November 2, 1955, p. 32.

93 *Ibid.*, May 20, 1957, p. 26.

94 *Ibid.*, November 2, 1955, p. 32.

95 *Ibid.*

96 'Fundamentalist Revival', *Century*, June 19, 1957, p. 749.

97 *Christianity Today*, August 19, 1957, p. 29.

98 'Needed: Evangelism in Depth', *Century*, June 26, 1957, p. 782.

99 'Fundamentalist Revival', *op. cit.*, pp. 749–751.

100 Arnold Nash, 'L'Affaire Graham', *Century*, June 26, 1957, p. 793.

101 'Mass Conversion', *loc. cit.*

102 'Fundamentalist Revival', *op. cit.*, p. 749.

103 Hordern, 'America's Religious Revival', *op. cit.*, p. 15; 'The Story of the C.A.M.' (pamphlet published by the Christian Amendment Movement, n.d.).

104 Samuel E. Boyle, 'Jesus Christ and the American Tradition', *UEA*, September 15, 1947, pp. 3–4.

105 Clarence H. Cramer, Royal Bob: *The Life of Robert G. Ingersoll* (Indianapolis: Bobbs-Merrill, 1952), p. 175.

106 'Christ is Our Moral Governor' (pamphlet published by the Christian Amendment Movement, n.d.), p. 7.

107 *Ibid.*

108 'Chaplaincy Under Fire,' *UEA*, February 1, 1956, p. 2.

[109] 'Under God,' *Time*, May 17, 1954, p. 101.

[110] *Ibid.*

[111] 'A Stamp for God', *Christian Life*, May, 1954, p. 45.

[112] 'In God We Trust', *UEA*, September 1, 1956, p. 14.

[113] 'In God We Trust', *Time*, August 6, 1956, p. 23.

[114] Hordern, 'America's Religious Revival', *op. cit.*, p. 15.

Index

DATE DUE

F			

DEMCO 38-297

Barclay, William
Educational Ideals in the Ancient
World

Bass, Clarence B.
Backgrounds to Dispensationalism

Battenhouse, Roy W. (ed.)
A Companion to the Study of
St. Augustine

Bavinck, Herman
The Doctrine of God
Our Reasonable Faith
The Philosophy of Revelation

Beardslee, John W., III (ed. & tr.)
Reformed Dogmatics

Beckwith, Isbon T.
The Apocalypse of John

Beecher, Willis Judson
The Prophets and the Promise

Berkhof, Hendrikus
Christ the Meaning of History

Berkhof, Louis
The History of Christian Doctrines
Introduction to Systematic Theology

Bright, John
The Authority of the Old Testament

Bushnell, Horace
Christian Nurture

Carnell, Edward John
A Philosophy of the Christian
Religion

Clark, Gordon H.
A Christian View of Men and Things
Thales to Dewey

Dargan, Edwin C.
A History of Preaching

Davies, J. G.
The Early Christian Church

Davis, John D.
Genesis and Semitic Tradition

Deissmann, Adolf
Light from the Ancient East

De Ridder, Richard R.
Discipling the Nations

Dodd, C. H.
The Apostolic Preaching and Its
Developments

Eck, John
Enchiridion of Commonplaces

Edersheim, Alfred
The History of the Jewish Nation
Prophecy and History

Ellis, E. Earle
Paul's Use of the Old Testament

Eusebius
The Proof of the Gospel

Farrar, Frederic W.
History of Interpretation

Frend, W. H. C.
Martyrdom and Persecution in the
Early Church

Gasper, Louis
The Fundamentalist Movement

Gerstner, John H.
Reasons for Faith
The Theology of the Major Sects

Goppelt, Leonhard
Apostolic and Post-Apostolic Times

Green, William Henry
General Introduction to the Old
Testament
The Higher Criticism of the
Pentateuch
The Unity of the Book of
Genesis

Henry, Carl F. H.
Aspects of Christian Social Ethics
Christian Personal Ethics

Henry, Carl F. H. (ed.)
Basic Christian Doctrines
Fundamentals of the Faith
Revelation and the Bible

Heppe, Heinrich
Reformed Dogmatics

Hillerbrand, Hans J.
The Reformation
The World of the Reformation

280.4
G294

LINCOLN CHRISTIAN COLLEGE

twin brooks series

Hort, Fenton John Anthony
Judaistic Christianity
Jerome
Commentary on Daniel
Kevan, Ernest F.
The Grace of Law
Klotsche, E. H.
The History of Christian Doctrine
Kuiper, R. B.
God-Centered Evangelism
Kurtz, J. H.
Sacrificial Worship of the Old
Testament
Kuyper, Abraham
Principles of Sacred Theology
Law, Robert
The Tests of Life
Lecerf, Auguste
An Introduction to Reformed
Dogmatics
Lightfoot, J. B.
The Apostolic Fathers
Longenecker, Richard N.
The Christology of Early Jewish
Christianity
Paul, Apostle of Liberty
Machen, J. Gresham
The Virgin Birth of Christ
Manson, T. W.
The Servant-Messiah
Mayor, Joseph B.
The Epistle of James
The Epistles of Jude and II Peter
McDonald, H. D.
Theories of Revelation
Meeter, H. Henry
The Basic Ideas of Calvinism
Niesel, Wilhelm
The Theology of Calvin
Orr, James
Revelation and Inspiration
Rackham, Richard Belward
The Acts of the Apostles
Ramm, Bernard
The Evangelical Heritage
Varieties of Christian Apologetics

Raven, John Howard
The History of the Religion of Israel
Sandeen, Ernest R.
The Roots of Fundamentalism
Seeberg, Reinhold
Textbook of the History of
Doctrines
Sherwin-White, A. N.
Roman Society and Roman Law in
the New Testament
Smith, David
The Days of His Flesh
Smith, James
The Voyage and Shipwreck of St.
Paul
Steinmetz, David C.
Reformers in the Wings
Stonehouse, Ned B.
Origins of the Synoptic Gospels
The Witness of the Synoptic Gospels
to Christ
Sweet, William Warren
The Story of Religion in America
Theron, Daniel J.
Evidence of Tradition
Trench, Richard Chenevix
Notes on the Miracles of Our Lord
Notes on the Parables of Our
Lord
Studies in the Gospels
Trueblood, David Elton
General Philosophy
Philosophy of Religion
Turretin, Francis
The Atonement of Christ
Van Til, Henry
The Calvinistic Concept of Culture
Vos, Geerhardus
The Pauline Eschatology
Westcott, B. F.
A General Survey of the History of
the Canon of the New Testament
Wilson, Robert Dick
Studies in the Book of Daniel
Young, Warren C.
A Christian Approach to Philosophy

BAKER BOOK HOUSE   BOX 6287   GRAND RAPIDS, MI 49506